THE ART OF
THE STONE AGE

FORTY THOUSAND YEARS OF ROCK ART

HANS-GEORG BANDI · HENRI BREUIL · LILO BERGER-
KIRCHNER · HENRI LHOTE · ERIK HOLM
ANDREAS LOMMEL

METHUEN · LONDON

FIRST PUBLISHED IN 1961

© HOLLE AND CO. VERLAG, BADEN-BADEN, GERMANY

PRINTED IN HOLLAND

Translated by Ann E. Keep, Dr. Phil.

The frontispiece represents the head and chest of a bull. The horns are in twisted perspective. Above, on the left, the head of a horse painted in black and brown. Aurignacian-Perigordian. Picture gallery, Lascaux.

1.1.

CATALOGUE No. 2/6229/1

LIST OF PLATES AND MAPS

MAPS

SOURCE OF COLOURED PLATES

LIST OF FIGURES WITH SOURCES

The following have kindly provided the figures in this volume: Konstanze Holm, Pretoria (Figs. 49—53), Greta Leuzinger, Zurich (Figs. 1—14, 37, 40, 42—45), Katharina Lommel, Munich (Figs. 54—66), Hannes Pixa, Baden-Baden (Figs. 36, 38, 39, 41, 46, 47).

CONTENTS

INTRODUCTION

World art does not start with the works of the advanced cultures of Mesopotamia and the Nile valley. Its roots lie much further back, in the earliest origins of human history. Works of art were already produced by prehistoric man, as they are by the primitive peoples that still exist in the world today. Fortunately for us many of these early works have been preserved up to modern times. In the majority of cases they are rock pictures executed by Stone Age hunters who were highly-specialized artists.

It may at first sight seem surprising that the publishers have decided to include the Stone Age in the series of volumes on the non-European cultures, when the description of the sites given here begins with those situated on our own continent. In coming to this decision they were guided by the consideration that for two reasons it would have been still less fitting to have treated this subject in connection with Western civilization: firstly because a great number of finds from other continents are also treated in these pages; secondly because the legacy of the European Stone Age peoples does not easily fit into the concept of Western culture.

Furthermore, this volume by no means covers the whole of Stone Age art. Only the rock art of this period is dealt with, and a comparatively limited section of it at that. The aim here has been to afford readers of the 'ART OF THE WORLD' series at least a glimpse of the artistic achievements of prehistoric peoples in different parts of the world and to open up a fascinating field of study which is generally bypassed or treated cursorily in other histories of art.

The study of prehistoric rock pictures is not only a fascinating subject but also a dangerous one: fascinating because it gives us an unexpectedly rich, realistic and colourful insight into cultures of which otherwise we have only the 'skeleton' (mostly stone implements), since everything else has vanished long ago; and dangerous because Stone Age rock pictures were never 'art for art's sake' but always an expression of certain attitudes of mind, and this readily leads to an excessively speculative interpretation. The prehistoric art to be discussed in these pages is the product of the so-called 'advanced hunter peoples'. Out of the primitive basic type of hunter culture, which survived for many millennia and spread over extensive areas of the globe, three paths of development gradually evolved:

one leading to hoeing of the soil; one to cattle-raising; and a third path, known as 'advanced hunter culture'. This type of culture, like the original primitive form, definitely still has an acquisitive non-productive character. But there is now marked specialization among the hunters, bringing with it significant cultural progress. On the other hand, this path of development led to a dead end, for in contrast to the two other types of economic activity, hoeing of the soil and pasturing cattle, which in combination led to settled agriculture, it did not evolve anywhere into a fully-developed culture.

The birth of 'advanced hunter culture' must be sought in the last phases of the Ice Age, some 50,000 years ago. Its demise can be observed in our own day, for there are still some peoples — the Bushmen in South Africa, for example — who are the last surviving practitioners of this once widespread mode of economic life.

With peoples in this stage of development their entire existence in all aspects — economic, social and spiritual — is dominated by hunting. Everything is focussed upon the quest for game. All man's thoughts and emotions are centred upon "the constant conflict, practical and spiritual, with animals. This leads to a conception of the relationship between man and beast as a very real unity of substance, that is to say, to a belief in the unity of the entire animal world and the interchangeability of human and animal forms of existence." [1] These far-reaching problems cannot be gone into in detail here, but it may be pointed out that in many places 'advanced hunters' had to their credit varied artistic achievements, a genuine 'ritual art' which gives us most interesting insights into the spiritual world in which these peoples lived.

We are concerned here with rock pictures, although the art of the 'advanced hunters' also comprises minor arts such as sculpture, engraved or painted decoration on movable objects, and much else besides. But one should not jump to the conclusion that all the rock engravings and paintings scattered over the entire globe are the work of 'advanced hunters'. Rock pictures can also be produced by peoples in other stages of cultural development, although in such cases one must frequently reckon with the possibility that influences or traditions derived from hunters play a certain role. Naturalistic works are found most particularly in the southern parts of the region inhabited by 'advanced hunters'. This fact will be illustrated in the various sections of the present volume. These sections do not amount to an exhaustive survey. Such a survey would have to comprise much more than the few glimpses given here of Franco-Cantabrian and Eastern Spanish art in south-western Europe, of the rock

paintings in North Africa (a region where pictures by hunters are interspersed with others by cattle-raisers, which are also treated here), of the rock art of South Africa, and finally that of Australia. Some other centres of rock pictures, principally in Africa and the Near East, have had to be omitted. Nor has it been possible to mention the rock art of the Arctic, although it may be pointed out here that in Scandinavia, in addition to engravings executed by agriculturists of the Bronze Age, there is also a very impressive widely diffused group of works by Stone Age hunters and fishermen. Other evidence of Arctic art is to be found in Karelia, Western Siberia and Central Asia. Finally, no attention has been paid in these pages to rock art in the western hemisphere, which also belongs in part to hunter culture.

Despite these limitations this volume will perhaps help to show that the 'ritual art' works of the 'advanced hunters', some of which date back to the Ice Age and some to more recent periods, are as impressive and beautiful as they are diversified and informative. The fact that the various regions of rock art are dealt with independently by different authors, and that each is alone responsible for the opinions expressed, shows how varied the approach to these problems can be. While some authors have kept rather to the traditional method of interpretation others have attempted to strike out along new paths. But all endeavour to introduce the reader to a subject which, owing to the magnificence of many of the works discussed, can also give something to those who are not so familiar with the mysterious world in which the minds of these hunter peoples moved.

Hans-Georg Bandi

[1] K. J. Narr, *Historia Mundi*, Vol. I, Berne, 1952, p. 517.

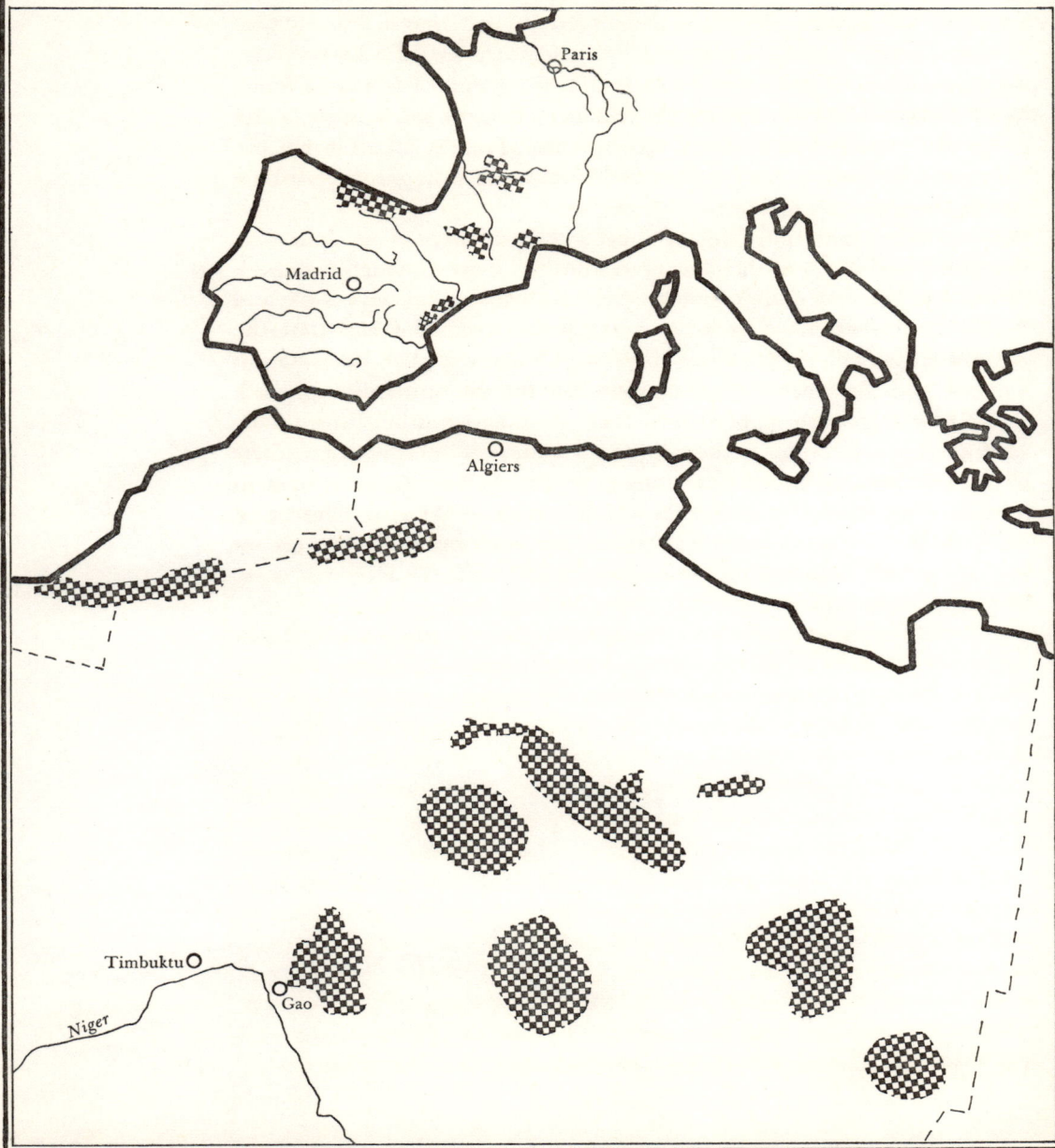

THE CHIEF CENTRES OF ROCK ART IN
SOUTH-WEST EUROPE AND NORTH AFRICA

FRANCO-CANTABRIAN ROCK ART

BY

H. BREUIL AND L. BERGER-KIRCHNER

At the close of the 19th century the entrances to caves in northern Spain and south-western France were rediscovered after they had remained sealed for thousands of years. In these caves lay hidden an undreamt-of wealth of artistic works dating from the Ice Age: magnificent polychrome murals and roof frescoes, decorated partly with figures of animals now long extinct, partly with vivid engravings and a vast number of curious signs. The disclosure of such an ancient prehistoric art came as a complete surprise to a world that had hitherto sought the origins of human artistic endeavour in the civilizations of Mesopotamia and Egypt. The discovery of Ice Age art had therefore to encounter a multitude of obstacles, and it was only a quarter of a century later that this art finally found acceptance.

In 1869 the entrance to the cave of Altamira was discovered by a man *DISCOVERY* hunting foxes in a tract of meadow land near the village of Santillana del Mar, in northern Spain. Ten years later Marcelino de Sautuola, a local nobleman, commenced excavations at Altamira. One day he took his little daughter Maria, then five years old, into the cave. While playing in a chamber some 30 yards from the entrance her eye was caught by the magnificent frescoes on the roof. Since Sautuola was the first man to have entered the cave he was convinced that no modern artist could have created these paintings. However, in the scientific world doubts were expressed as to their authenticity. At the Congress of Anthropology and Prehistoric Archaeology held at Lisbon in 1880 the Altamira paintings were dismissed as forgeries and were soon once again consigned to oblivion. In 1895 E. Rivière discovered paintings and engravings in the cave of La Mouthe in the Dordogne, and in the following year F. Daleau deciphered several engravings in the Pair-non-Pair cave in the Gironde. These pictures, partially covered by thick deposits, were the only ones that secured recognition by the experts.

It was only in the twentieth century, through the work performed by a *Recognition of* new generation of prehistorians, that Ice Age art came into its own. In *Ice Age art* September 1901 Henri Breuil, then a young man, in collaboration with

15

L. Capitan and D. Peyrony, discovered Les Combarelles near Les Eyzies, a cave lavishly decorated with engravings. The very next week the three explorers were able to report the discovery of the Font-de-Gaume cave, also situated near Les Eyzies in the Vézère valley. The very old sinter deposits that covered the engravings at Les Combarelles as well as the paintings at Font-de-Gaume gradually dispelled the doubts that had existed hitherto. The similarity between the frescoes of Font-de-Gaume and those of Altamira led the venerable prehistorian E. Cartailhac to revise his strongly held opinions and to recognize that the pictures originated from the Ice Age. With his *Mea culpa d'un sceptique* the debate as to the authenticity of this cave art was shelved.

In 1903 Peyrony disclosed further engravings at Bernifal and Teyjat in the Dordogne. 1906 is a key year: it was then that Alcalde del Rio and Padre Sierra discovered the famous caves of El Castillo, Covalanas and La Haza, as well as other caves in Cantabria, which were then studied by Breuil; in the same year F. Regnault came across ancient Aurignacian figures in the cave of Gargas in the French Pyrenees and Molard discovered magnificent animal paintings in black in the 'Salon Noir' of the gigantic cave at Niaux, which shortly afterwards were examined by Breuil and Cartailhac. Not long after this Dr. Jeannel drew attention to the paintings at Le Portel (Ariège). It was in 1912 that H. Obermaier and P. Wernert penetrated into the cave of La Pasiega, situated not far from Castillo. Already before the first world war publications began to appear, in the form of magnificent monographs, made possible by the generosity of Prince Albert of Monaco. In 1912 and 1914 Count Bégouen and his sons disclosed near Montesquieu-Avantès (Ariège) the two vast cave complexes of Tuc d'Audoubert and Trois Frères. 1940 was the year of the discovery of Lascaux, with its magnificent paintings, which were subsequently studied by Breuil and F. Windels. The most sensational discovery in the last few years was that of the cave of Rouffignac (Dordogne) in the summer of 1956. As happened a century ago, its paintings touched off a controversy with regard to their authenticity; it was only after a long debate among the experts that their Ice Age origin was conclusively established.

It is impossible to discuss within the framework of this volume all the numerous art stations discovered since the beginning of the twentieth century. An appendix at the end of this chapter, however, provides a summary of all the caves at present known for their mural art.

DISTRIBUTION   As the name indicates, Franco-Cantabrian art is fairly narrowly confined to certain regions in France and Spain. Apart from one or two offshoots three regions have achieved prominence as centres of Ice Age art: the first

16

in the south-west of France (the Dordogne and adjoining departments); the second in the Pyrenean region of southern France; and the third in the Cantabrian area of northern Spain. In France the border of the Franco-Cantabrian art region is formed in the north-east by caves situated in the departments of Vienne and Yonne, and in the east by the art stations located in the Ardèche and Gard valleys; there are none beyond the Rhône. In Spain the southernmost outposts are to be found in Andalusia (La Pileta). Several caves situated in central Spain (Casares) can be regarded as links between north and south. Completely isolated, on the other hand, are three caves at the extreme southern tip of Italy, in Sicily and the Aegadian Islands. Exploration carried out in Belgium, Germany and Czechoslovakia, as well as in the Balkans, has not as yet produced any notable results. The engraving of a stag found in one cave in Bavaria cannot be ascribed to the Palaeolithic age. Traces of painting in one cave in England are likewise of uncertain date.

The paintings and engravings in the Franco-Cantabrian caves were applied to the walls, which consist of limestone varying in type from one area to another. Only in exceptional cases do other types of rock serve as a surface. The question thus arises how these paintings have been preserved and what influences — physical, chemical and organic — they were exposed to during the course of the millennia. The effects of gravity were particularly important: in the innermost parts of the caves, as well as in open rock-shelters (abris), the overhanging rocks are continually collapsing, especially in stratified lime deposits. The constant changes of temperature are conducive to fissure of the rock, and this process of weathering is accelerated still further by earthquakes. The fallen boulders, decorated in part with paintings and engravings, are in the course of time covered over by further collapses of the roof, by sand and clay carried into the cave by the wind, and by the refuse left by human beings. In this way archaeological strata were formed. Sculptures embedded in these layers can be preserved so long as they are not destroyed by the action of water. Water acts in a cave in two ways: by infiltration (ground-water) and by condensation on the walls. Condensation is caused by changes of temperature and the constant stream of air flowing from the inner parts of the cave to the outside world. It attacks the calcareous walls and is one of the chief reasons for the destruction of Ice Age mural paintings. Ground-water, on the other hand, by percolating through fissures in the rock, causes the formation of fantastic bizarre-shaped stalactites and stalagmites hanging from the roof or rising up from the floor. In the same way calcareous layers are deposited by ground-water on the cave walls, covering the

CONDITIONS
REQUIRED FOR
PRESERVATION

DISTRIBUTION OF ROCK ART IN
SOUTH-WEST EUROPE

1. Cf. also Map p. 23
2. Cf. also Map p. 72
3. Cf. also Map p. 22
4. Arcy-sur-Cure
5. Angles-sur-Anglin
6. Sallèles-Cabardès
7. Aldène
8. Los Casares
9. La Cala
10. Ardales (Cueva Trinidad)
11. La Pileta
12. Las Palomas
13. Levanzo
14. Addaura
15. Romanelli

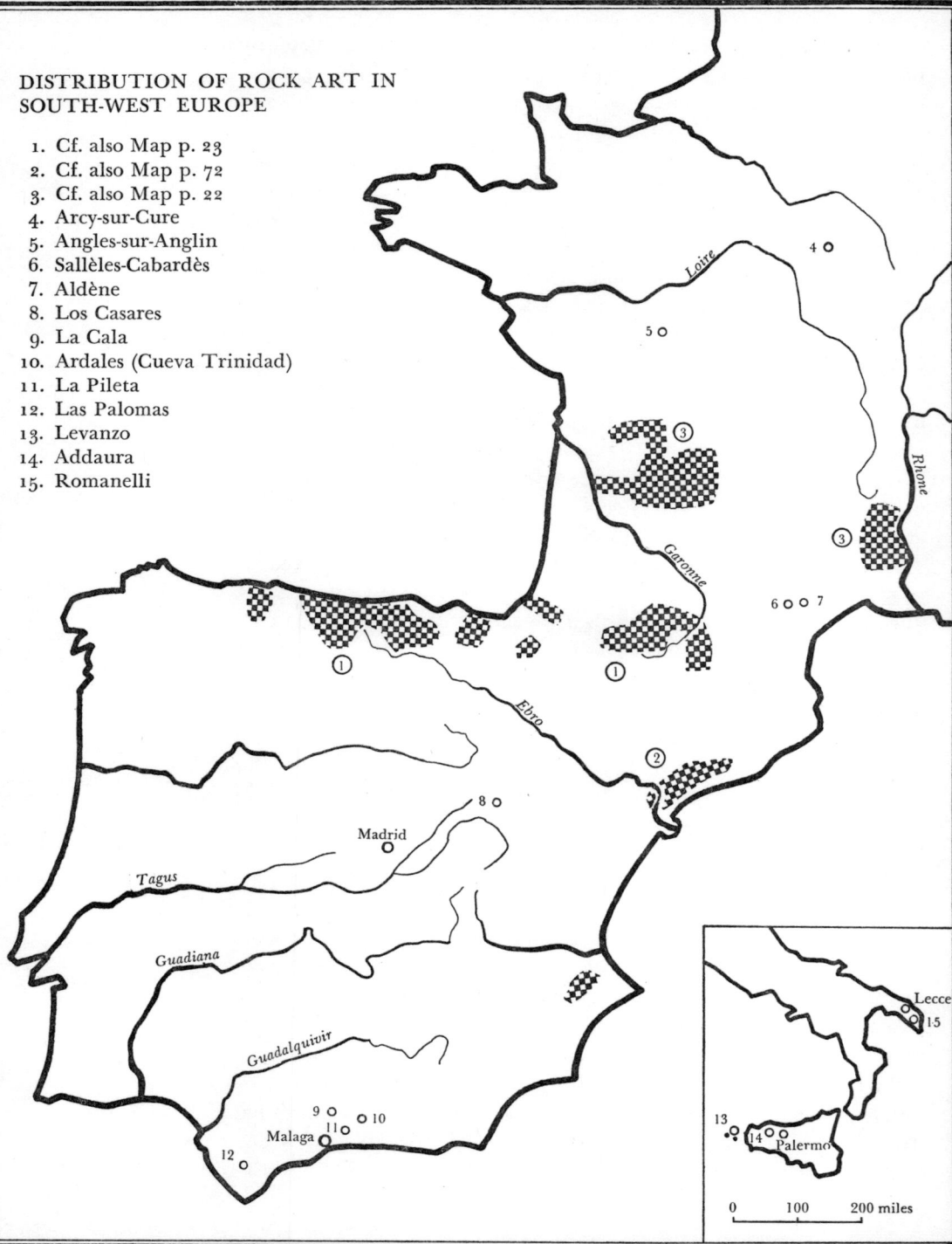

Loire

Rhone

Garonne

Ebro

Tagus

Madrid

Guadiana

Guadalquivir

Malaga

Lecce
15

13
14 Palermo

0   100   200 miles

paintings; this can provide evidence as to their antiquity. This sinter deposit also contributes to the preservation of the paintings. There are, of course, cases where the sinter formation may become so thick that a painting or engraving can no longer shimmer through. Even if the depositing of sinter has ceased and paintings are to be found beneath it, this is a guarantee of their antiquity. But if, on the other hand, the depositing of sinter is still in progress this merely proves that the paintings to be found beneath the deposit do not originate from recent times. At Lascaux the walls of the picture gallery are covered with a fine bright sinter deposit upon which the pictures were later superimposed. The depositing of sinter had already ceased during the Ice Age.

Cave walls, like all other rock surfaces, are also exposed to biological and chemical processes: in lighted parts lichens grow on dry and sometimes on wet rock, algae and mosses on rock that is permanently damp. This vegetation can often help to destroy the paintings. On a completely dry wall oxydization is always found on the surface, causing the natural colour of the rock to change, often to a darker colour, and this in turn in many places limits the extent to which the paintings are visible.

Deposit is an important phenomenon to be found in caves. It is of the greatest significance in dating pictures and sometimes in their preservation. As has already been mentioned, the floor of the cave is raised up by falls of the roof, drifts and human settlement — the latter, however, only takes effect at the cave entrance — with the result that in several caves extensive deposits form. Walls decorated with paintings are thus partly covered over. At several art stations this deposit can also consist merely of sand or clay. At Pair-non-Pair deposits reached almost up to the roof; walls decorated with engravings disappeared below it, but the paintings retained their original brilliance remarkably well. The strata of the deposit helped to establish the date of the paintings they had covered over. *Deposit*

Since the discovery of Franco-Cantabrian cave art scholars have been largely concerned with the question of ascertaining the age of the various works. How could the great antiquity of Ice Age art be authenticated? What evidence is there that these paintings and engravings do not originate from the last few centuries? AGE AND DEVELOPMENT

As has already been mentioned, in the course of an immense length of time the walls were exposed to the action of water, causing the surface to erode or leaving calcareous deposits on the paintings. In addition to this the rock was affected by chemical processes, which caused the colour of the engraved picture to change, thus indicating great antiquity.

Another characteristic feature of this art is that in most cases the animals represented belong to species that are either extinct or are no longer to be found in Europe. Pictures of animals such as reindeer, mammoths, rhinoceroses, musk-oxen, bisons and saiga antelopes — the latter, however, depicted only once, in Combarelles — which inhabited the Franco-Cantabrian area during the late Ice Age prove that this form of art, too, must be assigned to that era, i.e. that it must originate from the last glaciation, which ended about 10,000 B.C. The antiquity of cave art is also attested by the fact that the pictures were repeatedly covered by strata whose age can be established exactly from the finds embedded in them. At Pair-non-Pair the bones of Ice Age animals, as well as remains left by humans beings contained in the layers covering the engravings, have enabled them to be dated to the Aurignacian period, an early stage of cultural development when the first pictures were produced. Works of art found below a layer can either be older than that layer or contemporaneous with it, but never more recent. The same applies to boulders decorated with paintings which have fallen into the deposit, such as have been recovered, for example, from Aurignacian deposits at Sergeac in the Dordogne. At Altamira, El Castillo and Gargas small objects of art have also come to light in the deposits. These, and also the works of mural art, express the creative power of the Ice Age artist. In most cases they are reliefs or engravings on horn, antler, bone or small slabs of stone; the minor arts, however, also comprise figures sculptured in the round, in stone, ivory and baked clay. If such small contour drawings are found in the layer this is a guarantee of their antiquity, and stylistic comparisons can be drawn with mural paintings. But the different styles correspond to different eras and stages of development within Franco-Cantabrian cave art. This is in turn attested by the frequent superposition of paintings on top of one another. It is clear that the most recent figures are superimposed upon all the others and that the oldest pictures are to be found in the deepest strata. Such layers of pictures are to be met with in many caves. By means of these, and the criteria mentioned above, Breuil has succeeded, in the course of a long life devoted to exploration and study, in reconstructing the chronology or sequence in which Ice Age works of art appeared.

Breuil distinguishes between two major periods: Aurignacian-Perigordian and Solutrian-Magdalenian. These cycles correspond to the archaeological division of the late Ice Age into three main cultures: Aurignacian (after the type-site in the Haute Garonne), Perigordian (after the district of Périgord), Solutrian (after the type-site of Solutré in the department of

Saône-et-Loire), and Magdalenian (after the type-site of La Madeleine in the department of the Dordogne).

It was not until the beginning of the Upper Palaeolithic, which occurred some 30,000 years ago during the last great glaciation in Europe, that the first signs of man's artistic endeavours appeared. According to Breuil the oldest examples of this art are representations of hands, dating from the Middle Aurignacian. Such paintings of hands, which occur at Gargas, El Castillo and other caves, are outlined in red and black and stand out brightly against their rock backgrounds. The origin of figurative art must, however, be seen rather in the lines or incisions drawn on clay with several fingers or pronged palette-knives. These 'macaroni', as they are called, to be found on many cave walls, which at first are merely a chaotic tangle of lines, form the earliest 'pictorial writing'; they probably also date from the Middle Aurignacian. In the case of Aurignacian man this was probably at first a simple act of emulation, which later evolved into ever more complicated forms, until eventually from the jumble of meandering lines there developed a purposeful figure: though at first still clumsy and amateurish, in the course of time man succeeded in creating a simple but distinct image of an animal. Fingers were soon replaced by an engraving tool, by means of which lines could also be cut into the hard rock. Altamira and Gargas yield fine specimens, in which the distinct contours of animal heads suddenly stand out from the tangle of lines cut into the clay. These attempts are followed by polychrome line drawings of animals no longer executed with the fingers but with brush-like implements. From Castillo and Font-de-Gaume we have animal pictures painted in this way in red and yellow — though rarely in black. They are often found together with simple hut-like figures known as tectiforms. Apparently more recent in date are the animal figures where the contour is drawn with wide lines; in many cases the strokes are jagged, and the bodies of the animals are occasionally outlined by a row of closely-spaced dots (Covalanas, Altamira and El Castillo). The colour, originally limited to the contour line, now begins to cover the body of the animal — at first only certain portions, but soon, as this technique develops, the entire body. Representations of this kind, painted in red, are to be found at Altamira and Le Portel (Ariège), while black and sepia ones may be seen at Font-de-Gaume and Lascaux. Breuil assumes that this is the origin of the gradual development of bicolour painting, as is suggested by the caves of La Pasiega (Santander) and Pech-Merle (Lot). Painted boulders of this kind found in the Aurignacian and Perigordian strata of Sergeac confirm that this dating is correct. The

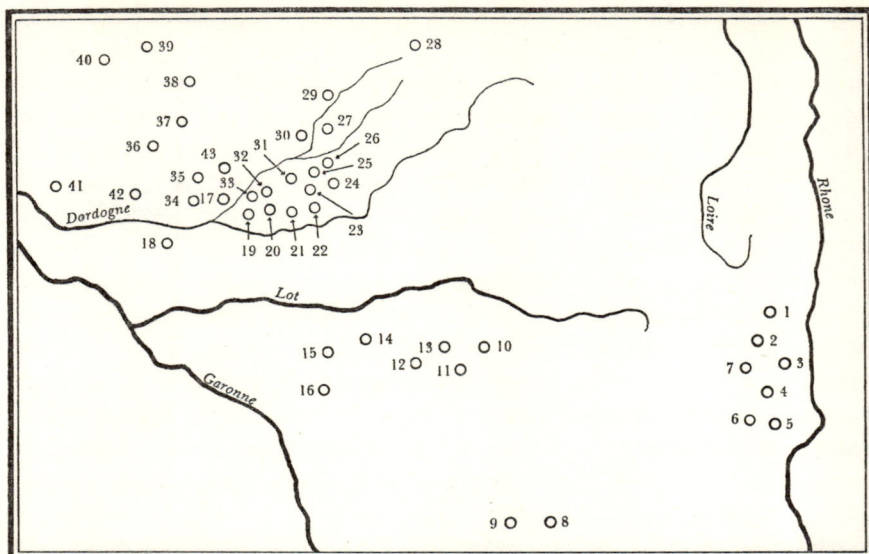

Rock art areas in the Dordogne

1. Ebbou
2. Le Colombier
3. Le Figuier
4. Chabot
5. Bayol
6. Baume-Latrone
7. Oullins
8. Aldène
9. Sallèles-Cabardès
10. Sainte-Eulalie
11. Cantal
12. Pech-Merle
13. Marcenac
14. Les Merveilles
15. Cougnac
16. La Magdelaine
17. Gorge d'Enfer
18. Jean-Blancs
19. Font-de-Gaume
20. La Mouthe
21. La Calévie
22. Bernifal

23. Beyssac
24. Commarque
25. La Grèze
26. Laussel
27. Lascaux
28. La Sudrie
29. Belcayre
30. Sergeac
31. Cap Blanc
32. Les Combarelles
33. Croze à Gontran
34. Barabao
35. La Ferrassie
36. Rouffignac
37. Fourneau du Diable
38. Teyjat
39. Roc de Sers
40. Chaire à Calvin
41. Pair-non-Pair
42. Le Gabillou
43. Laugerie Basse
    Laugerie Haute

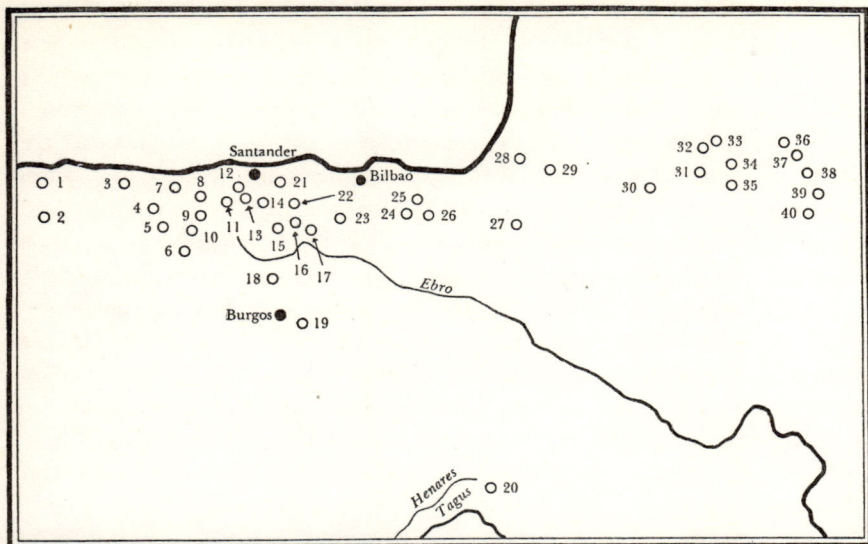

Rock art areas in the Pyrenees

1. El Cueto	22. El Castillo
2. Peña de Candamo	La Pasiega
3. Pindal	Las Monedas
4. Buxu	23. Salitré
5. Mazaculos	24. Sottarriza
6. La Meaza	25. Santimamiñe
7. Quintanal	26. Venta de la Perra
8. Bolado	27. Berroberia
9. La Loja	28. Isturitz
10. La Clotilde	29. Etcheberriko
11. San Antonio	30. Labastide
12. Santian	31. Gargas
13. Las Aguas	32. Montespan
14. Altamira	33. Marsoulas
15. La Haza	34. Tuc d'Audoubert
16. Covalanas	35. Les Trois Frères
17. Hornos de la Peña	36. Mas d'Azil
18. Penches	37. Le Portel
19. Atapuerca	38. Bédeilhac
20. Los Casares	39. Ussat
21. El Pendo	40. Niaux

large red animal figures at Lascaux with their black and dark brown heads must also be assigned to this period. A particularly characteristic FIG. 7 feature of Perigordian art at Lascaux is the 'twisted perspective' of the horns or antlers of bovidae or cervidae — i.e., these are not represented in profile, as is the case with the remainder of the body, but instead are viewed from the front. The technique of engraving develops on lines parallel to painting in this period. In the first stage drawings are executed on wet clay with the fingers; but soon there develop figures of animals depicted in a forceful naturalistic style. The legs are still rudimentarily suggested and the technique of drawing is still stiff, but all the potentialities are already at hand that are later to lead to splendidly life-like engravings of animals. Breuil also ascribes to the Perigordian period engravings in which the lines, at first shallow, gradually become deeper — as do those at Altamira, Pair-non-Pair and La Grèze (Dordogne). These form a transition to the magnificent bas-reliefs in the Dordogne and Charente area.

Solutrian-Magdalenian Up to the present day we know of no paintings that could unequivocally be ascribed to the Solutrian period. The early Magdalenian goes back to line drawings in black, which are frequently sketchy (Altamira, El Castillo, Le Portel and Niaux). To this group also belong the black tectiforms at Altamira. In the subsequent stage of development the line becomes wider and blurred; fine contour drawings executed with masterly skill are created; once again there is partial filling in, and the animals' coats are suggested by firm brush-strokes. This stage is best exemplified at Niaux, Pech-Merle and Le Portel. The body comes to be modelled more and more fully by application of colour, and is filled in with thin red and brown paint, or with black and red dots, as at Pech-Merle. The most advanced stage of Ice Age art, polychrome painting, has thus been reached. After fumbling beginnings it attains a magnificent peak of achievement, the first climax in the history of art, in the roof frescoes of Altamira, with their fine animal figures in shades of red and brown, outlined in black and accentuated by means of a burin. But Magdalenian art has now passed its zenith; it seems as though the Magdalenian artists had exhausted their powers. Ice Age art ends in an era of imitative work, of small line drawings which gradually become more and more stylized and schematized, until it eventually ceases completely in the Franco-Cantabrian area.

Parallel with the development of painting one can observe an efflorescence of modelling in relief after the middle Solutrian and during the early Magdalenian. Magnificent examples are to be found at Roc de Sers

(Charente) and Cap Blanc (Dordogne). The twisted perspective has here been abandoned. Engravings executed with masterly skill are super-imposed upon older ones dating from the Perigordian. An animal's coat is suggested by fine hatching. The most splendid animal figures from this period are furnished by the 'sanctuaire' of the Trois Frères cave (Ariège). At Tuc d'Audoubert (Ariège) and Montespan (Haute Garonne) the Mag-dalenian artists utilized the clay in the caves to create naturalistic works of animal sculpture.

Before going on to discuss the implements and materials used in the execution of rock paintings a few words may be said with regard to the problem of lighting. Frequently the paintings are situated in dark lateral passages, often at an immense distance from the entrance to the cave, as is the case, for instance, at Niaux or Bédeilhac (Ariège). Often it is a hazardous undertaking to walk about in a cave — for example, in Tuc d'Audoubert or Montespan. A light, as well as some sort of ladder or rope, are necessary to penetrate into certain caves. The problem of the lighting used by the artists cannot be answered simply. A few cupel-shaped lamps have been found, the best known of them at La Mouthe (Dordogne), which contained remains of some fatty substance. In the Pyrenean caves, particularly at Trois Frères, slabs of schistous sandstone have been discovered which are scorched at one end and coated with a carbonized mass. Presumably these slabs also contained a greasy substance, provided with a wick; this object must have been held in the hand by the opposite end and have served as a kind of torch. The use of torches is also suggested by the remains of charcoal that are to be found every-where in the caves. There is no doubt that the men who frequented the large caves were able both to provide lighting and to re-light a flame if it was put out by a draught or a drop of water.

For the various branches of Ice Age mural art a variety of instruments and materials were required. Paintings were occasionally executed with dry crayon, but usually with a liquid paste.

After the end of the Mousterian period, the last phase of Lower Palaeo-lithic culture, the strata often contain fragments of pigment. From these it appears that the Ice Age painter made most frequent use of ochre, from which he could obtain shades of colour ranging from a yellowish red through red to brown; in addition to this he used red chalk. Manganese ore and charcoal provided him with black for his palette. White was probably never used, while green and blue are entirely lacking in Ice Age painting. Violet tones have only been observed at Altamira. Red ochre has even been found sharpened into crayons, which we

IMPLEMENTS
AND TECHNIQUE

Mousterian

25

may assume were used in the manner of pastels. As a rule, however, the colours were ground to a fine powder to which oily or greasy substances were later added. Blood and albumen may have been used as binders. The paste thus made was then applied to the rock surface. Fingers, frayed twigs or tufts of feathers may have served in place of a brush. Occasionally the paint was also blown directly on to the wall with the mouth, a practice still found among Australian aborigines today. The distribution of fine grains of pigment over the surface of many paintings bears witness to the use of this technique.

The engravings were cut into the rock by means of flint burins, such as are to be found in large numbers everywhere. In the case of some high reliefs which were cut deep into the stone stronger tools were required. Finds in early Magdalenian strata in the Dordogne point to the use of enormous stone picks.

ORIGIN AND
SIGNIFICANCE
OF ICE AGE ART

The origins of art in the Late Ice Age are shrouded in the deepest obscurity and the present state of our knowledge allows us to give only an outline sketch here. The development of art must undoubtedly have been preceded by the notion of the similarity between two living beings, whilst impulses must also have radiated from the oldest of the arts, that of drama. For already in his dances primitive man imitated living creatures, i.e., he copied their habits, gestures and mimicry. As is the case among primitive peoples still today, the mask or its image can become a completely independent being conferring magic powers upon its wearer.

Another impetus towards artistic creation may have come from the realm of hunting. Every day the Ice Age hunter came across the tracks left in the soil by wild animals, which could be imitated artificially. This may have induced man first to reproduce his own hands, and this may in turn have given him the idea of drawing lines on the clay with his fingers or painting on a rock wall with fingers steeped in clay. At first purely accidental, such action will soon have acquired a purpose: a tangle of lines will gradually have led to arabesques and winding meanders, and at some point from these designs the silhouette of an animal will have been born.

Homo sapiens

The birth of art occurred in the Upper Palaeolithic age, some 30,000 years ago, when the last great glaciation spread over Europe. A new race of man, the so-called *homo sapiens,* immigrated into this part of the world, superseding the older and more primitive human types. This man must have had latent within him the talent necessary in order to produce works of art.

During the last Ice Age man lived amidst an environment dominated by mighty wild beasts, including mammoths, rhinoceroses, bisons, aurochs,

Polychrome standing bison, with hind quarters of three other bisons. Magdalenian. Detail from roof paintings in the picture gallery at Altamira.

wild horses, musk-oxen and reindeer, not to mention cave-bears, tigers and lions. Throughout his life man received strong visual and dynamic impressions from the dangers to which he was exposed in his daily struggle with these animals. From this also resulted his unique knowledge of the animal world, which alone was capable of inspiring artists to reproduce these creatures in monumental and lifelike form.

The representation of animals on the walls of caves in France and Spain could, however, not have derived merely from the inspiration of a few individuals. This was no 'art for art's sake', although pure delight in beauty should not be excluded; but ultimately, as was the case also in later epochs, it existed against the background of the religious and social obligations and interests of the community to which the artist belonged. Ice Age art gives profound expression to the social and religious structure of the culture of the hunters who lived during that period. For the tribe to survive a certain stock of wild animals was always essential. There had to be sufficient quantities available, and it was a matter of concern that the stock of animals, decimated by hunting and natural causes, should continually be replenished. As in all hunter cultures, recourse was had to magic, to the performance of death and fertility rites. This is the only explanation for the fact that the paintings are located deep in the interior of caves and are often superposed on one another. For Ice Age man, as for hunter peoples of the present day or those that died out not long ago, the governing factor will have been similar: by confining the animal within the limits of a painting one subjected it to one's power in the hunting grounds.

It may be assumed that the Ice Age artists, who were trained in a kind of 'art school', were simultaneously the tribal magicians and the only men privileged to have access to the subterranean art stations. Here they performed the magic rites essential to the survival of the tribe.

SIX LARGE CAVES   We will now turn to the six caves at Altamira, Font-de-Gaume, Les Combarelles, Lascaux, Niaux and Trois Frères, which contain the finest works of Franco-Cantabrian art. Brief mention will be made of caves and rock-shelters in France, Spain and Italy.

Altamira   This cave is situated 19 miles from Santander, not far from the small town of Santillana del Mar in northern Spain. With its splendid frescoes it still takes pride of place, alongside Lascaux, among all the Franco-Cantabrian art stations — just as it did when it was first discovered almost a hundred years ago. Altamira extends for 300 yards into the heart of a limestone massif, but the famous paintings are to be found in the so-

Fig. 1 — Hind. Engraving. Altamira. Length 7 ft. 4½ in.

called 'picture gallery' only about thirty yards from the entrance. Its height is in some parts no more than six or seven feet, so that one can best view the paintings when lying down. This explains why the child Maria Sautuola was the first to notice them. In the deep interior of the cave there are other paintings in black and red, as well as engravings originating from different periods, distributed irregularly over the walls.

The frescoes on the roof of the picture gallery are better preserved than any of the others. There are 25 polychrome figures here, most of them painted in red ochre, and the others in brown and black. The animals are painted almost life-size and measure fifteen yards in length. They are mainly bisons, their contours being accentuated in parts by engraving. Between them other animals can be identified with slightly modelled body surfaces and contour lines in black, superimposed on even older pictures. The roof is covered by numerous signs, partly club-shaped and partly scalariform. On the right-hand side of the frieze there are to be seen several unfinished polychrome paintings, as well as older animal figures in a light shade of red, groups of dots and a small series of painted human hands.

PLATE P. 27

The technique of these polychrome paintings attains a higher degree of perfection than any others in Franco-Cantabrian art. For painting the bodies of the animals the artists made use of charcoal and ochre, which afforded them shades of colour ranging from yellow through red to brown. Remains of pigment sharpened like crayons have been found in the archaeological strata of the cave. The outline of the pictures was first of all drawn with a fine black line. In this way the artist obtained a rough sketch which he could now proceed to fill in with colour and model. Shortly before the work was completed certain details such as the eye, horns, nostrils and parts of the hooves were accentuated with a burin, which in most cases was also used beforehand to make the contour line wider. After the colour had been applied, the paintings must sometimes have been washed and scraped to produce finer shadings of colour and still more delicate and harmonious effects. With such simple means the Ice Age artist was able to model the surface of the body, and to distribute light and shade by delicately contrasting the colours. He succeeded in depicting the animals in their habitual attitudes: here we see almost life-size bisons, some standing erect, while others are portrayed lying on the ground, galloping at full speed, or slowly stealing along. But the artists did not rest content with this. There is another factor that contributes to the moving vigour of these animal figures. The roof of the large chamber is not flat and smooth, but has bulges, small protuberances and uneven patches. With the aid of paint the artist was able to incorporate the natural relief of the rock into the bodies of the animals in such parts as the head, rump or crupper, thus making them extremely realistic. At Altamira the representations are mostly of bisons, followed by wild horses, hinds, stags, ibexes and wild boars, less frequently by aurochs, and extremely rarely by elks and wolves.

PLATE P. 31   All these animals are painted in a naturalistic style, and with elaborate care and accuracy. The bisons range in length from 4 ft. 6 in. to 6 ft. The magnificent hind to the left of the series of frescoes is 7 ft. 4 in. in length.

One would look in vain for scenic compositions at Altamira. These are almost completely absent from Franco-Cantabrian art. Each animal portrayed on the roof of the gallery forms an entity of its own; although they are sometimes depicted in groups side by side, there is no scenic connection between the individual animals.

Superpositions are rarely to be found in the gallery. The polychrome figures constitute the most recent layer in the Altamira paintings. In

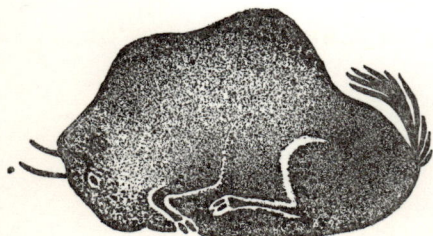

Fig. 2 — Crouching bison. Painting. Altamira. Length 5 ft. 1 in.

30

Head and neck of a polychrome hind. Below, on the right, small bison in outline. From the picture gallery, Altamira. *Length of hind 7 ft. 4½ in.*

many places they have been painted on top of older figures and are not themselves covered by paintings or engravings. At the most some of the comb-shaped red signs between the polychrome paintings may be thought to date from the same period, or to be more recent.

The polychrome paintings are the work of the Upper Magdalenian period, which may be dated circa 12,000 B.C.

Altamira also harbours some extremely fine engravings; one may merely mention the magnificent heads of hinds, bisons and stags, all of them belonging to the later Magdalenian period.

Font-de-Gaume Font-de-Gaume, one of the most lavishly decorated art stations on French soil, is situated in the Beune valley, a side-valley of the Vézère, approximately half a mile from Les Eyzies. A narrow corridor measuring over 100 yards in length, it extends deep into the mountain and has several lateral galleries branching off from the main passage. The main gallery in parts reaches the considerable height of 23 to 26 ft. The first pictures are found 70 yards from the entrance at a spot where daylight no longer penetrates. Some works nearer the entrance may possibly have been destroyed in the course of time by atmospheric influences. At Font-de-Gaume some 200 pictures can be deciphered, though at times only with difficulty. Among the best representations is one of the finest friezes of the cave: a series of polychrome bisons, on some of which small, very delicately engraved mammoths are superimposed. These animal pictures are accompanied by tectiforms, which are unfortunately in a poor state of preservation. The bisons are painted in red and brown, the horns, eye, dorsal line and muzzle being accentuated by means of deeply engraved strokes. 16 feet further along one may discern parts of a fine frieze continuing along the left-hand wall as far as the 'chamber of small bisons'. At one point there is a rendering of two magnificent reindeer facing one another. From their antlers and their demeanour they appear to be male and female: the buck seems to be scenting the head of the hind. In this case, too, use was made of red and brown to fill in the bodies and of the burin to accentuate the contour lines. Another frieze of polychrome bisons adorns the right-hand wall of the main gallery. This also comprises fine reproductions of several small horses, a wolf and a reindeer. In the 'chamber of small bisons' the walls and roof are covered with pictures of these animals. Some of them are painted in a uniform black shade, or in brown, and there are also figures painted in more than one colour. The remains of oxen painted in black and brown seem to date from an earlier epoch. After this chamber the main gallery comes to an end in a narrow corridor, the walls of which are covered with a variety of polychrome

THE STONE AGE

ART OF THE WORLD

A SERIES OF REGIONAL HISTORIES

OF THE VISUAL ARTS

I. INDIA by Hermann Goetz

II. INDONESIA by Frits A. Wagner

III. AFRICA by Elsy Leuzinger

IV. CHINA by Werner Speiser

V. THE STONE AGE by H. G. Bandi and others

pictures. Noteworthy among them is the engraved figure of a feline animal facing several horses, and particularly that of a rhinoceros, a typical denizen of Europe during the Ice Age, reproductions of which are rarely met with in cave art. The woolly-haired rhinoceros is outlined in red, the hair being suggested by hatching along the contour line. The horn is clearly visible. This figure is undoubtedly from the Aurignacian period. On the right-hand wall of the main gallery there is also a picture of a black reindeer that is worth mentioning, although its head can hardly be identified; to the right of it there follows a bison, likewise painted in black, the hind quarters of which are formed by the relief of the rock. In Font-de-Gaume tectiform signs are repeatedly found in various shapes, some painted and others engraved. According to Breuil these may be renderings of Palaeolithic dwellings, the roofs of which were covered with branches or dried grass.

PLATE P. 34

The works of art at Font-de-Gaume derive from several prehistoric periods during which changes took place not only in the human settlement but also in the fauna and flora of the area. There are numerous superposed pictures at Font-de-Gaume, making it possible to distinguish clearly the chronological sequence of the various styles of painting. This shows that the cave was frequented by human beings during all periods of the Upper Palaeolithic. Breuil's summary of the animal types depicted at Font-de-Gaume is of interest: according to him there are 80 bisons, 40 wild horses, 23 mammoths, 17 reindeer and cervidae, 8 aurochs, 2 rhinoceroses, one or two felines, one wolf and one bear. Breuil believes that rhinoceroses, felines, bears and ibexes inhabited the Dordogne area during the first third or quarter of the Upper Palaeolithic; the aurochs was extant from the beginning but not permanently; the reindeer was likewise extant during all periods, whereas the bison was only seldom featured at the beginning, but predominates over the other animals towards the end. The rhinoceros, feline, cave-bear and possibly also the ibex became extinct before the end of the Ice Age or else migrated to other areas; the mammoth reappeared from time to time after periods of absence, and horses were particularly plentiful at the beginning of Ice Age art. Breuil dates the pictures to the early and middle Magdalenian period, while some of them may already belong to the Aurignacian-Perigordian cycle.

Les Combarelles

The cave of Les Combarelles is situated in a precipitous limestone rock face not far from Font-de-Gaume, only a few miles from Les Eyzies. The cave consists of two low narrow galleries, which meet in a fairly spacious antechamber. It is, however, only the left-hand gallery that has yielded mural art of importance. The cave extends for over 250 yards into the heart of the mountain; at one time it was a subterranean stream, which had, however, dried up by the time of Ice Age man. Les Combarelles is one of the few caves where finds are restricted to engravings, the traces of painting being quite insignificant. The first of the pictures, which number several hundreds, adorn the walls some 75 yards from the entrance. It is difficult to pick out the individual figures from the vast tangle of lines and strokes. Out of 300 pictures 291 have been deciphered, while some 100 representations have only been preserved in part and can no longer be identified. Breuil puts the number of figures counted at Combarelles at 116 horses, 37 bisons, 19 bears, 14 reindeer, 13 mammoths, 9 ibexes, 7 head of cattle, 5 stags, 3 hinds, 5 lions, 4 wolves, one fox and 39 figures of human beings.

When one examines the pictures at Combarelles in greater detail the contours and lines suddenly come to life, and there appear magnificent animal figures that rank among the finest products of the Ice Age.

Black bison. On the left a reindeer walking away. Magdalenian. From the main gallery, Font-de-Gaume.

Drawn in a flowing style, the majority of the pictures probably belong to the Magdalenian period, but at the same time one should not overlook the more ancient and rigid pictures dating from the Aurignacian.

Some of the engravings of mammoths and horses are magnificent. In the case of the horses alone Breuil distinguishes between four different species. An enormous bear conveys an impression of great strength. The splendid feline, now famous, can easily be identified, despite a thick covering of calcareous deposit. Its hind quarters are raised up; the upper part of the thigh is vigorous and muscular, the shoulder-blades project outwards, and the body is squat and strong. The head, as well as the chest, paws and stomach are all worked in bas-relief. There are some other pictures of felines at Combarelles, but an exact identification of these animals is usually very difficult, since they really resemble lions rather than tigers and are rarely portrayed in Franco-Cantabrian art. Mention may also be made of a striding reindeer and a mammoth with thick fur and an involute trunk.

The human beings depicted at Combarelles, though no more than mediocre from an artistic point of view, are all the more significant from the standpoint of cultural history. As is the case in other caves, they give the impression of men wearing animal masks. Among the most grotesque figures is a human silhouette with a mammoth's head and greatly elongated arms, which may perhaps suggest tusks. Elsewhere a male figure appears to be following a woman, and the head of a bearded man is distinctly discernible. There must be some deeper reason for the fact that these figures of human beings are always represented in an unskilful manner, whereas elaborate care is bestowed upon the pictures of animals. One of the reasons may be the great reluctance of primitive man to depict his own image and thus place himself in the hands of a magic-working enemy. In the majority of cases, however, the idea was to represent masks used in hunting or rites which personified mythical beings and were connected with some magic cult. Scenes of a phallic

Fig. 4 — Lion. Wall engraving. Les Combarelles. Length 2 ft. 3½ in.

Fig. 3 — Horse. Wall engraving. Les
Combarelles. Length 2 ft. 9½ in.

nature are rare but, where they occur, according to
Breuil, they may bear relation to magic fertility rites.
All the finest engravings at Combarelles are assigned
by Breuil to the early and middle Magdalenian
period. Combarelles serves as a perfect illustration of
the fact that the cave could not possibly have been used
for human habitation. Leaving the entrance out of account, the narrow
interior of the cave is dark and damp, and settlement there can never have
been feasible. The pictures on the walls will therefore not have been drawn
for decorative effect or purely for their own sake. Only a few members of
the tribe could have been present in the narrow corridor at the same time.
Combarelles shows more clearly than many other caves that the pictures
must have been produced as part of some magic ritual performed by a
few select representatives of the tribe.

Lascaux Lascaux was not discovered until the relatively recent date of 1940. For
this reason it appears to surpass everything previously attained in Franco-
Cantabrian mural art. The pictures are in a wonderful state of preservation, and the dazzling brilliance of the colours is hardly credible to an
observer coming from caves in which the paintings have already faded.
The pictures in the vast chamber and the adjoining gallery are applied
upon a light shimmering ground which sets off in strong contrast the
various shades of red, yellow, brown and black.
The cave is situated in a limestone massif above the Vézère valley, just
over a mile from the village of Montignac. Directly upon entering we
find the picture gallery, which measures 33 yards in length and 11 yards
in width; its walls are adorned right up to the roof with magnificent animal
paintings. At the end of the chamber a small gallery opens up, which
continues in the same direction as the chamber and loses itself in the
inner depths of the mountain; its walls and roof are also decorated with
magnificent frescoes. On returning to the main chamber one's eye alights
upon the opening to a gallery in the right-hand wall, leading to a part
of the cave situated at a somewhat higher level: this part of the cave has
numerous engravings. Right at the rear the 'apse' of the so-called 'nave',

Two small horses, with hind legs of a third animal. Above, on the left, part of a black cow, painted over an older figure in red, is just recognizable. Aurignacian-Perigordian. Lascaux. *Width 5 ft. 6 in.*

an extension of the gallery in the shape of a chamber, leads to a shaft some 23 feet deep through which the visitor clambers down into a lower gallery. In this part one of the few narrative compositions of Ice Age art has been discovered: a badly wounded bison, its flank pierced by a lance, its horns lowered ready for the charge, and before it, sketched as always with a few strokes, the figure of a man is seen prostrate on the ground; in the foreground is a bird on a perch, and to the left a rhinoceros can be seen moving away. The whole composition is drawn in black, with the lines slightly blurred. It has been interpreted in many different ways; it is probably either a tragedy of the chase or a scene of a magic ritual character.

Of the paintings in the picture gallery and the adjoining gallery the finest examples may be mentioned here. The large chamber is also referred

to as 'the chamber of the aurochs' after the very striking figures portrayed here. Three gigantic pictures of such aurochs and parts of a fourth animal form the decoration around the walls. These figures, measuring up to 18 ft. in length, are unique phenomena in Ice Age art. The contours are painted in black, with flowing lines; the inner surface of the bodies is filled in with black colour, or black dots, particularly along the belly-line, the muzzle and legs. The horns and hooves of the aurochs are twisted round and treated in the same plane as the body, i.e., the painter could not as yet visualize them in normal perspective, but represented them in twisted perspective, this being a characteristic feature of the Aurignacian-Perigordian style. These aurochs overlap with an older group of wild oxen, painted over evenly in dark red. Stylistically the so-called 'unicorn', the most curious animal at Lascaux, must be ascribed to this group of aurochs. It is the first figure on the left-hand wall of the large chamber. The contour lines are rugged and sharp, the body and legs are powerful, and the animal gives the impression of being with young. It bears most resemblance to an ox or a rhinoceros, but the small head, from which two long straight shafts protrude, belongs wholly to the realm of legend. The chest and back are dappled and the tail is quite short. This is either some mythical animal or a human being in animal disguise. It is not the

Fig. 6 — 'Swimming stags'. Lascaux. Length of frieze 16 ft. 4 in.

only mythical creature to be found in Franco-Cantabrian art, but probably the most striking one.

Between the two aurochs that face each other on the left-hand wall there are several small stags with fully-developed antlers; they too are painted in dark red, and seem to be contemporaneous with the small oxen. Superposed on the aurochs nearest to the unicorn is a fairly large horse, with the body painted in a dark reddish brown, but the head, mane and legs in black. In front of it, and opposite the head of the second ox, are the head and back of a similar horse. Below these horses we can see a group of relatively small, very dark galloping horses, which resemble the black ponies in the adjoining gallery. Here the shaggy horses are topped by a large cow that appears to be leaping towards a lattice-like sign. It is painted in black over an older figure in red. The superimposition of the two colours gives the animal an almost polychrome character. Also worthy of note in this gallery are the very fine horses with small dark heads and bodies painted in light red, on some of which the hair is indicated, as well as several cows in reddish brown. In between them are remains of older figures as well as a great number of these lattice-like signs in several variations. Were they supposed to suggest traps or game preserves?

PLATE P. 3

PLATE P. 37

Fig. 8 — Large cow. Painting in red and black. Lascaux. Length 9 ft. 2¼ in.

FIG. 6 In the lateral gallery engravings prevail, although paintings are not infrequent. The picture of several stags swimming has become famous: the animals appear to be crossing a river one behind the other; only the contours of the heads, in black, with gigantic antlers, and parts of the necks are shown. (The herd measures 16 ft. 6 in. in width). On an opposite wall there are several wild horses and two fine bisons in dark brown, the flank of the animal on the left being in red; the animals stand with their hind legs opposite one another.

Prominent among the engravings in this part of the cave is a mighty stag. Also noteworthy are an elaborately engraved head of a horse and a very fine lion. The outlines of the black horses and polychrome lattice-like signs are engraved.

At Lascaux, in addition to the well-known painting techniques in which the artist employs his finger or a brush, finely pulverized pigments were

Two black bisons with black and red arrows drawn on their bodies. Above, on the left, a third bison, of which the dorsal line is formed by a rock ledge. Below, on the left, a large horse, and in the centre a small equine animal. Salon noir, Niaux. *Length of bisons 3 ft. 11 in. and 4 ft. 2 in.*

blown on to the rock. If one examines the contours of many animals exactly, one can see that these consist of round spots which merge into one another. This technique, hitherto only known from silhouettes of hands, was chiefly employed for the colouring of horses' manes. The 'twisted perspective', a feature absent from Magdalenian and Upper Solutrian art, shows that the Lascaux pictures can be assigned to the later Aurignacian-Perigordian period, an attribution also borne out by other stylistic features. The art of this epoch reaches its zenith at Lascaux, and attests — apart from some paintings, where primitive features are still evident — to a masterly skill in the execution of the pictures, which occasionally attain monumental proportions. The variety of the techniques that follow upon one another at short intervals suggests that these experienced and imaginative artists must have been possessed by a kind of creative frenzy. The art of Lascaux is indeed great, and in its way perfect.

This gigantic cave, overlooking a valley in the Pyrenees, is situated 2½ *Niaux* miles from the small town of Tarascon-sur-Ariège. Tourists and local inhabitants have flocked to visit it since the 17th century, and have left their names upon its walls. The paintings in the famous 'salon noir' were discovered by Dr. Garrigou as early as 1866, but no special significance PLATE P. 40 was attached to them. It was not until 1906, after Ice Age art had been recognized as authentic, that attention was once again paid to these black line paintings, which are in an excellent state of preservation.

Passing along a narrow corridor, the visitor to Niaux arrives at the first chamber, which has a small lake, usually filled with water. 668 yards from the entrance a corridor leads into a vast chamber, the roof of which gradually becomes lower. In this part of the cave one may already find a number of varied signs, such as red and black dots or groups of lines. The visitor proceeds through chambers of red and yellow marble, which is often brightly polished; elsewhere stalactites may be seen cascading down from precipitous walls and roofs that lose themselves in the darkness. After a chamber filled with various sorts of sand, the visitor finds himself in the 'salon noir', which has the finest pictures in the cave. It was at this

Fig. 9 — Bison with arrows drawn on. Niaux. Length 3 ft. 3 in.

Head of bison, engraved in clay. Magdalenian. Niaux. *Total length of animal 1 ft. 10¾ in.*

spot that one of the explorers, Molard, came across flint implements and remains of bones in a state of decomposition. All the pictures are drawn in a wonderful flowing style with black contour lines; the hair of the animals is indicated by hatching, and the horns and hooves are rendered in natural perspective. These pictures, of the bisons in particular, as well as those of the horses, ibexes and stags, are among the finest examples of Magdalenian art. Breuil assigns them to the middle and late Magdalenian periods. The figures of an earlier date were drawn in the linear technique. Later, as the style became more fluent, artists also made use of rock projections to model animal bodies in relief. The most important group of pictures in the 'salon noir' is that of several bisons, which appear to have been pierced by arrows — apparently connected with a magic hunting rite. A rare feature in Franco-Cantabrian art are the engravings at Niaux, cut into the clay. Thus on the floor of the 'salon noir' the discovery was made of engravings of a particularly fine bison as well as two trout, one of the best renderings of fish handed down to us from the Ice Age. At the end of the 'salon noir', which is situated 840 yards from the entrance, the cave continues into the innermost recesses of the rock, where one still finds some remains of bison figures in black, as well PLATE P. 42 as a few signs and animal pictures in red. Right at the end of the cave of Niaux there is a placid lake; not the slightest movement of air ripples its calm surface.

This cave is situated near Montesquieu-Avantès, on the estate of Count *Trois Frères* Bégouen. In 1914, two years after the discovery of the cave of Tuc d'Audoubert (see below), Henri Bégouen and his three sons discovered the second of the two great art stations on their land: the cave of the Three Brothers, or Trois Frères. Deep in its interior, in a chamber known as the 'sanctuaire', are the most important paintings of the cave. This chamber, the floor of which drops steeply, has on its walls a vast number of overlapping engravings, partly originating from the Aurignacian and Perigordian, and partly from the best phases of the Magdalenian period.

Fig. 10 — Ibex. Niaux. Length 1 ft. 8½ in.

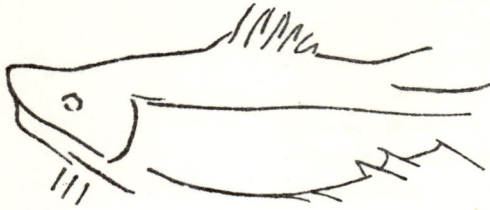

The lines of the engravings are often cut deep into the rock, so that the dark incisions stand out like cameos against the light background. Here Breuil has made copies of some magnificent bison figures, mighty stags, a large number of reindeer, bears' heads, horses, ibexes, and at the entrance to the 'sanctuaire' two large lions' heads, viewed from the front, which suggest two guardian figures. On the right-hand wall of the chamber lies a mammoth drawn in an archaic manner, with the dorsal line breaking off sharply, and a bear pierced by many holes, with blood pouring forth from its muzzle. In other parts of the cave explorers came across a rendering of two snowy owls from the Aurignacian period.

In one part of the 'sanctuaire' one can distinguish a bison with human hind quarters and behind it a dancing figure wearing a bison's head, but depicted in an erect attitude. This is presumably a human being in animal disguise, who is shown holding a longish instrument in his hands and putting it to his mouth. This may possibly be a flute. There are several 'magician' figures of this type in the 'sanctuaire'; between the animal paintings there are also small distorted human faces, which Breuil interprets as animals' souls. It is here, too, that we find the most curious rendering of man-and-beast in Ice Ace art: the 'magician of Trois Frères', who looks down from a height of 13 feet on one wall of the 'sanctuaire', seemingly ruling over the whole vast concourse of animals and half-human, half-animal creatures.

One stag has a long beard hanging right down to its chest and small round eyes staring from its face; its forelegs are raised up and its hind legs perform a dance; the genital organ is clearly marked and the head is crowned by gigantic antlers. Black brush-strokes serve to accentuate the individual parts of the body, but the contours, on the other hand, are engraved. The Magdalenian artist may have regarded this figure as the focus of all his paintings. Was it the Great Spirit, master of the animals, who disposed of all matters pertaining to hunting and fertility?

The vast cave of Baume-Latrone is situated some 8½ miles from Nîmes on the left bank of the river Gard. Its paintings were discovered in 1940. All of them are housed in a chamber situated 260 yards from the entrance. First of all a number of representations of human hands, mainly left hands, were noticed on the roof of this chamber. Soon explorers also observed the curious paintings. They are animal figures, quite archaic in style, drawn on the wall with fingers dipped in clay, recalling those found in the Andalusian cave of La Pileta. We can distinguish some six or seven elephants measuring up to 4 ft. 9 in. in length, as well as a rhinoceros and a snake. The trunks of the elephants are rendered by strange zigzag lines; the snake is 9 ft. 9 in. long, and its head resembles that of a bear with its jaws opened in a threatening manner. At Baume-Latrone there are also some representations dating from a more advanced phase of development, executed in a linear style, but both they and the paintings done with the fingers may probably be ascribed to an early stage of the Aurignacian.

Elephant, drawn with several fingers. Early Aurignacian. Baume-Latrone.

Chabot In 1878 the teacher L. Chiron discovered the cave of Chabot, situated near the town of St. Martin d'Ardèche. In an antechamber where daylight could still penetrate the explorer came across numerous deeply-incised engravings. But it was not until Ice Age art had found recognition that they were brought to notice and deciphered. They are engravings of mammoths; in 1928 Breuil discovered more figures of horses, ibexes and mammoths, all of them archaic in style. Similar engravings are to be found in the adjoining cave of Le Figuier. Here, as at Chabot, Upper Palaeolithic strata were encountered.

Ebbou The pictures at this cave, also situated in the Ardèche gorge, were discovered by Abbé Glory in 1946. In addition to the representation of a hand in red near the entrance, Glory came across 70 engravings in a chamber 71 yards long and about 16 yards wide; he was able to identify 24 horses, 12 aurochs, 2 bisons, one mammoth and several ibexes. Each of these figures has only one pair of legs; the horns of the aurochs are depicted in twisted perspective, and a sense of perspective is also lacking in the treatment of the stags' antlers.

While dealing with Ebbou mention may also be made of engravings in a similar style found in the Ardèche caves of Colombier and Oullins. Not far from the Pont-du-Gard, approximately 6 miles north-east of Nîmes, Abbé Bayol found in a cave which has been named after him a line drawing of an ibex in red as well as several representations of hands. These paintings and other remains of red pigment point to an archaic style.

Le Portel This cave is situated close to the farm of that name, not far from the railway-station of Varilhes. The paintings were discovered in 1908 by Dr. Jeannel. The owner of the cave, M. Vézian, carried out several excavations in the course of which he recovered finds dating from the middle Magdalenian period. It is not easy to gain access to the cave; it is entered through a narrow low corridor which descends sharply; the floor is damp and clayey, and it is only at the back of the cave that it becomes more even and easier to walk upon. It is here that the paintings are to be found; they are in a corridor 65 yards long leading into some vast chambers, from which several galleries branch off. At the rear of the first corridor on the left-hand wall there are various niches in which several signs in red have been observed, one of which could be the representation of a large hand. Next to it is a recumbent red reindeer, painted in a linear style, with the antlers shown in 'twisted perspective'. The right-hand wall has several almost faded fragments of pictures, the head of a bison outlined in black, an owl with a large round head and disproportionate body, and a fine black pony.

46

Two bisons. On the left, hind quarters of a third animal. Magdalenian. Breuil gallery, Le Portel.

In the following left-hand gallery there are two pictures of human beings with grotesque faces. There are also some fine horses painted in a soft brown colour; their archaic style recalls the dappled horses of Pech-Merle as well as some figures at Lascaux. The central gallery, named after F. Regnault, contains a small horse painted in red and a badly drawn ox. Almost all the pictures in this part of the cave are painted either in black or sepia, and judging from their style may be dated to the Aurignacian-Perigordian period. Figures of horses predominate, but bisons are no rarity. The finest representations of horses at Le Portel are located at the rear of this gallery; they are painted in black, with the paint encroaching upon the inner surface of the animals' bodies, giving the effect of modelling; this makes it possible to attribute it to the middle Magdalenian. Further along is the Breuil gallery, named after its discoverer, where numerous scratches testify to the fact that it was once inhabited by cavebears. On the right-hand wall in the front part of the gallery there are several engravings executed in the Magdalenian style, among them a fine rendering of a bison and one of a horse pierced by an arrow. The picture of two bisons facing each other may be accounted one of the finest works at Le Portel. They are outlined in black, and the body of the animal on the right shows a tendency towards modelling through the spreading of the paint inwards. The horns are drawn in natural perspective. Breuil dates these animals to the early Magdalenian.

Thus the two great art cycles are clearly represented in this cave: relatively early Aurignacian-Perigordian and early Magdalenian.

Tuc d'Audoubert

On the estate of the Bégouen family near Montesquieu-Avantès there is, as well as Trois Frères, the vast cave of Tuc d'Audoubert. The three Bégouen brothers penetrated into the cave, which is watered by a small stream, the Volp, by means of a home-made canoe. The Volp flows into the open out of one chamber of the cave after having cut its way for just over a mile through the subterranean rock, and it was thus that the cave was formed many millennia ago, before it was frequented either by cave-bears or by man. It was from this chamber that the explorers succeeded in penetrating into the cave. In one small gallery they came across fine engravings of horses and bisons, a small reindeer, and several arrows and club-shaped signs. But the most significant works were found deep in the interior of the upper cave: in the centre of the last chamber, 765 yards from the entrance, were two unique sculptures of bisons, propped against a ledge of rock. They are male and female: the bull is depicted following the scent of the cow. Both sculptures, fashioned by the artist in the soft clay of the rock floor, have something fascinatingly lifelike about them and thousands of years ago must undoubtedly have served a purpose in some fertility rites performed here in the interior of the cave. There is another characteristic which marks this chamber out as a place of worship during the Ice Age: in the clay floor marks were found left by human feet, which judging by their size must have been those of youths no more than 15 years of age. These footprints, the surface of which was covered and protected by a hard coating of clay, automatically bring to mind the initiation ceremonies that play so important a part in tribal life, when the youth who has attained manhood is accepted into the adult community. Visitors to the cave, which incidentally is not greatly frequented owing to the difficulty of access to it, report that they experienced an eerie and stirring feeling when they entered this ancient place of worship of Magdalenian man.

PLATE P. 62

Montespan

The cave complex of Montespan extends for over half a mile as the crow flies between the villages of Ganties and Montespan. The galleries measure in all some 2750 yards in length. The cave is watered by a small river, the Hountao, which makes movement within it extremely difficult. The engravings and sculptures were discovered in 1923 by the explorers N. Casteret and H. Godin. Parts of the cave are today permanently under water, which was probably not the case during the drier Magdalenian era. The upper part of the cave, in the direction of Ganties, yields the first engraving after 230 yards. This is a rearing horse; there are also figures of three horses, a mule and a bird. The horns of the 8 bisons are curved and rendered in natural perspective. In another dry gallery several interesting engravings can be noted, e.g.: a fine horse's head with a mane elaborately engraved in clay and a delicately curved neck-line. Further along on the right-hand side the wall gives the impression of being perforated by spearheads, and other similar holes, cut rather crudely deep into the clay, pierce the horse depicted close by. Undoubtedly we have here traces of some magic practice: weapons must have been thrown at these animal pictures to ensure the success of a hunting expedition.

Back view of a headless bear, modelled in clay. Montespan. *Length 3 ft. 7¹/₃ in.*

The second part of the cave, situated at a lower level, is of greater significance from an artistic point of view but is only accessible if the visitor is inclined to take a bath in the icy water of the river. After covering a distance of some 110 yards he finds himself in a gallery which is no longer under water. On the walls of this gallery, which measures 175 yards in length, numerous engravings are distributed irregularly. Owing to the damp they are not in a good state of preservation. Breuil mentions 4 complete horses, 4 bisons and one bovine animal. In addition to these he deciphered several heads of bisons and horses. All the engravings at Montespan date from a relatively early Magdalenian period.

But the highlight of this cave, as at Tuc d'Audoubert, are the clay sculptures. There are several less significant specimens, such as the horses, that should rather be classified as bas-reliefs; there are some sculptures which have been called lion statues; others have deteriorated so badly that they have completely lost their shape, and now only a heap of clay remains to testify to their past existence. But one small, relatively low chamber contains a sculpture modelled in the round representing a bear, of which the head, however, is missing. This sculpture measures 2 ft. in

PLATE P. 49

height and 4 ft. 8 in. in length. The animal is rendered squatting, with its front paws stretched out and its hind legs pulled up under its belly. It is covered with a thin layer of sinter deposit. In the middle of its neck is a large hole, probably made for a wooden plug with which a real bear's head must have been affixed on top instead of one also modelled in clay. When the wood rotted the bear's head fell to the ground; the remains of this were found below the sculpture by the explorer Casteret. Once again the heavy perforation of the body is striking. This may probably be attributed to spears having been hurled at it as part of a magic rite.

From an artistic point of view this statue is of less value than those of Tuc d'Audoubert, but it is unique for the light it throws upon the magic rites practised by the Magdalenian hunters. It supplied Breuil with a solution to the problem why the figure of the bear at Trois Frères is studded with holes.

Gargas This cave is situated on the parish boundary between Aventignan and St. Bertrand de Comminges. The hill into which the cave extends lies above the left bank of the Garonne. Gargas is a great tunnel with several chambers. It was used at different times by man as a shelter. Since the 19th century it has frequently been visited by tourists. From 1887 onwards F. Regnault made excavations in the cave and within a short space of time he found numerous skeletons of cave-bears and other animals that

Red and black silhouettes of hands. Early Aurignacian. Gargas.

had met their end there. The excavations revealed a constant succession of Aurignacian and Perigordian strata.

A particular feature of this art station is the wealth of silhouettes of human hands to be found there. Shortly after entering the cave, in the first chamber, one's eye is caught by the silhouettes of human hands in black and red scattered over the wall on the left. Some of them, especially those near the entrance to the cave, are much faded, but in the interior, on the other hand, they are in a good state of preservation. There are also a great number of representations of hands on the walls of the three adjoining chambers. There are some 18 art stations in the Franco-Cantabrian area in which it has been possible to identify this curious element of Ice Age art. But nowhere are they so numerous as here at

PLATE P. 51

Gargas. The hands painted in red, black and yellow are the only coloured representations to be found in this cave, which is almost permanently damp. Two types of representations of hands may be distinguished in Ice Age art: one of these is the negative, or silhouette of the hand, such as is to be found at Gargas. This type is produced by the artist pressing his hand against the wall and blowing pigment from his mouth, or through a tube, on to the surrounding surface. In this way a sort of shadow-figure or silhouette is formed, i.e. the light colour of the hand stands out clearly against the brightly-coloured background, the fine-grained texture of which can only have been produced by blowing. Much less frequent, by contrast, are positives of hands. These were produced by the artist dipping his hand in paint and stamping it on the wall. Curiously enough, this very ancient custom of depicting hands is not restricted to Franco-Cantabrian Ice Age art, but is also found in numerous hunter cultures in America, Africa and Australia. It presumably served primitive man as a sort of personal symbol, a kind of signature which defined his relationship with other members of the tribe or with supernatural forces.

More than 150 representations of hands have been identified at Gargas. Those in red are frequently superposed by black ones, and are inferior in execution; they certainly date from an earlier period. In the case of hand silhouettes, it is generally the left hand that is shown, whereas in the case of positives it is generally the right hand. One explanation for this could be that, when making a negative, the pigment or the container for it was held in the right hand — assuming that Ice Age man was right-handed as we are today — and thus only the left hand was free for application, whereas to make a simple impression the free right hand could easily be used.

A unique feature at Gargas are the numerous representations of mutilated hands, i.e. in many cases one or more finger-joints are missing. In various parts of the cave representations have been noted of one particular mutilated hand. This custom is also found among several primitive peoples, who cut off parts of their fingers as a sacrifice or to signify mourning. Representations of mutilated hands have even been found in caves in southern Australia.

Besides these representations in colour at Gargas one may also find here another typical characteristic of the most ancient stage of artistic evolution: 'macaroni', which are, of course, only to be found on the clay walls and roof of the cave. The surface of these arabesques cut in the clay has been faultlessly oxydized and covered with a delicate film, which makes it possible to distinguish them from engravings made at a later date. This again illustrates distinctly the process whereby the first animal figures developed out of a tangle of lines; though still primitive, they are already inspired by a powerful sense of realism. A third group of figures comprises engravings where a burin was already used to cut the lines into the rock. From a stylistic point of view these representations of wild horses, ibexes, stags, oxen, bisons, mammoths and one marsh-bird are stylistically akin to the engravings in schist slabs excavated in Perigordian strata not far from the cave entrance.

This extensive tunnel cave has become famous through the excavations *Isturitz* carried out there by E. Passemard and the Comte de St. Perrier, who in the interior of the large north-west chamber found a great sequence of strata comprising all the cultures of the Upper Palaeolithic. In the Magdalenian strata in particular very fine portable art objects were discovered. In the centre of the chamber there stands an imposing stalagmite pillar with bas-reliefs cut by Magdalenian artists into its soft tuff. According to the evidence of the deposits that partially cover these reliefs they derive from the early Magdalenian and Upper Solutrian. In a general survey which he has made Breuil draws attention to a reindeer facing left; below this is a horse, whose body was completely buried by the layer, and below this animal a bear facing left in the same manner as the horse. On the left of the frieze there is a mighty reindeer superposed by two smaller stags.

This cave is situated to the west of the market town of Cabreret, over- *Pech-Merle* looking the Sagne, a small river. The exploration of this vast cave was undertaken between 1920 and 1922 by Abbé Lémozi and A. David, a local man. From the entrance, which was made at the time, the visitor soon passes a small low chamber, known as the 'ossuaire' (ossuary), in which the explorers came across the remains of bones of cave-bears. On the roof of this chamber very many faded silhouettes of human hands in red and series of red dots can be identified; there are also a number of 'macaroni' cut into the soft clay, and a very beautiful rendering of a large stag with impressive antlers. The 'great gallery' of Pech-Merle measures 153 yards in length and in some parts is 22 yards wide. Bizarre stalactite formations endow these chambers with a singular charm. It was here that Lémozi discovered the finest paintings and engravings. Noteworthy are three female figures of which copies were made by Breuil in 1924. They were drawn on the clay with the artist's finger; the women have pendulous breasts, their arms are summarily indicated, and they appear to be in a crouching attitude. Only one leg is shown, and in two figures the hair at the nape of the neck forms a queue. Not far away one can make out an enormous animal between the arabesques cut into the clay, which Breuil has identified as either a bison or a musk-ox. Above it is the seated figure of a man with no head, presumably holding an arrow in his arm. Some 33 yards from these very early Aurignacian figures one comes to the most accomplished pictures in the cave. Here the south wall of the 'great gallery' forms a hollow between two projections, known as the 'chapel of the mammoths'. The drawings in black stand out with wonderful clarity against the delicate reddish background of the rock. There are about ten mammoths, four head of cattle, two or three bisons and one horse. Below these pictures there are groups of red dots undoubtedly originating from the Aurignacian. The animals belong to one of the final phases of the Perigordian or to an archaic phase of the Magdalenian.

Frieze with black horses and black silhouettes of hands. Aurignacian-Perigordian. Pech-Merle. *Width of frieze 11 ft. 1¾ in.*

The twisted perspective occurs only in rudimentary fashion. The violent movement of a mammoth rearing in flight, seemingly seeking to escape from the deep abyss, has an affinity rather with the Perigordian style. The movements of the other animals are also portrayed in a vigorous realistic way, as at Niaux, Breuil is inclined to take the view that they were executed by an artist in an archaic style.

Almost opposite this 'chapel of the mammoths' is the 'chamber of black hands', where the paintings are completely different from those just mentioned and must certainly date from an earlier period. The frieze is situated 104 yards from the modern artificial entrance and is 11 feet wide and 6 ft. 3 in. high. The visitor finds himself confronted with two large horses framed by broad black lines, their bodies filled in with black dots. Their manes are painted in uniform black and the heads are strikingly small. To depict the head of the animal on the right the artist utilized a natural relief in the rock. Both horses are shown in foal. Along the dorsal line of the animal on the right a pike has been drawn in red, its back studded with small red dots. Below the horses are remains of an older animal figure in red. The two horses are framed by six elaborately executed silhouettes of hands in black. They represent left as well as right hands. According to Breuil this ensemble dates from the Aurignacian-Perigordian period. In another part of the 'great gallery' the silhouette of a hand in red, formed by 12 red dots, has been discovered. The small village of Sergeac is situated on the left bank of the Vézère, *Sergeac* not far from Montignac; close by, in a calc-spar, are the rock-shelters of Sergeac. The strata they contained were all from the Upper Palaeolithic and harboured paintings, engravings and sculptures. The rock-shelter of Blanchard, excavated between 1909 and 1911, yielded an inventory typical of the Aurignacian period, such as a boulder on which vulvae were incised; on another boulder are two bovidae outlined in black on a red ground. On the same side of the rock is the shelter of Castanet, in which several Aurignacian strata were unearthed. In the rock-shelter of Labattut several lumps of rock have fallen to the Perigordian level; they might therefore date from this period, but could equally well be older. In any case there is enough evidence at Labattut to permit the finds to be dated. On one of the boulders is a horse, represented in high relief; its four legs are suggested and it has a small head. Stylistically it brings to mind the pictures of horses at Lascaux. The finest figure is that of a stag of which only the head, neck and dorsal line have been preserved. The contours of the animal are drawn with superb skill in a flowing style, and the fine antlers are delineated in detail. There is undoubtedly a close affinity between these paintings and those at Lascaux and the Cantabrian caves, as well as those of the Spanish Levant.

Reverdit The rock-shelter of Reverdit, with its high reliefs, gives some useful guidance in determining the chronology of the Magdalenian period. The wall bears traces of a frieze which, however, has almost been destroyed by vegetation. One horse and three bisons may still be identified. Of greater importance are those parts of the frieze which are covered by deposit. Tools have been found here which may have been used to carve the reliefs.

Laussel A few miles from Les Eyzies is the small château of Laussel, near which is the rock-shelter of that name. Laussel contained several Upper Palaeolithic layers and five large bas-reliefs on stone slabs were excavated from refuse of the Perigordian period. The famous Venus of Laussel is one of the finest female figures known to Ice Age art. This sculpture once adorned a block of calcareous rock in the rear of the rock-shelter, from which it has been hewn out and transferred to a museum. The breasts are fully developed, as is the case in all Aurignacian sculptures of this kind; the hips protrude, and at shoulder level she appears to be holding in her right hand an incised bison's horn; the left hand is stretched out across the stomach. The face, turned towards the horn, is round and devoid of detail, and the hair too is shown in outline, resting upon the shoulders. The figure was elaborately worked and stands out from the stone in full plastic relief. Traces of ochre indicate that it was once coloured red; this is borne out by the evidence of other female statuettes dating from the Perigordian era.

Three other female figures found at Laussel are very similar to the Venus, but are somewhat smaller and have no horns in their hands. There is also a very beautiful male figure in profile, extraordinarily slender and shown without any genital organs. The man wears a girdle round his waist and appears to have once held an arrow or bow in his arms.

Cap Blanc Only half a mile below the small château of Laussel is the rock-shelter of Cap Blanc, situated in a part of the country that offers abundant evidence of Ice Age art. In 1911 the discovery was made here of two Magdalenian layers superposed upon one another, both belonging mainly to the early Magdalenian. The rock-shelter, which is 49 feet long, harbours a magnificent frieze of horses as well as figures of bisons. This monumental frieze, which extends along a wall at the rear of the rock-shelter, constitutes a highlight of Ice Age relief modelling. The finest animals measure up to 11¾ in. in depth. The figures are executed in a wonderfully plastic manner;

Horse. Magdalenian. From the large frieze at Cap Blanc.

unfortunately, however, some of them have deteriorated through weathering. The eyes are round and deeply incised; the bodies are fairly slender; the thigh-joints and parts of the chest provide distinct evidence of modelling; the manes are suggested by light hatching. Like the other bas-reliefs of the Dordogne and the Charente, that of Cap Blanc is dated by Breuil to the early Magdalenian.

In 1904, in the course of an excavation in the small cave of La Grèze, *La Grèze* Dr. Ampoulange discovered in a hollow in the left-hand wall, hidden beneath deposit, the famous engraving of a bison. The animal measures 23½ in. in length and is depicted entirely in profile, with the horns turned to the plane of the body. The outline is drawn sharply and distinctly; only one foreleg and one hind leg are visible, but no hooves. This work presumably dates from the Perigordian, although no typically Perigordian tool was found in the layer that covered it.

This cave is situated not far from the small town of Le Bugue. It has been *Barabao* known for a long time to the local population. The entrance is relatively large, but as one proceeds further the going becomes very difficult owing to masses of fallen rock and clay deposit. The paintings in the cave, which were discovered a short while ago, were examined in 1951 by Breuil and Windels, and later by Abbé Glory. With a certain amount of difficulty it is possible to identify some fairly large animal figures engraved in the soft clay walls with the artist's finger or a stick. There are 12 to 15 pictures, mainly of horses and oxen. Elsewhere a bison and a rhinoceros were deciphered. The figures vary in size between 3 ft. 3 in. and 6 ft. 6 in.; they are drawn with rugged strokes but nevertheless display a vigorous naturalism. Breuil ascribes them to the Aurignacian-Perigordian period.

Teyjat The cave of La Mairie is situated in the middle of the village of Teyjat, near Varaignes on the border between the northern Dordogne and Charente. In 1903 Peyrony went to Teyjat, where he discovered some magnificent engravings of animals on a yellowish stalactite column. Fragments of this pillar were unearthed during excavations made in late Magdalenian strata. At that time Breuil deciphered about 19 reindeer or remains of such animals, 10 stags, 3 head of cattle, 3 bisons and 2 bears. The cattle are arranged to form a scene: an ox follows a cow and behind the ox there trots a second ox. The outlines are drawn in the finest fluent Magdalenian style, individual details being carefully accentuated and the horns rendered in natural perspective. Some of the reindeer may be reckoned among the most magnificent engravings in Ice Age art; there is a delightful composition in which the female reindeer is rendered lying beside her calf. The bodies of the bisons are brilliantly portrayed, but the heads are drawn with curious indecision. It is gratifying to find that at Teyjat the pictures correspond in style to finds recovered from the layer. The figures at Teyjat are small, some no bigger than those found on portable art objects.

Rouffignac The cave of Rouffignac, which stretches for more than 6 miles, has for four centuries been an object of attraction to visitors, who have written their names in soot on its walls. In 1956 the owners of the cave, the Plassard family, invited two French prehistorians, L. R. Nougier and Romain Robert, to examine several figures which it was believed could be detected among the countless names. A large number of figures were discovered, either engraved or painted in black. On 17th July Abbé Breuil was also asked to verify their authenticity, and his verdict was positive.

The entrance to the cave, which faces south-west, affords access to a long gallery extending in an east-west direction, the floor of which is covered with a very slippery mass of mud (it has now been paved with stones). In an adjacent gallery, which runs from north to south and has many ramifications, the floor gradually becomes more solid. Here are the first of the extremely large number of pictures to be found in the main gallery and in the front part of several transverse galleries. They appear on walls and roofs. In certain parts the figures are amassed together. In this connection mention may be made of two herds of mammoths facing one another, each with a male animal in the lead. Very close to a steep drop, by way of which one reaches a lower level of the cave, is a part of the roof with exceedingly fine paintings of mammoths, ibexes, bisons and rhinoceroses.

Unique in Ice Age art, in Breuil's estimation, are the three paintings of woolly-haired rhinoceroses discovered on the right-hand wall of the Breuil gallery. All these figures, which are outlined in black and are

Head of rhinoceros, outlined in black. Early Magdalenian. Rouffignac.

sometimes accentuated by engraved strokes, are ascribed by Breuil to an early phase of Magdalenian. Whereas at Rouffignac representations of mammoths and rhinoceroses predominate, there are only few bisons and horses, and aurochs and cervidae are conspicuous by their complete absence — a fact presumably connected with totemistic differentiation between individual tribes.

In one lateral gallery in the eastern part of the cave Nougier and Robert discovered a large section of the roof where the clayey surface is covered with countless 'macaroni'. In the front part of the chamber-like extension they are in an excellent condition, but their state of preservation deteriorates as one proceeds further to the rear, until only traces of drawings done with the fingers are to be seen; the changes that have affected the surface of this part of the roof are attributed by Abbé Breuil to a warm current of air that was able to penetrate into the cooler interior of the cave through an old opening which is now sealed off by scree. Among the 'macaroni' very large representations of snakes stand out which recall similar figures drawn with the fingers at Baume-Latrone. The antiquity of the drawings indicates that this part of the cave was already frequented in the days of Aurignacian man. The number of works of art at Rouffignac is astonishingly large. Since Breuil discovered and examined the site 47 engraved and 31 painted mammoths have been identified (a figure that may well be subject to augmentation), and in addition 17 bisons, 11 ibexes, 10 rhinoceroses, 9 horses and a few unidentifiable figures. Some of the pictures are as much as 6 ft. 6 in. in length.

Pair-non-Pair   This cave is situated above the right bank of the lower Dordogne, not far from Bourg-sur-Gironde. In 1883 F. Daleau observed engravings on the walls but paid little attention to them. Only after he had heard of similar discoveries at La Mouthe (1895) did he begin to take an interest in the works he had then observed. In 1896 he deciphered a horse that happened to be located in a position where the light was good. Excavations in the cave revealed a massive sequence of strata, more than 13 ft. 6 in. thick, mainly consisting of Aurignacian and Perigordian layers, which completely covered all the engravings. One of the finest works to have come to light from the excavated part of the cave is a small horse in a frieze on the right-hand wall, lying with its head turned to the rear; it was called 'Agnus Dei' on account of the suggestive parallel with Christian iconography. It has delicately engraved contours, a small head, a large eye and a delicate mouth. The forelegs are clearly marked, whereas only one hind leg is shown. In another frieze, also on the right-hand wall, it is possible to identify a feline, facing to the right with the head shown full-face; its hind quarters are superposed by an enormous mammoth, whose sharply sloping dorsal line is clearly visible; only one tusk is engraved in the small head. Nearby two bear's heads can be distinctly picked out. In addition to this right-hand wall there is a lateral gallery which harbours a wealth of engravings. The innumerable overlapping lines here are certainly confusing. The frieze is well illuminated by the daylight from the entrance. Superposed upon the engraving of a stag one can decipher a rhinoceros' head with a single horn and the turned-up snout characteristic of this animal. Next to it is another bear's head, and not far from this a horse with a sweeping neck-line. The engravings at Pair-non-Pair, which are exceedingly numerous, are ascribed to the Aurignacian-Perigordian culture on the evidence of the deposit that covered them.

In the course of excavations in the large rock-shelter of Roc de Sers, some *Roc de Sers* 9 miles from Angoulême, Henri Martin discovered between 1927 and 1929, one after the other, some very fine bas-reliefs hewn into several boulders. All these boulders were raised out of an Upper Solutrian layer, with the side that had been worked facing downwards; some of them had been smashed, and some boulders were even found on the slope in front of the rock-shelter, giving the impression that once in prehistoric times an iconoclastic storm must have raged here, as a result of which this place of worship was destroyed. Presumably the stone slabs were placed in a raised position on a semi-circular pedestal at the rear of the shelter. Among the animals represented it is easy to identify six horses, three or four bisons, partially incomplete, and several ibexes. The finest specimens are two male ibexes charging each other with lowered horns. On another stone slab a musk-ox is depicted chasing a small man carrying a stick across his shoulder. The horses are without exception shown with short legs and in foal. These reliefs, produced at the end of the Solutrian period, are masterpieces in no way inferior to the bas-reliefs at Cap Blanc or the equally fine frieze of horses at Chaire à Calvin (Charente) dating from the early Magdalenian. In this connection one may also mention a frieze with bas-reliefs at Angles-sur-Anglin (Vienne dép.), discovered in 1949

Fig. 12 — Ibexes butting one another. Bas-relief. Le Roc de Sers. Length of animal on right 1 ft. 9½ in.

61

Bison, sculptured in clay. Magdalenian. Tuc d'Audoubert. *Length of animal approx. 2 ft.*

by S. St.-Mathurin and D. Garrod; it yielded fine pictures of bisons, horses and ibexes, some of which were still on the wall whilst others had fallen into deposit dating from an advanced phase of the Magdalenian period. Noteworthy, too, here are the torsos of three life-size female figures.

La Magdelaine This cave is situated on the right bank of the Tarn, not far from the town of Montauban. In 1952 M. Bessac discovered at La Magdelaine a fine rendering of a mare and one, less successfully executed, of a bison. Both animals may be ascribed to the Magdalenian period. The explorer also discovered two naked female figures, represented in a naturalistic style, facing each other on the right and left side of the chamber. According to Breuil these figures originate from the early Magdalenian. This early date is also suggested by fragments of other pictures surrounding the 'Venus' figures. Breuil has drawn attention to the fact that these female figures are not present in deep caves where no daylight penetrated; all such examples, from the Perigordian figures of Laussel to these Magdalenian figures at Angles-sur-Anglin, are to be found in rock-shelters which were once frequented. This leads Breuil to assume that Palaeolithic man did not represent 'Venus' figures at places of worship.

Not far from the railway-station of Gibaja, in the mountainous country of Cantabria, lies the village of Ramales. Just over a mile above this village are the caves of La Haza and Covalanas, situated in a broad rocky ravine. Both caves were discovered by Alcalde del Rio and Padre Sierra in 1903. From the entrance to Covalanas, which is 5½ yards wide, two galleries branch off, only one of which, however, can boast of paintings. These are to be found on the right-hand wall of the right-hand gallery, 82 yards from the entrance. After two hinds in a very imperfect state of preservation one comes across a whole herd of these animals: one hind is depicted with its head turned to the rear, another has its head turned to the right, and a third follows immediately behind. All of them are outlined in red and executed in a peculiar manner: the contours consist of spots, which in parts merge into one another. Presumably these were applied with a tampon. The three following hinds were painted in the same technique; one animal is caught very well in the act of flight. Another frieze comprises four hinds surrounding a horse with an elongated body. This manner of painting is a variant, somewhat blurred and flowing, of the linear stroke. Breuil assigns these paintings at Covalanas to a phase of the Cantabrian Perigordian.

CAVES IN SPAIN
Covalanas

Some 9 miles from Santander is the small castle of Santian, near which lies the cave of that name. It consists of one single gallery 224 yards long. The drawings are on the left-hand wall 142 yards from the entrance. Here two rows of curious signs were painted in red. They appear to depict human arms and hands; others end in something rather like a trident, while other types again are club-shaped. Breuil assumes that these 15 signs originate from a very early phase of the Magdalenian period and that they may possibly bear some relation to the red signs on the roof of the picture gallery at Altamira; but it is also possible that they are connected with representations of hands.

Santian

15½ miles south of Santander, near Puente-Viesgo, there rises up a steeply-sloping limestone massif, in which there are a number of caves. The most important one, El Castillo, was discovered by Alcalde del Rio in 1903 and examined by Breuil three years later. The excavations at the entrance carried out by H. Obermaier and P. Wernert between 1909 and 1914 proved fruitful, revealing a sequence of strata some 56 ft. thick, which yielded evidence of all the Upper Palaeolithic cultures.

El Castillo

Proceeding through a large vestibule one reaches a spacious hall which continues to the left in several chambers; the floor shows numerous traces of frequentation by late Ice Age man. On the right-hand side of the gallery the visitor comes across engravings and paintings, as well as the well-known frieze of hands. The traces of scratches made by cave-bears before the advent of man are older than the representations of hands and the groups of dots to be found close beside them. During earlier ages daylight must still have penetrated into the large chamber, until this became impossible owing to the ever-increasing deposit, and in the Magdalenian period it was already shrouded in darkness. Breuil has put the number of well-preserved hand silhouettes at 44, 35 of which are of left and 9 of right hands. All the representations are surrounded by red pigment which has been blown on to the wall; none of them are of mutilated hands.

Another group of representations comprises animal figures with linear outlines in red and yellow, which are to be found on the same parts of the wall as the renderings of hands. The former are often superimposed upon the latter and must therefore be more recent. It is, however, uncertain how much time elapsed between them. These animal figures are mainly of bisons, among which Breuil includes a horse and the head of a hind. The third group consists of paintings with outlines drawn with broader flowing strokes. Bisons painted in this style were also superposed upon the silhouettes of hands. The fourth group comprises paintings in black, which are chiefly to be found at the rear of the chamber. The older paintings were executed with fine strokes, but later the strokes became broader, as is clearly shown by the hind's head and the horse. Many sketches of cattle and ibexes in black were drawn in cursory fashion but with a sure touch. The paintings are definitely early Magdalenian; to the late Magdalenian periods belong several bisons in black, where some attempt has already been made to model the bodies with paint. Two of the representations of bisons resemble the fine polychrome pictures at Altamira. The painter here made use of the red colouring of the faded hand silhouettes and added some black paint. With these efforts, however, polychrome painting at Castillo came to an end.

The engravings in this cave are also of special artistic value: from the Aurignacian period we have the head of an ibex and several inferior pictures of horses. But magnificent Magdalenian engravings of stags and hinds, with the body surfaces filled in with hatching, are, however, a frequent feature at Castillo; they correspond completely to the portable art objects unearthed in the early Magdalenian layers. There are also beautiful engravings of cattle and several bisons from the later phases of the Magdalenian period.

This cave, which was discovered by H. Obermaier and P. Wernert in 1911, *La Pasiega* is situated in the same massif as El Castillo, not far from Puente-Viesgo. The entrance in use nowadays leads into a small chamber whence gallery 'A' leads deeper into the interior of the cave and is in turn connected with three other galleries, which in ancient times could be entered from outside. Only the third gallery 'B' is of importance. It yielded several paintings of the Aurignacian-Perigordian era. The oldest find is probably a black painting of a hand of the positive variety. Engravings are rare in Pasiega and are not elaborately executed. Breuil describes red, yellow and black paintings of horses, hinds and bisons, followed by figures of hinds, horses and a stag outlined with red dots; he also lists several club-shaped signs and tectiforms. In Pasiega only two large bisons and a black stag seem to originate from the Magdalenian era.

The entrance to the cave of Pindal, which is much exposed to rain and *Pindal* wind, is situated above the shore of the Gulf of Biscay, not far from the small village of Pimiango. From the entrance, situated on a rock terrace, access is gained to a large straight gallery, nearly 400 yards in length and varying between 11 and 22 yards in width. The first pictures are to be found 120 yards from the entrance. Almost all of them are scattered over the right-hand wall. One that is familiar is the elephant of Pindal: this is an enormous creature, rendered in a posture of repose, its contour FIG. 13 indicated by a fine red line; the forehead is high and bulging; the trunk hangs down, involute only at its extremity; the legs are long and the hooves mushroom-shaped. It differs from the Ice Age representations of mammoths by having no long thick fur and by its shorter tusks. In the centre of the body there is a large red spot. Does this perhaps indicate the position of the heart?

Nearer the entrance an engraving of a fish has been discovered, superposed on a series of dots. Breuil has identified this as a tunny-fish and has ascribed it to an advanced phase of the Magdalenian period. Below it is a large engraved bison. To the right is a series of dots in red and black, arranged horizontally. Beneath a bison painted with a broad red line are six club-shaped signs. The style in which this animal is painted suggests late Magdalenian.

The art station of Buxu is situated to the north of the village of Cardes *Buxu* in the Libas valley. The cave consists of a corridor 87 yards long. 66 yards from the entrance engravings have been found of horses, cervidae and ibexes. In Buxu there are also representations in black: 15 tectiforms of

a type found as well at Altamira. Breuil assigns the engravings and paintings at Buxu to the early Magdalenian.

Peña de Candamo   This cave was discovered in 1914 and studied by J. Cabré in 1915.
From a spacious vestibule the visitor gains access to a point, still
illuminated by daylight, where there are some painted red signs similar
to those at Santian and Altamira. The entrance corridor now becomes
narrower and descends fairly sharply to the interior of the cave. In
a large chamber are a great number of engravings and paintings.
Archaic animal figures recall the paintings at Covalanas and La Pasiega.
At first they are executed with delicate strokes, later with wider red or
dark lines; sometimes the contours of the bodies of the animals consist
of single dots. The representations are of aurochs and horses. According
to Breuil they originate from different Perigordian periods. Superposed
on them are various engravings of horses, bisons and stags. The antlers of
the latter are still rendered in twisted perspective. However, the technique
of filling in and modelling the bodies with striation is somewhat reminiscent of the engravings of the last stage of the Solutrian at Altamira and
those of the early Magdalenian period at Castillo, and so we are presumably
dealing with a retarded style — i.e., twisted perspective, an element of
Perigordian art, is in this case found right up to the early Magdalenian.

Los Casares   Between the Cantabrian mountain range and the Mediterranean coast-line
there are several caves, such as Penches and Atapuerca in the province of
Burgos, which contain paintings of no importance. On the other hand,
significant works have been found in Casares, a cave in the heart of Spain
situated directly on the Aragon border.

Casares, 2½ miles to the north of the town of Riba del Saelices, was
partially excavated by J. Cabré in 1934. He succeeded in deciphering a
large number of very fine engravings in an advanced Perigordian style.
Cabré recorded 15 horses, 10 aurochs, 9 stags, 4 ibexes, 2 lions, a rhinoceros, a glutton and a wolf. There are some older engravings with shallow
incisions beneath these pictures which are engraved more deeply. Among

them are several striking anthropomorphous representations with grotesque faces partly resembling fish and partly toads. These creatures may perhaps have served a purpose in some water-rite: one of the figures seems to be diving into the water. Only a few of the pictures at Casares are painted in black.

The southernmost offshoots of Franco-Cantabrian art in Spain are to be found in the caves of La Pileta and Ardales in Andalusia, not far from Malaga. It was in 1911 that the Englishman W. Verner announced the discovery of the large cave of La Pileta in the Serranía de Ronda. This cave, like Baume-Latrone, harbours very ancient rock art from the Aurignacian period. From multilinear arabesques drawn with the fingers

La Pileta

Group of hinds, painted in red. Parts of the contours are stippled. Cantabrian Perigordian. Covalanas.

there developed the first attempts at animal paintings in yellow, red and black. The head of an ibex and of an ox have been deciphered. The representations in yellow are in several places superposed by other paintings and are the oldest finds in this cave. Somewhat more recent in origin are the figures with linear outlines not unlike those that frequently appear in Cantabrian caves. Breuil records in this group ibexes and hinds in yellow and cattle, horses and hinds in red. The numerous representations in this cave may originate from post-glacial periods.

CAVES IN ITALY

Levanzo

In 1950 the first engravings executed in the Franco-Cantabrian style to be discovered in Italy were found in a cave on the small island of Levanzo, which belongs to the group of Aegadian Islands off the west coast of Sicily. These engravings are without exception well preserved and are to be found in the heart of the cave. They are covered with a dark patina. Here, too, Ice Age fauna are depicted as well as a series of curious anthropomorphous creatures, probably also in this case men in disguise performing a dance.

FIG. 14

The finest image of an animal, one of the best representations in the whole of Ice Age art, is the rendering of a wild ass turning its head to the rear as though catching a glimpse of something; this is an immensely vigorous and animated engraving with lines cut deeply into the rock. The explorers also observed an ox following a cow, similar to that at Teyjat, a stag with undeveloped antlers, a small stag with very elongated forelegs and a poorly executed rendering of a small horse. As elsewhere in Franco-Cantabrian art, this southernmost offshoot manifests the same sort of superpositions, the same rather chaotic arrangement of paintings on the cave walls, and the same sureness of hand in applying a naturalistic style.

Romanelli

This cave, discovered as early as the beginning of this century by Baron G. A. Blanc, stands outside the framework of Franco-Cantabrian art, since in this case we have a semi-naturalistic style. Only the rendering of an ox bears a remote resemblance to Franco-Cantabrian animal pictures. The main find at Romanelli, which is situated not far from Castro-Marnio in Apulia, consists of stylized female figures, geometric motifs, bands of parallel lines, and scaliforms. Breuil deems it possible to see certain affinities with the old Perigordian figures in the Franco-Cantabrian area, an argument that seems to be corroborated by two engravings found on small stone slabs depicting a feline and a wild boar.

Addaura

In 1952 Signora Bovio Marconi reported the discovery of a small cave at the foot of Monte Pellegrino, to the west of Palermo. At Addaura,

Fig. 14 — Small wild ass. Levanzo. Height 9¾ in.

which is no more than about 20 feet long and 20 feet wide, sinter deposits broke loose from the walls as a result of the explosion of an American ammunition depot located in the shelter, thereby exposing the engravings beneath, which had hitherto lain hidden. Stylistically these pictures are akin to those at Levanzo. Apart from two fine representations of cervidae and several horses rendered in Magdalenian style Addaura yielded a very animated group of human figures, depicted naked with some of them wearing masks. Two men appear to be engaged in a wrestling-bout, while two others lie sprawling on the ground. Both the discoverers and Breuil think it possible that these two men are committing suicide by strangulation. Their legs, which are bound together, fettered and bent far back, seem to be pulling tight a cord placed around the victim's neck.

Whereas the animal figures at Addaura are undoubtedly related to Magdalenian art, the representation of the human figures approximates greatly to the human image as portrayed in the art of the Spanish Levant. Niscemie, another shelter to the south-west of Monte Pellegrino, harbours   *Niscemie* animal pictures in the same style as at Addaura. In Niscemie there are equine animals and an aurochs with horns drawn in perspective, which again points to the Magdalenian era.

This selection of Ice Age cave art in France, Spain and Italy is designed to convey an impression of the advanced level of artistic achievement attained by Palaeolithic man in Europe. As already mentioned, it has not been possible to consider the minor arts in this connection.

Towards the end of the Magdalenian period the ice slowly retreated to the Alps and the Arctic and with the changes that now occurred in the flora and fauna the post-glacial climate created new conditions for human existence. This, however, also eliminated the prerequisites for the naturalistic cave art that flourished during the Ice Age. The art stations sank into oblivion: roof falls, landslides and deposit blocked the entrances to the caves until, after the lapse of millennia, they were by chance once again opened to human eyes.

We now know of almost 120 stations of Ice Age art in the Franco-Cantabrian area. This figure, however, does not include all the caves in which early Palaeolithic paintings and engravings are to be found. The cave of Rouffignac in the Dordogne was only located a few years ago, and one may reckon with the discovery of more unknown art stations in the future.

FRANCO-CANTABRIAN ART STATIONS
WITH DATES OF DISCOVERY

FRANCE

RHÔNE VALLEY

Ebbou (Vallon-Ardèche) 1946
Le Colombier (Virac-Ardèche) 1947
Oullins (Garn-Ardèche) 1951
Chabot (Aiguèze-Gard) 1878
Le Figuier (Saint-Martin-Ardèche) 1888
Bayol (Collias-Gard) 1927
Baume-Latrone (Gard) 1940
Sallèles-Gabardès (Aude) 1947

PYRENEES DISTRICT

Aldène (Hérault) 1926
Niaux (Ardèche) 1906
Bédeilhac (Ariège) 1907
Ussat (Ariège) 1921
Le Portel (Ariège) 1908
Les Trois Frères (Ariège) 1914
Tuc d'Audoubert (Ariège) 1912
Mas d'Azil (Ariège) 1902
Marsoulas (Haute-Garonne) 1897
Montespan (Haute-Garonne) 1923
Gargas (Hautes-Pyrénées) 1906
Tibiran (Hautes-Pyrénées) 1951
La Bastide (Hautes-Pyrénées) 1932
Isturitz (Basses-Pyrénées) 1913
Etcheberriko-Karbia (Basses-Pyrénées) 1950

LOT

Pech-Merle (Cabrerets) 1922
Marcenac (Cabrerets) 1920
Sainte-Eulalie (Cabrerets) 1920
Cantal (Cabrerets) 1920
Les Merveilles (Rocamadour) 1922
Murat (Rocamadour) 1914
Cougnac (Gourdon) 1953

DORDOGNE

Lascaux (Montignac) 1940
Sergeac (St. Léon) 1909
Belcayre (Thonac) 1934
Laussel (Marquay) 1908
Cap Blanc (Marquay) 1909
Beyssac (Sireuil) 1915
Nancy (Sireuil) 1915
Commarque (Sireuil) 1915
La Grèze (Marquay) 1904
Bernifal (Meyrals) 1903
La Calévie (Meyrals) 1903
La Mouthe (Les Eyzies) 1895
Les Combarelles (Les Eyzies) 1901
Font-de-Gaume (Les Eyzies) 1901
Gorge d'Enfer (Les Eyzies) 1912

Oreille d'Enfer (Les Eyzies) 1932
Jean-Blancs (Bourniquel) 1911
Laugerie-Haute (Les Eyzies) 1864
Laugerie-Basse (Les Eyzies) 1864
Croze à Gontran (Les Eyzies) 1913
La Ferrassie (Les Eyzies) 1898
Château-la-Tour (Sarlat)
La Sudrie (Villac) 1937
Barabao (Le Bugue) 1951
Le Gabillou (Sourzac) 1940
Teyjat (in Teyjat) 1903
Fourneau d. Diable (Bourdeilles) 1919
Rouffignac (near Rouffignac) 1956

GIRONDE

Pair-non-Pair (Marcamp) 1881

CHARENTE

Roc-de-Sers (Sers) 1881
Chaire à Calvin (Mouthiers) 1926

VIENNE

Angles-sur-Anglin
(near Angles-sur-Anglin) 1949
La Marche (Lussac-les-Châteaux) 1937

YONNE

Arcy-sur-Cure
(Grotte des Mammouths) 1946

TARN

La Magdelaine (Penne) 1952

AIN BASQUE PROVINCES

Berroberia (Pamplona) 1929
Santimamiñe (Vizcaya) 1916
Venta de la Perra (Vizcaya) 1904

SANTANDER

Sottariza (Gibaja) 1906
La Haza (Ramales) 1903

Covalanas (Ramales) 1903
Salitré (Miera) 1903
El Pendo (Camargo) 1907
Santian (Puente Arce) 1905
La Clotilde (Reocin) 1906
Hornos (San Felice de Buelna) 1903
Altamira (Santillana) 1879
Castillo (Puente Viesgo) 1903
La Pasiega (Puente Viesgo) 1911
Les Aguas (Novales) 1909
La Meaza (Comillas) 1907
Les Monedas (Puente Viesgo) 1952

ASTURIAS (OVIEDO)

La Loja (Panes) 1908
Pindal (Riba de Deva) 1908
Mazaculos (Riba de Deva) 1908
Quintanal (Balmori) 1908
Buxu (Cangas de Onis) 1916
El Cueto (Lledias) 1936
San Antonio (Riba de Sella) 1912
Bolado (Llanes) 1912
Peña de Candamo (San Roman) 1914

OLD CASTILE

Atapuerca (Burgos) 1910
Penches (Burgos) 1915
Los Casares (Guadalajara) 1934

ANDALUSIA

La Pileta (Malaga) 1911
Ardales (Malaga) 1918
La Cala (Malaga) 1908
Palomas (Cadiz)

OTRANTO   **ITALY**

Romanelli (Castro-Marino) 1904

SICILY

Levanzo (Levanzo I.) 1949
Addaura (Palermo) 1953

Rock art areas in the Spanish Levant

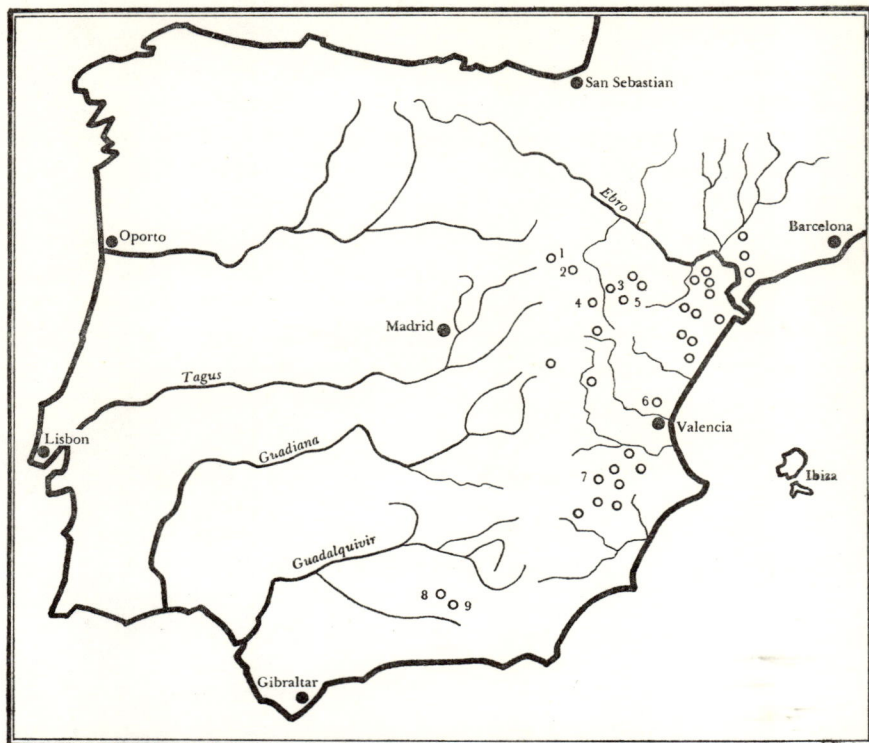

1. Els Secans
2. Val del Charco del Agua Amarga
3. Gasulla gorge
4. Valltorta gorge
5. Morella la Vella
6. Cuevas de la Araña
7. Alpera
8. Cueva del Santo
9. Cogul

THE ROCK ART OF
THE SPANISH LEVANT

BY

HANS-GEORG BANDI

The rock pictures of the Spanish Levant constitute the most vigorous works of art bequeathed by the prehistoric peoples of Europe. They are to be found in the hilly and mountainous hinterland of the coastal area that extends from the province of Lérida in the north to the province of Murcia in the south, or in other words from the Pyrenees to the Sierra Nevada. In contrast to the Franco-Cantabrian engravings and paintings they are not located in the interior of deep caves, hidden from human eyes: they are to be found beneath overhanging ledges of rock or shallow rock-shelters, in natural niches often situated at the foot of precipitous cliffs and separated from the bottom of the barren valleys by boulder-strewn slopes that can only be climbed with difficulty. Many of these niches are visible from afar, since owing to their ochre patina they stand out against the rest of the rock, which is generally grey.

Many of the eastern Spanish paintings were long familiar to the local population, and already before the turn of the century a note was published on one niche containing pictures situated near Albarracín (Teruel prov.). However, it was not until the beginning of the present century that they came to the attention of scholars. In 1903 J. Cabré Aguiló, a photographer, came across several frescoes in the vicinity of Calapatá, not far from Cretas (Teruel prov.): they comprise three stags and an aurochs painted in red. Cabré, however, did not realize the significance of his discovery until several years later, when he heard of the Ice Age cave paintings in the north of Spain. In 1907 news of this find reached H. Breuil, who at once took a keen interest in it. With this Spanish Levantine art came to the notice of international scholars, who without delay set about the task of studying it systematically. In this connection it was by no means unimportant that the controversy as to the authenticity and antiquity of the Franco-Cantabrian cave paintings had by this time already been concluded and that the significance of these Ice Age works had, after some curious false trails, at last been correctly assessed. From then onwards information about the rapidly mounting number of

DISCOVERY
AND STUDY

discoveries made in this field was provided by several scholarly monographs and also by numerous articles and papers, particularly in the leading French specialist journal *L'Anthropologie*. We can only go into this question quite briefly and have to rest content with singling out individual art stations. Cogul, situated to the south of Lérida, is an important site which was discovered at an early date; it houses the famous 'Dancing Women', a painting in red and black, about which the first scholarly work appeared as long ago as 1908. Even greater significance attaches to the find of rock paintings made in 1910 near Alpera, situated west of Almansa (Albacete

Hunter running, and holding bow and arrows. The head, still visible in 1915, is hardly recognizable today. The figure was added at a later date to the neck of a large wild ox, but this animal has now almost entirely faded. Cueva del Charco del Agua Amarga, Teruel prov. *Scale approx. 1:6.*

prov.). Special mention should be made in this connection of a large painted frieze in the Cueva Vieja, which consists of a jumble of human and animal figures. In 1913 other important paintings were discovered at the Cueva del Val del Charco del Agua Amarga, near Alcañiz (Teruel prov.) and in 1914 at Cantos de la Visera on Monte Arabí near Yecla (Murcia prov.). 1914 was the year of the discovery of an important site containing many paintings near Minateda (Albacete prov.), on the railway-line between Madrid and Cartagena, and named after that town. These figures, of which there are several hundred, include a particularly large number of human beings on a frieze 60 feet long at the mouth of the Barranco de la Mortaja; according to H. Breuil they belong to 13 different periods of painting, so that this station possesses a special importance for the dating of eastern Spanish rock pictures according to their style.

PLATE P. 74

In 1917 new paintings were found near Morella la Vella (or Vieja, Castellón prov.) and especially in the Valltorta gorge between Albocácer and Tirig (Castellón prov.), some 25 miles from the coast. As in most other sites, the Valltorta gorge, a barren rocky valley, has not just one but several rock-shelters — 15 in all, which contain a large number of paintings. The most important are Cueva del Civil, Cueva de los Caballos (where the pictures, like many others in this region, appear to have long been familiar to the local population), Cueva Mas d'en Josep and Cueva Saltadora. The Valltorta gorge is one of the richest art stations of the Spanish Levant. The study of the various niches and their pictures is closely associated with the name of H. Obermaier.

PLATE P. 78

PLATE P. 83

Among the discoveries during the following two years mention must be made of the pictures at Els Secans near Mazaleón (Teruel prov.) and at the Cuevas de la Araña near Bicorp (Valencia prov.), where there is a famous scene of two honey-gatherers climbing up by means of a rope to the hiding-place of some wild bees (Fig. 29). Another delightful station is Tormón in the Olivonas valley near Albarracín (Teruel prov.), which was explored by H. Breuil and H. Obermaier in 1926; it contains a number of pictures of human beings, wild oxen, wild horses and stags, painted in red and black.

PLATE P. 86

Other sites with paintings of great significance were discovered in the early 1930s in the Barranco de Gasulla near Ares del Maestre (Castellón prov.), not far from the Valltorta gorge: the Cueva Remigia and the Cingle de la Mola Remigia, with several niches containing pictures. There are hundreds of human and animal figures, painted in red, black and brown, on a rock ledge comparatively high up the right-hand side of the barren valley. Here, too, H. Obermaier, in collaboration with H.

Breuil and J. B. Porcar, played a leading part in recording and evaluating the pictures. In the course of his work in the Gasulla gorge, Porcar discovered not far away in the barren little valley of 'Les Dogues' a singular scene of warriors in combat.

No group of rock pictures as large as that found in the Gasulla gorge has been discovered since that time. But a number of smaller sites that have come to light during the past two decades show that the discovery of Spanish Levantine art is not yet at an end. Among the new sites we may mention the Abrigo del Arquero and the Cueva de Doña Clotilde near Albarracín (Teruel prov.), an area where, as has been stated, niches containing pictures had previously been discovered; also El Mortero and Cerro Felio near Alacón (Teruel prov.), Cueva del Polvorín (Castellón prov.) and several sites in the Barranco de Llort near Rojals (Tarragona prov.). We can take it for granted that further discoveries will be made in future. The number of sites on the Spanish Levant containing paintings so far mentioned in the literature on the subject totals about 50 — and in many places several niches have been listed under the same name. They are spread over the high-lying hinterland of the eastern Spanish coast, which suggests that this mainly rocky area was the home of one particular group of people.

TECHNIQUE The majority of the works in the Spanish Levant are paintings; engravings are very rare. As a rule the paintings are monochrome, polychrome pictures appearing only in exceptional instances. The range of colours is limited: in most cases the prevailing colour is reddish (from light red to reddish brown), but black and sometimes white were also used. Natural pigments, such as manganese, haematite, limonite, ochre, red chalk and charcoal were employed. Tests carried out by K. Herberts show that the colours were probably applied in the form of a thin liquid. It was thus a glazing technique, whereby the pulverized pigments were apparently mixed not only with water but with a slightly sticky substance such as diluted blood, melted honey, albumen or vegetable juices, which acted as a binder. The paint must have been applied to the yellowish or greyish-blue rock in several stages with the aid of simple brush-like implements. An unfinished representation of a human figure at Cueva del Civil (in the Valltorta gorge) shows that the contours were apparently drawn first: we have here the outline of a leg, of which only a small part has been filled in with paint (Fig. 15). It is also clear from some pictures that the inner surface was first painted with a watery glaze, usually grey, and that the final colour was only applied later, for the two coats do not always coincide completely. It is, of course, impossible to say whether this procedure was always quite so complicated, but in some cases it can be seen very distinctly. Finally, it may also be mentioned that sometimes — as, for example, in the case of a male figure from Tormón (Teruel prov.) — the inner surface is filled with a striped design (Fig. 16) instead of being painted all over in monochrome, and that in exceptional cases figures painted in two or more colours occur. On the other hand, there are several pictures in which the outlines are engraved.

Fig. 16 — Man with bow. Painting in red. Tormón, Teruel prov. After H. Obermaier. Scale approx. 1 : 4 · 5

The preservation of the paintings in eastern Spain presents a particular problem. The fact that the pictures survived for several millennia — the question of their antiquity will be discussed below — is astonishing, considering that they were only to a very limited extent protected by overhanging rocks, and not everywhere at that.

PRESERVATION

This can only be explained by the fact that the climate of eastern Spain is very dry. Another factor may have been that in the course of time a thin sinter deposit was formed by the percolation of water through the rock, which constituted a binding element similar to the calcium hydrate of the mortar in frescoes, and also formed a protective film. It is all the more regrettable that many of the pictures in this veritable 'archive' of art have suffered greatly during past decades, whereas generally speaking they were in an excellent state of preservation right up to the time of their discovery — apart from some minor damage caused by flocks of sheep or goats or by shepherds passing away their time. On comparing the present condition of the paintings with early photographs it can be seen that the reproductions are in general wonderfully accurate, but, on the other hand, it is striking how many of them can scarcely be made out any longer. The reason for this undoubtedly is that the paintings are sprinkled, dabbed or rubbed with water by visitors to bring out the colours. The mere mechanical aspect

Fig. 17 — Archer. Alpera man. Painting in dark red. Cueva Saltadora, Valltorta gorge, Castellón prov. After H. Obermaier. Scale approx. 1 : 2 · 5

77

Wild goat. To judge from the unnatural posture of the legs, the animal has probably been killed. Morella la Vella (or Vieja), Castellón prov. *Scale approx. 1 : 3.*

of such treatment must inevitably cause damage, and in addition to this it enables dust to settle on the damp parts; but probably the most dangerous consequence of all is the chemical process that takes place when water is applied: the oxygen contained in the water seems to act on the limestone. Nowadays the state of preservation is unfortunately so bad in many places that the paintings are hardly visible unless the visitor sprinkles water on them himself, even though he realizes that this has a detrimental effect. Finally, it may be mentioned that the paintings have suffered greatly here and there from the actions of irresponsible persons and souvenir hunters. Unfortunately it is an almost impossible undertaking to try to prevent these abuses. Most of the niches in eastern Spain where paintings are to be found are situated in very isolated areas, and could only be protected by a railing, which would cost a great deal and probably be an eyesore as well, so that control and safety are not really feasible. This is not altered by the fact that only a small number of tourists go and see these paintings: experience teaches that the 'water treatment' applied during the last fifty years or so has caused very considerable deterioration; and anti-social elements feel safer in remoter places than at sites where they might be reprimanded by other visitors. On the other hand, the question of restoring certain paintings deserves to be examined. This applies, for instance, to the 'Dancing Women' at

Fig. 18 — Archer. Cestosomatic man. Painting in black. Cueva del Civil, Valltorta gorge, Castellón prov. After H. Obermaier. Scale approx. 1 : 4

Cogul, where the figures can just be made out when the rock is sprinkled with water; we possess reliable information about the state of this work when it was discovered. Here and at many other sites expert restoration would surely produce results as rewarding as, for example, in the case of Roman frescoes. If nothing is done, in a few years' time we shall only be able to point out sections of rock where some beautiful dancing scene or other interesting painting could once be seen.

The paintings of the Spanish Levant are mostly small, the individual figures being no larger than a man's hand. Human and animal figures are combined to form scenic compositions. This is the main difference between Spanish Levantine and Franco-Cantabrian mural art, since the latter, as is well known, consists mainly of naturalistic single animal figures, frequently drawn on a large scale.

In the rock paintings of eastern Spain the animals are almost without exception depicted in a manner very true to life, but mostly very reduced in scale. If they measure as much as 30 in. in length, as is the case, for example, with some of the wild oxen at Tormón (Teruel prov.), they may be considered quite large. With a good many of the animals their characteristic features are brought out distinctly, showing how keenly these hunter artists observed their quarry and how accurately they recognized their peculiarities.

It is rather a different matter as regards the human figures: although they also display a naturalistic conception, they are frequently subject to very definite tendencies towards stylization. According to P. Wernert, at least four groups can be distinguished: the 'Alpera type', identified by its close adherence to nature and accurate proportions (Fig. 17); the 'cestosomatic type', with exaggeratedly long body, round head, broad, almost triangular chest, narrow hips and long, fairly thick legs (Fig. 18); the 'pachypodous type', with a comparatively short body, large head in profile, short slender torso and excessively thick legs (Fig. 19); and finally the 'nematomorphous

STYLE

79

Fig. 19 — Hunter. Pachypodous man. Painting in dark red. Cueva de los Caballos, Valltorta gorge, Castellón prov. After H. Obermaier. Scale approx. 1 : 4

type', with figures reduced almost to linear dimensions and stylized in such a way that their bodies are composed of no more than a few straight and curved lines (Fig. 20). This reduction or enlargement of the body, or parts of the body, in the

Expressionism manner of *ombres chinoises,* is frequently called Expressionism, and it is believed that artists who employed this method wished to suggest certain ideas of movement or force. But we must also reckon with the possibility that it was only at the beginning that the method of depicting human figures was consciously conceived and that subsequently the same methods were adhered to purely on traditional grounds. Nor can it be determined conclusively whether these various types constitute different stages in the same tendency of stylistic development or whether they denote ethnographical or anthropological differences. In this connection it is noteworthy that no scenic compositions are known in which more than one of the types of human being mentioned appears. But in any case these figures, even where they intentionally or unintentionally depart to some extent from nature, can produce an extremely lively effect. Finally, it ought to be mentioned that in these human figures the face has a certain tendency to portraiture, and that importance is often attached to the rendering of head-dress, body ornaments, weapons, and — more rarely — other articles of equipment or clothing; we shall come back to this point later.

SUBJECT-MATTER When the paintings are grouped scenically, which, as has already been stated, is frequently the case, they mainly depict the events of the chase. They portray the hunters and their quarry in a variety of situations. In one instance we see some men following an animal's tracks, which are clearly indicated; we may suppose that the hunters must have been very experienced, for the tracks cannot have been very distinct on this dry stony terrain. Sometimes the stalkers have already succeeded in bringing their quarry to bay and have just dealt the *coup de grâce*. In pictures where the hunter is shown running after game at full speed — as, for example, in the painting at Agua Amarga (Teruel prov.) — this appears to represent the chase. Particularly frequent are the pictures showing the *battue:* in many cases men and animals have been combined to form extremely animated groups. How magnificent are, for instance, the ibex or wild goat chase painted in red (Fig. 22) at the Cueva Remigia (Gasulla gorge), and the stag stalk at the Cueva de los Caballos (Valltorta gorge). In both cases a number of archers are lying in wait for the game, startled by invisible beaters, and overwhelming it with a hail of arrows. Whereas in scenes of the chase the representations of the running hunters are especially striking, here we are particularly impressed by the terrified animals, whose sole concern is to escape and who rush to their doom by coming within range of the arrows of the waiting hunters. The representations of human beings here deserve attention, for the line-work of the lurking hunters, shooting their arrows from tautly-drawn bows, is in many cases very fine. The fact that hunting involved danger can be seen in pictures where the hunter is pursued by a wounded animal. One such scene (Fig. 23) is known to us from the Cueva Remigia (Gasulla gorge).

Another interesting insight into the life of those who created eastern Spanish art is afforded by representations connected with warlike episodes. *Battle-scenes* Particularly delightful are, for example, the so-called 'advancing warriors' from the Cingle de la Mola Remigia (Gasulla gorge): five men, some of them shown bearded, are marching one behind the other with a long stride, each holding several arrows in one hand and holding up a bow in the other (Fig. 24); this may represent a war-dance. Some other pictures, such as those from Morella la Vella (Fig. 25) and from the rock-shelter of Les Dogues, near Ares del Maestre, depict lively scenes of men engaged in a fierce battle, some of whom are wounded. Cueva Saltadora (Valltorta gorge) contains a picture, painted in light red, of a warrior in flight: struck by several arrows, he collapses and thereby loses his head-dress (Fig. 26). Obermaier has called attention to certain representations from the Cueva Remigia to which a somewhat different significance must be

Fig. 20 — Archer. Nematomorphous man. Painting in light red. Cueva de los Caballos, Valltorta gorge, Castellón prov. After H. Obermaier. Scale approx. 1 : 2

attached. The same motif, reiterated several times, depicts a group of men, drawn in a rather schematic manner, brandishing their bows as if expressing joy; on the ground before them lies an individual who has been struck by several arrows (Fig. 27). These seem to be regular scenes of execution, although it is, of course, difficult to determine whether those executed were prisoners of war or offenders belonging to the same tribe as their executioners, and whether they are being sacrificed or punished. In any case it is obvious that these pictures testify to the existence of definite juridical conceptions.

The pictures so far mentioned by no means exhaust the subject-matter treated in the scenic rock pictures of eastern Spain. Mention has already been made of the honey-gatherers in the Cuevas de la Araña near Bicorp, who are warding off a swarm of wild bees (Fig. 29) and also of the so-called 'Dancing Women' of Cogul, where a group of women, some painted in red and some in black, are shown surrounding a small man; this picture may depict a ceremonial dance. At Minateda a mother can be seen walking and leading her child by the hand, and at Alpera there are two women who seem to be chatting to one another. There are several curious an-

PLATE P. 96

thropomorphous figures, half-human and half-animal, which may be identified as spirits of wild animals, or bush spirits, or possibly masked dancers. It is difficult to interpret some representations of insects, such as the spider painted in dark red, surrounded by a swarm of flies, to be

PLATE P. 93

found in the Cingle de la Mola Remigia (Gasulla gorge).

The pictures also give us important information about the weapons, equipment, clothing, ornaments and hair-dress of the prehistoric inhabitants of eastern Spain. By far the most important hunting weapon was undoubtedly the bow and arrow, depicted very frequently. Some of them appear to have been simple bows, as illustrated in the picture of a hunter at the Cueva Vieja, Alpera (Albacete prov.), or 'reflex' bows of various sizes (Fig. 28). Various types of arrow can also be distinguished according to their different heads and feathering. Spare arrows are sometimes carried in quivers, probably made of leather. It is likely that javelins were also used, but on the basis of these pictures it is difficult to distinguish them from arrows. A figure in the Cuevas de la Araña has been identified by K. Lindner as a lasso-thrower, but it may be a man brandishing his bow (Fig. 30). Other weapons and articles of hunting equipment have not been authenticated; there are also no indications whatsoever of fishing-tackle.

PLATE P. 96

But there are some pictures illustrating the use of containers and pouches, presumably made of leather or wickerwork (perhaps in some cases from clay). Noteworthy, too, is the use of ropes or leather straps for climbing.

Archer taking aim. The bow, drawn taut with one arm, is only faintly recognizable in the left-hand part of the picture. Cueva del Civil, Valltorta gorge, Castellón prov. *Scale 1 : 3.*

Fig. 21 — Boar hunt. Painting in dark red. Cueva del Val del Charco del Agua Amarga, Teruel prov. After H. Obermaier. Scale approx. 1 : 4

The male figures are frequently depicted completely naked, but there are a few pictures (for example, that at Els Secans, Teruel prov.) in which a proper pair of breeches can be identified. In various places loin-cloths and waist-bands have been indicated, and one archer at Mas d'en Josep (Valltorta gorge) is depicted with a cape, the fringed ends of which hang down his back (Fig. 31). These articles of clothing must presumably have been made of beaten-out bark cloth, very fine wickerwork, leather or hide, since the art of weaving can scarcely have been known. We have a relatively good idea of the head-dress that seems to have been generally worn by men. In many cases feathers were either placed loosely in the hair or combined to form an ornament. Other figures are depicted wearing caps of various shapes, some resembling animals' ear-flaps; a fine example of this (Fig. 33) is to be found in the Cueva Vieja, Alpera (Albacete prov.). Quite often the men wear ornaments, mostly knee-rings, but also — less frequently — armlets; some of these must probably be interpreted as insignia of rank or honour. Finally, the paintings show that men wore their hair either short or hanging down to their shoulders; beards and moustaches were not infrequent. The women seem usually to have been dressed in bell-shaped skirts falling from their hips, whereas the upper part of the body was left naked; this is how they are represented performing a dance at Roca dels Moros, Cogul (Lérida prov.) (Fig. 34). Some of the women adorn their arms with armlets or arm-bands; their hair hangs down loosely.

SIGNIFICANCE From what has been said it follows that, seen as a whole, the paintings of the Spanish Levant (which, of course, do not consist exclusively of masterpieces but also include works of lesser merit) affords us a very interesting insight into this epoch of Iberian prehistory. But what was the significance of these rock paintings? What motivated these hunter artists to produce paintings in some of the rock niches in their hunting-grounds? One explanation is that they were pictorial narratives, i.e. that certain incidents, such as important battles, successful hunting expeditions or memorable feasts were recorded for the benefit of contemporaries, or possibly of posterity. This idea should not be dismissed out of hand. And yet there are reasons for believing that matters are not so simple as all this. It is especially remarkable that these pictures are generally found concentrated in one particular niche, although very similar rock formations, in some cases even more suitable for painting, were available close by. But while these show no sign whatever of having been used, the niches with paintings in many cases boast of a great number of works, which were, moreover, produced at different periods and are therefore in part superposed upon one another. What is the reason for the apparent preference given to certain places? How can one explain the mystery of their continuous use, in some cases for many generations? M. Almagro argues that they were places of worship, sanctuaries which were constantly frequented because magic powers were ascribed to them or to the pictures they contained. He points out that at Cogul, for example, Iberian and Latin votive inscriptions suggest that the niches were for a long time famed

Fig. 22 — Ibex hunt. Painting in light red. Cueva Remigia, Gasulla gorge, Castellón prov. After J. B. Porcar, H. Obermaier and H. Breuil. Scale 1 : 5

Fig. 23 — Hunter pursued by wounded wild ox. Painting in dark red. Cueva Remigia, Gasulla gorge, Castellón prov. After J. B. Porcar, H. Obermaier and H. Breuil. Scale 1 : 3

85

From top to bottom: hind facing backwards; stag; wild goat. Second niche of pictures, Cuevas de la Araña, Valencia prov. *Scale 1 : 2·5*

Fig. 24 — *Warriors advancing (or dance scene?).*
Painting in greyish-black. Cingle de la Mola
Remigia, Gasulla gorge, Castellón prov. After
J. B. Porcar, H. Obermaier and H. Breuil.
Scale approx. 1 : 3

for their supernatural powers. Curiously enough, it can actually be proved in some cases that the pictures were occasionally 'restored' in prehistoric times by the application of a new coat of paint. In this connection M. Almagro refers in particular to the bovidae at Tormón near Albarracín and the 'Dancing Women' of Cogul. But there are, however, other paintings which have been subjected to minor alterations, such as the 'stags' at the base of the large frieze in the Cueva Vieja near Alpera; here one can unmistakably trace older figures of wild oxen to which antlers have subsequently been added.

We should also consider in this connection the existence of anthropomorphous figures, which must be identified as the spirits of wild animals, or bush spirits, rather than as masked men, and also the picture of spiders surrounded by small insects in the Cingle de la Mola Remigia, in the Gasulla gorge, and in the Cuevas de la Araña near Bicorp. These are surely more than the product of some hunter passing the time while waiting for game to appear.

All this suggests that we are not simply dealing with pictorial narratives

PLATE P. 93

Fig. 25 — *Archers fighting. Painting in dark*
red. Morella la Vella, Castellón prov. After
F. Benitez. Scale 1 : 1·5

about contemporary events. On the contrary, it seems that we have here, in some scenes at least, mythical incidents or conceptions derived from totemism. Possibly the hunting scenes are not renderings of one particular hunt, but the repetition of some primeval event. But, however this may be, the methods employed, the weapons, articles of clothing and ornaments represented in the pictures must correspond to a large extent with those in use at the time when the pictures were painted. The pictures thus do afford us an interesting insight into the life of the people who created Spanish Levantine art.

In conclusion it should be stated that great caution is necessary in interpreting the subject-matter of these paintings. It would be just as erroneous to regard everything simply as contemporary pictorial narrative as it would be to write all the pictures off as 'magic'. Only a thorough analysis of each scene can lead to plausible results. There is much of which we shall probably never be able to grasp the original meaning.

DEVELOPMENT The rock paintings of eastern Spain were not all produced at the same time; on the contrary, they must have appeared in some kind of sequence. This is shown not only by the fact that the paintings are frequently superposed, i.e. that the older pictures are partially or completely covered over by more recent ones, but also by the stylistic modifications that can be observed when one compares those of earlier and later date. On the basis of observations made by H. Breuil at Minateda, as well as his own experiences, H. Obermaier advanced the view that the eastern Spanish paintings show a trend of evolution, which led at first to ever greater perfection of style and technique but finally to decadence through excessive schematization.

DATING This brings us to the question of the antiquity of Spanish Levantine art. Briefly, the problem which has to be solved is whether the eastern Spanish paintings, like the Franco-Cantabrian ones, originate from the end of the Ice Age, or whether they are of more recent date, i.e. whether they belong to the Upper Palaeolithic or to a later cultural epoch. The main reasons why this question is more difficult to answer than in the

Men with bows. Cingle de la Mola Remigia, Gasulla gorge, Castellón prov. *Scale approx. 1:2.*

case of Franco-Cantabrian art are: firstly, that the fauna depicted are mostly species that could live both in cold and warm climates; secondly, that we do not have any products of the artistic crafts, i.e. engraved or sculptured objects, corresponding stylistically to the mural paintings and found in strata of ascertainable date; and thirdly, that the eastern Spanish rock paintings do not occur in caves which can be proved to have remained intact from the end of the Ice Age until they were rediscovered in our own day.

Opinions are therefore very divided as to the antiquity and cultural attribution of the Spanish Levantine paintings. H. Breuil, H. Obermaier and a number of other scholars have pointed to the affinity with Franco-Cantabrian art and on these grounds are disposed to date them to the Ice Age and the Upper Palaeolithic. Several Spanish authors, on the other hand, have occasionally expressed the view that this is 'Neolithic art'. Nevertheless, this point of view has generally not been expressed in a categorical fashion, and these writers are often in two minds as to whether it is Mesolithic or Neolithic. An unequivocal opinion is voiced by M. Almagro, who in an excellent concise summary written in 1954 states that these paintings date from a post-glacial period "in which they were definitely produced by Mesolithic hunters who for a long time retained their backward way of life in the wild mountainous areas of eastern Spain." But he recognizes that there was a considerable overlap with Neolithic cultures. Despite this there is no need "to deny all points of contact and affinity which suggest that they were based upon Ice Age rock art. They could have been produced by Perigordian man, who belonged to a culture which was widely disseminated in Spain and formed the basis of the whole Upper Palaeolithic and Mesolithic, and which without doubt also lives on in the background of the present-day populations of the Iberian peninsula." The evidence of a considerable number of excavations shows that towards the end of the Palaeolithic offshoots of Franco-Cantabrian art reached eastern and southern Spain. This is borne out by the rock paintings in the cave at Pileta and two other sites in the province of Malaga, as well

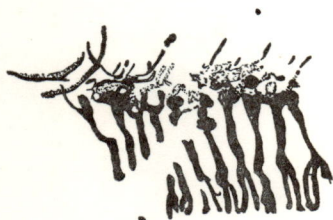

Fig. 27 — 'Execution'. Painting in red and black. Cueva Remigia, Gasulla gorge, Castellón prov. After J. B. Porcar, H. Obermaier and H. Breuil. Scale 1 : 2 · 7

Fig. 28 — Archer with reflex bow. Painting in black. Cueva Vieja, Alpera, Albacete prov. After J. Cabré. Scale approx. 1 : 2 · 5

as by products of the artistic crafts brought to light at Parpallo (Valencia prov.) and other caves. This affords a weighty argument against ascribing Spanish Levantine art to the Upper Palaeolithic. For it is more than unlikely that two different styles of Ice Age art should have co-existed side by side in eastern Spain, and not in any other region.

Furthermore, it may be mentioned that the arguments adduced in support of the view that they date from the Ice Age are unconvincing. It is true that there do exist stylistic affinities between the animal pictures of the Spanish Levant and those of Franco-Cantabrian art which point to some possible connection. But this by no means implies contemporaneity; it can just as easily be a case of influences having been handed down from one period to another. The latter hypothesis is all the more probable since eastern Spanish paintings contain numerous other elements which are completely absent from Upper Palaeolithic art.

The attempts made with the aid of certain animal figures to prove that the art of the Spanish Levant has its roots in the Ice Age are also highly arbitrary. Scholars believed that they could in some places identify figures of rhinoceroses, bears, lions, reindeer, bisons, wild asses and saiga antelopes. But these pictures are all of dubious antiquity, and M. Almagro has been able to show that in many cases the evidence rests upon supplementary drawings which differed in style from the originals to which they were added. There is also the possibility that isolated remnants of Ice Age fauna could continue to exist for a comparatively long time in the mountainous districts of eastern Spain; this is at least more than likely in the case of some of the animals mentioned, especially bears. And if the identification of the animals at Minateda as rhinoceroses is correct, they could well belong to the hairless African species, about which information may somehow have reached eastern Spain. Finally, one must also not exclude the possibility that animals may have been painted which were only known from legendary tradition.

It is in any case certain that, wherever the identification of the species is quite clear, these animals lived in the Spanish Levant at the end of the Ice Age and that they could also exist there for a certain length

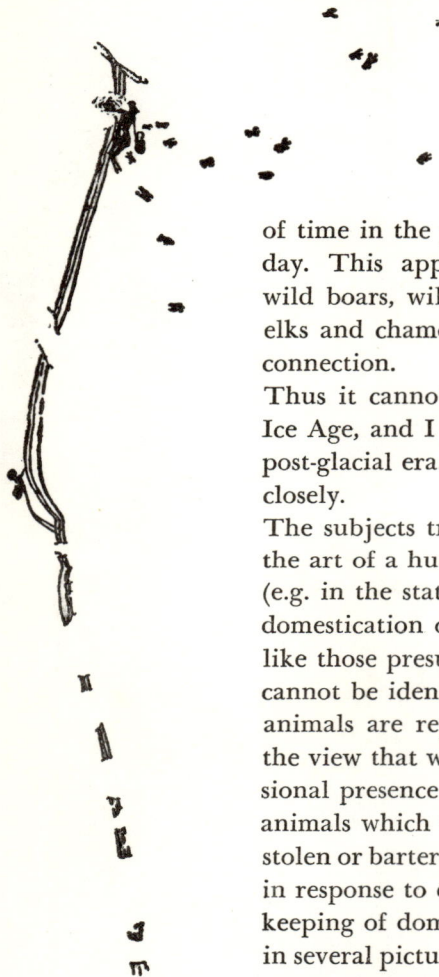

of time in the post-glacial period, some of them even up to the present day. This applies chiefly to common stags, wild goats, rock deer, wild boars, wild oxen, and less frequently to wild horses, fallow deer, elks and chamois; birds and insects may be left out of account in this connection.

Thus it cannot be proved that Spanish Levantine art dates from the Ice Age, and I personally am convinced that its origin goes back to the post-glacial era. We shall now attempt to define this period a little more closely.

The subjects treated in these paintings make it quite plain that this is the art of a hunter people. To the argument that some figures or scenes (e.g. in the station of Villar del Huomo, Cuenca prov.) suggest that the domestication of animals was practised it may be said that all of them, like those presumed to date from the Ice Age, are open to question and cannot be identified for certain. And even if in some instances domestic animals are represented, this in my opinion by no means contradicts the view that we are dealing here with the art of hunters, since the occasional presence of such animals can be explained otherwise: they can be animals which the hunters had seen among neighbouring tribes, or had stolen or bartered from them. It is even possible that in this hunter culture, in response to external influences, the first steps were being taken in the keeping of domestic animals. As for the dog which seems to be depicted in several pictures, e.g. the stag chase in the Cueva Vieja, Alpera (Albacete prov.), it is not surprising that it should be present in a post-glacial hunter culture. We have authentic evidence that it appeared in the Mesolithic period in other districts (Maglemosian culture in northern Europe, Natufian culture in Asia Minor).

DISTRIBUTION   Further evidence may be adduced from the distribution of Spanish Levantine paintings. We have seen that they occur almost exclusively in the mountainous hinterland of the coastal area and are not to be found in the strip of land along the coast itself. This suggests that this was an area to which the hunters in question were forced to retire by the advent of other peoples. This is also indicated by the fact that no discovery has been made of any fishing scenes or renderings of boats, which is most remarkable in view of the proximity of the sea; we must at any rate reckon with the possibility that the coastal area was under the control of other tribes. Against this the argument may be advanced that the absence of such representations was due to the fact that the myths express-ed in these rock paintings for some reason or other bore no relation to the sea. But since the rock paintings certainly often manifest a mixture of mythical tradition and present experience, I attach no great signif-icance to this argument.

Spider surrounded by flies. Cingle de la Mola Remigia, Gasulla gorge, Castellón prov. *Scale approx. 1 : 1·5.*

Fig. 30 — 'Lasso-thrower'. Painting in red. Cuevas de la Araña, Valencia prov. After E. Hernandez-Pacheco. Scale approx. 1 : 2

Thus we have now already obtained two clues to the age of our paintings: they appear to be post-glacial and to be the product of hunters. The question thus arises as to how long people with such an acquisitive mode of existence lived in the mountainous hinterland of the eastern Spanish coast. This cannot be easily ascertained: firstly, because we know relatively little about the Mesolithic cultures of this area; and secondly, because we have no reliable indications as to how quickly they came within the sphere of the Neolithic culture which established itself in the Iberian peninsula towards the end of the fourth millennium B.C.

In the realm of eastern Spanish rock paintings various groups of Epipalaeolithic finds have been discovered. Some of them were excavated stratigraphically in the area of, or close to, niches containing pictures — for example, at Cueva de Doña Clotilde, Cocinilla del Obispo and Prado del Navazo near Albarracín (Teruel prov.), Cueva de la Rabosa or de los Melones in the Valltorta gorge, and Roca des Moros near Cogul (Lérida prov.). Others were found at open stations. They manifest the tendency, characteristic of the Mesolithic period, to produce, in addition to rather badly-worked flint implements of normal size, small stone objects, often geometrically-shaped, which are mounted in frames of wood or bone. It is more than probable that the people who produced these stone implements may also be regarded as the creators of the Spanish Levantine paintings. They may simply be descendants of the Upper Palaeolithic population of the same area. But we must also reckon with new influences introducing fresh elements, the most likely area from which they could have originated being that of the Capsian culture in North Africa. These innovations could in theory include not only the differently-shaped microlithic flint implements, but perhaps also the ideas expressed in the paintings. When these influences began to exert themselves upon the

Fig. 31 — Archer with shoulder-cape and loin-cloth or girdle. Painting in dark red. Mas d'en Josep, Valltorta gorge, Castellón prov. After H. Obermaier. Scale approx. 1 : 2·5

indigenous Epipalaeolithic or post-glacial tribes cannot as yet be determined. It may have taken place some time between 8000 and 5000 B.C. But one would have to make a thorough study of all the Epipalaeolithic material, supplemented by further finds, in order to establish whether the external influences appeared at once or gradually. The compilation of accurate maps could perhaps also show whether the Epipalaeolithic and Mesolithic hunters lived at first in the proximity of the coast and were then gradually pressed back into the mountainous hinterland, and whether an explanation based on cultural differences can be given for the absence of analogous pictures in the south of the Iberian peninsula. Without these essential prerequisites it is difficult to say anything about the date when paintings appeared for the first time in Spanish Levantine style. If this genre has its roots partly in the art of the last phase of the Ice Age (we shall come back to this point later), it must be assumed that it is very old indeed. On the other hand, its location in the mountainous hinterland seems to suggest that it developed at a relatively late date. The almost complete absence of clothing in the pictures of human beings, to which we have already referred, also seems to indicate a markedly warm period (climatic optimum 4th-3rd millennium B.C.?). In this connection it may be added that according to some scholars the bell-shaped skirts which can easily be identified in pictures of women presuppose not only the use of home-made (or, more probably, bartered?) woven cloths, but may possibly also point to influences radiating from the Minoan civilization in Crete. This, however, would suggest a surprisingly late date. We are just as much in the dark as regards the date when eastern Spanish art came to an end. For we do not know whether rock art continued until the end of the old hunter culture; nor do we have any sure indication as to the date when the Mesolithic population became assimilated or was wiped out by the cave or Almerian cultures, or by a Neolithic facies derived from them, as they gradually spread towards the interior. Presumably this took place in the main some time during the 3rd millennium B.C., with remnants surviving for a little longer.

Fig 32 — Man with knee-breeches. Painting in dark red. Els Secans, Teruel prov. After H. Obermaier. Scale approx. 1 : 3

Below, on the right: an anthropomorphous figure (possibly the spirit of a wild animal or a man with an animal mask); above, on the right: wild goat (?); below, in the centre, a receptacle (a small basket or bag) over six horizontal arrows; above, on the left, man with bow. Cingle de la Mola Remigia, Gasulla gorge, Castellón prov. *Scale 1 : 1·8.*

ORIGIN   A final point to be considered in connection with Spanish Levantine art is the question of its origin. We are faced in particular with the following problem: do any connections exist with Franco-Cantabrian Ice Age art, or could an individual rock painting style have developed in the Epipalaeolithic and Mesolithic cultures of eastern Spain independently from the Upper Palaeolithic tradition? And, irrespective of the question whether they were based on ancient traditions or not, did external influences play a part in the development of Spanish Levantine art? It has already frequently been pointed out that the paintings of the Spanish Levant bear some resemblance to the Franco-Cantabrian pictures. This is in fact the case with some of the animal pictures. Consider, for instance, the stag at Labattut (Dordogne dép.), which we have had occasion to mention, and which may possibly bear comparison with one of the cervidae at the Cueva Remigia (Castellón prov.); or the wild

96

oxen at Lascaux (Dordogne dép.), which distinctly resemble those at Roca dels Moros near Cogul (Lérida prov.). But these similarities are rather of a general nature and only concern animal figures. In spite of this one would not be wrong in assuming that Upper Palaeolithic

Fig. 33 — Man with bow and cap. Painting in red. Cueva Vieja, Alpera, Albacete prov. After H. Obermaier. Scale 1 : 4 · 5

traditions played their part if one knew for certain that Spanish Levantine art had already appeared in an early phase of the eastern Spanish Mesolithic; all the more so since there is authentic evidence of Franco-Cantabrian minor arts in the eastern Spanish area, most notably the painted and engraved stone slabs from the cave of Parpallo (Valencia prov.). If this were not so, we should have to assume that traditions which had fallen into oblivion for a long period of time suddenly burst into life again later, which is highly improbable.

It is, however, certain that, animal figures apart, eastern Spanish rock painting follows an individual style markedly at variance with that of earlier Ice Age art. In theory, the new elements — i.e. the entire art of the Spanish Levant — may possibly have developed independently on the spot. But before we discuss this point we must still deal with the question whether any links can be established with other areas.

Apart from several rather peculiar human figures at the cave of Addaura (Monte Pellegrino, near Palermo, Sicily) there is nothing in Stone Age Europe that could be related to Spanish Levantine art. It is therefore necessary to look towards Africa. We have already mentioned (in connection with the question of the origin of the microlithic element in the inventory of post-glacial stone implements in eastern Spain) the probability that African impulses could have played at least some part in the development of the eastern Spanish style. There are, moreover, doubtless some resemblances between the paintings of the Spanish Levant and certain rock pictures on the Dark Continent. According to K. J. Narr a more recent pictorial style can be traced from South Africa through Southern Rhodesia and East Africa to eastern Spain. The same author therefore speaks of a 'Eurafrican hunter culture', the last remnants

Fig. 34 — Two figures from the 'Dancing Women'. Painting in black. Cogul, Lérida prov. After J. Cabré. Scale approx. 1 : 8

of which can be found today with the Bushmen and some other non-Negro peoples in Africa. There are, indeed, as has been observed long ago, startling resemblances between the eastern Spanish paintings and those of South Africa. The great distance which separates these two areas can to some extent be reduced by finds in the same style in Rhodesia, East Africa, Egypt and the central Sahara. But there is as yet no convincing evidence of a link across North Africa; although this region, too, can boast of extensive centres of rock paintings, they differ from those in other regions. Nevertheless, there is a certain probability that connections do exist, despite the distance involved, between the Iberian peninsula and the southernmost parts of Africa. We have not as yet any detailed information about these connections, which can only be identified indistinctly. Only a series of stylistic comparisons will make possible some progress in solving this question. Serious difficulties also exist in that the dating of the relevant pictures in rock strata in Africa is just as uncertain — if not more so — as the dating of the Spanish Levantine paintings. Consequently it is not easy to answer the question whether the style of eastern Spanish rock pictures developed on the spot or whether it can be traced back to African impulses. For it is just as feasible that the influences radiated from the Iberian peninsula to Africa as from south to north. The circumstance that the Mesolithic groups of eastern Spain were probably influenced by the Capsian culture of North Africa is of no particular significance; in any case, there are as yet no indications that a new style of painting was introduced to the Spanish Levant from the Capsian area. Nevertheless the possibility remains that the basic ideas of eastern Spanish rock painting have their roots in Capsian culture. It is, however, strange that similar paintings are non-existent in the south of the Iberian peninsula. Must we therefore reckon with influences introduced into the Spanish Levant not by way of Gibraltar but directly from North Africa?

Thus we see that connections between eastern Spain and the African centres of rock art are quite probable. But it is still an open question whether the impulses came from the Iberian peninsula or from Africa. The origins of Spanish Levantine art are therefore still shrouded in mystery. Further research is required before this problem can be solved.

Fig. 35 — Stag hunt. The animal to the left of the stag may be a dog. Painting in black. Cueva Vieja, Alpera, Albacete prov. After J. Cabré. Scale approx. 1 : 8

98

THE ROCK ART OF THE MAGHREB AND SAHARA

BY

HENRI LHOTE

By the Maghreb we understand Morocco, Algeria and Tunisia, the region once called by the Arabs 'the island of the Maghreb'. The backbone of the Maghreb is the High Atlas mountain range. The most important specimens of rock art are to be found south of the Atlas mountains, and those situated in the north are only of secondary importance.

By the Sahara we understand the desert area extending south from the Saharan Atlas to the grass steppes of the Sudan. Our region of study also embraces the Fezzan, Tibesti, Borku and Ennedi regions, although the last-named district forms part of the Sudanese steppe. We shall not consider here the deserts of Egypt and the former Anglo-Egyptian Sudan, although these regions also contain rock engravings.

The first discoveries of prehistoric works of art were made in the Maghreb and the Sahara at a time when the origin of mankind was still in fierce dispute and no one dreamed of the existence of prehistoric art. In 1847 officers of General Cavaignac's expedition against the Ksour tribes in the mountains of southern Oran chanced to come across large rock engravings at Thyout, Moghar and Tahtani. The figures depicted elephants, lions, antelopes, bovidae, ostriches, gazelles, he-goats and human beings armed with bows, several of whom were linked to one another by their genital organs. The discoverers had no doubt that these were ancient works, dating from an era before the Arab invasion but after the time of Carthage. They concluded that they were the work of idolaters believing in fetishes, who had been brought to the oases of southern Oran in caravan expeditions from the south of Africa; they assumed that the artists must have been Tuareg. For the first discovery of rock drawings in the Sahara we are indebted to the German scholar Heinrich Barth; in 1850, during the course of the famous journey that was to take him from Tripoli to Timbuktu by way of the Fezzan and the Chad, he discovered near Tel Issaghan in the Fezzan several rocks bearing engravings of human beings with animal heads and a herd of cattle. When, following the track along the Aïr massif, he reached the

DISTRIBUTION

DISCOVERY

99

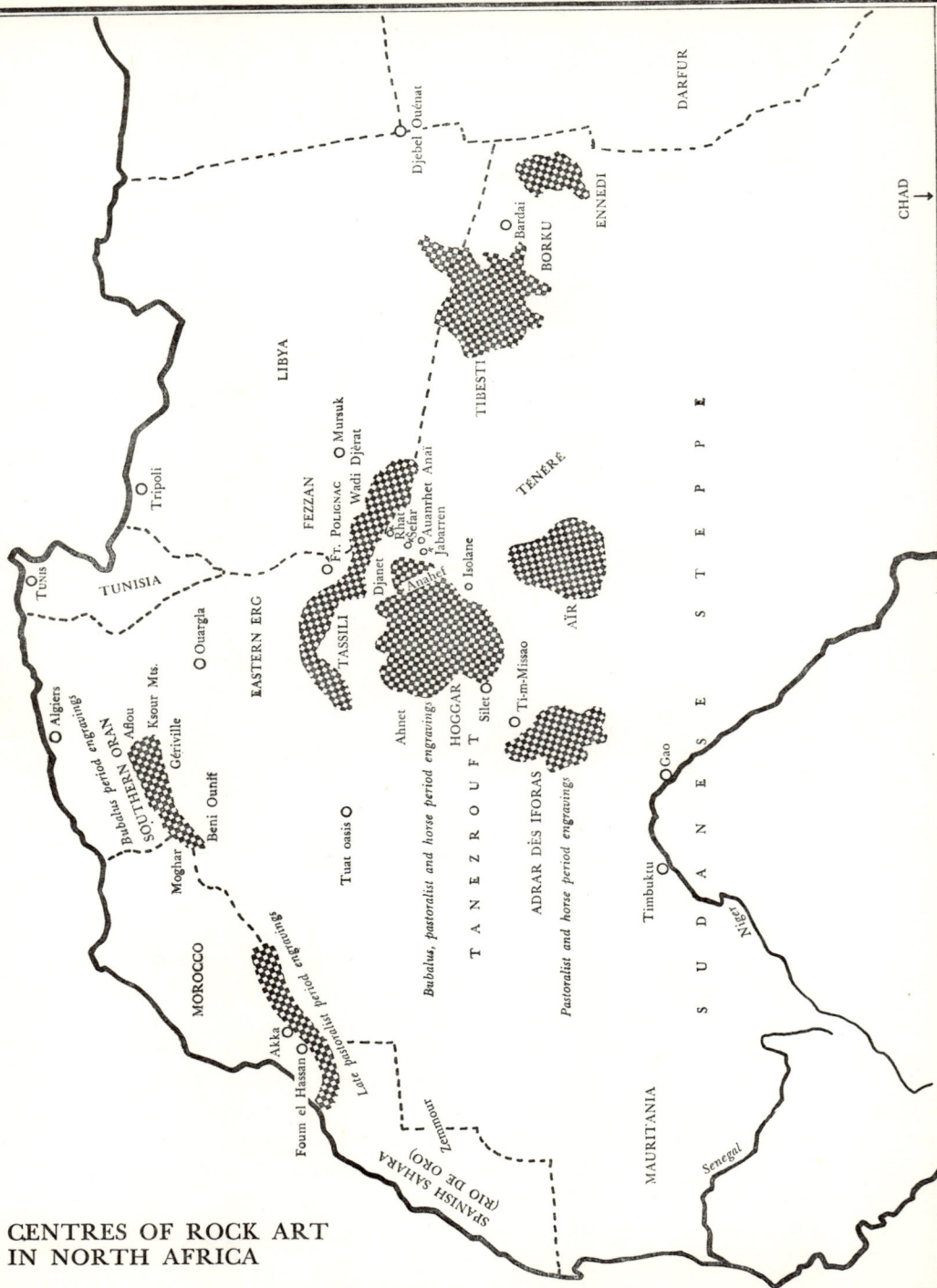

CENTRES OF ROCK ART
IN NORTH AFRICA

springs of Isolane in the southern part of the Anahef he found further animal engravings and written characters, the products of the Tuareg.[1] Barth recognized these engravings as of high quality, the handiwork of skilled draughtsmen. He believed that they showed affinities with Egyptian art and that they must have originated from the Carthaginian epoch. Already at that time he also came to the interesting conclusion that the animals depicted on the rocks bore witness to the fact that the climatic conditions were once completely different from those of the present era, and that the population of those days must have been familiar with cattle-raising.

Change of climatic conditions

In 1860 a French scholar, Henri Duveyrier, found inscriptions in the Tassili and reported that, according to information supplied by the natives, there were other engravings, representing carts drawn by oxen, near Anaï in the Fezzan.

In 1869 Dr. Nachtigal explored the Tibesti, where he came across engravings of cattle: he identified these as animals which the natives had seen in the south, and did not ascribe them to an early period. In 1887 Erwin von Bary mentioned rock engravings, representing human beings, horses and camels, near Dokou in the Aïr massif.

Finally, the explorer F. Foureau, during the course of various journeys undertaken between 1893 and 1899 in the central Sahara, as well as in the Aïr massif, discovered a large number of engravings — both in the Tassili and in the Aïr massif.

Already at that time it was recognized that the rock engravings were distributed over a wide area and could be found in all the larger massifs. This fact was to be corroborated by numerous scholars, travellers and officers who visited the region once the occupation of the Sahara by the French and the Fezzan by the Italians made it safe to do so. In southern Oran, in addition to the rock drawing sites at Thyout, Moghar and Tahtani, others were found at Bou Alem, El Richa, Mouchgueug, Chebkha Dirhem and elsewhere — in other words, the whole region from Béni-Ounif to Aflou can boast of very fine large engravings.

The first important discoveries in the Sahara were made in the Hoggar, whereas the great finds of rock drawings in the Fezzan were only later discovered by Italian explorers and analysed by Frobenius. In this region the discovery was made for the first time of representations of war chariots drawn by horses; these were new elements which had no connection with the finds of engravings made earlier and must be dated to a more recent period.

Whilst performing his military service in Ahnet, the western part of the

Th. Monod

Hoggar, Professor Th. Monod discovered, over a period of 18 months, a large number of engravings which he subjected to careful study. The publication of the results of his investigations furnished valuable material of fundamental importance for all later research.

Several years later a French lieutenant named Brenans discovered in the Wadi Djèrat, a valley in the Tassili-n-Ajjer massif, a vast complex of engravings which apparently showed analogies with the fine pictures of the Fezzan and southern Oran. Among them were war chariots superior in style to those of the Fezzan. There were overhanging rocks covered with paintings from the same period, depicting chariots, human beings and animals.

After Nachtigal a geologist named Dalloni recorded in the Tibesti a large number of other engravings, while British archaeologists accompanying Prince Kemal el Dine found engravings and paintings, mainly of cattle, at the Djebel Ouénat. Later Professor Th. Monod and some French officers were to discover a further vast quantity of engravings and paintings there.

On the Ennedi plateau, too, paintings were found, and not long ago some engravings as well.

A most useful detailed inventory of the rock engravings of this massif has just been completed by a colleague of mine, M. Bailloud.

The exploration of Upper Egypt and the Sudan likewise yielded nu-

Fig. 36 — Horse with human figure in double triangle style and Libyco-Berber characters. Tit, Hoggar

102

merous specimens of engravings and hieroglyphs dating from different periods, of which some definitely originate from pre-Pharaonic times. The first discoveries of rock engravings in the west were reported from southern Morocco in 1875 by Rabbi Mardochée ben Serour; the figures were of elephants, rhinoceroses, horses and human beings. In 1884 Dr. Oskar Lentz made similar discoveries in the region of Foum el Hassane. Since that time exploration has been carried on by French archaeologists and we now know of a large number of sites containing rock pictures. In the Atlas mountains of Marrakesh engravings of chariots were found on Talaat-n-Iisk at a height of over 7000 ft.

In Rio de Oro Spanish explorers have discovered engravings akin to those in southern Morocco.

At Zemmour horizontal shelves of rock have been found covered with small engravings of no great antiquity; at this spot 107 schematically drawn chariots have been recorded.

The exploration of Mauritania has been carried out by Professor Th. Monod, who has registered 1846 engravings and several paintings. Paintings were also discovered in the Adrar region of Mauritania by Mlle. du Puigaudeau and Mlle. Marion Senones. The Aïr massif, situated south-east of the Hoggar, was thoroughly explored by the Englishman FIG. 36 Fr. Rodd, who discovered some particularly fine engravings of horses and camels as well as Libyco-Berber hieroglyphs. Other engravings from this area were brought to notice by M. Nicolas.

The massif of the Adrar des Iforas, situated south-west of the Hoggar, yielded even more finds than the Aïr. Here a number of sites were identified by some officers, as well as by M. Zohrer of the Ethnographical Museum at Neuchâtel, Switzerland.[2]

To sum up briefly, all the mountainous regions of the Sahara contain rock engravings or paintings — often both together — and today, although an inventory of them has not yet been completed, we know of more than 30,000 engravings; in the Tassili alone there are more than 15,000. No other part of the globe can boast of such an important and varied wealth of rock art as this part of Africa, which paradoxically enough is at the same time the largest desert on earth.

Already at the time of the first discoveries it became apparent that not DATING all the engravings originated from the same period. It did not take long to realize that there were marked differences in style, technique and patina, and that in many groups of pictures we find animals depicted which are nowadays extinct in the Sahara, such as elephants, rhinoceroses, large buffaloes (bubalus antiquus) and cattle, while in others we

Group of rhinoceroses and ostriches. The inner surface of the figures is polished. Semi-naturalistic style. *Bubalus* period. Wadi Djèrat, Tassili. *Length 4 ft. 10¼ in.*

find specimens of present-day fauna such as horses, camels and moufflons. Striking variations are also evident in the portrayal of human beings, who are, moreover, armed with different kinds of weapons: axes, boomerangs, bows, javelins, swords and fire-arms.

The techniques of line engraving are particularly varied, and a study of these can in itself enable us to draw valuable conclusions. *Technique*

In the case of the oldest engravings, i.e. those with a very dark patina, the contour is usually formed by a deeply incised line, a groove which in cross-section has the shape of a levelled-off V or a U. This groove can be almost half an inch wide and is polished quite smooth; it is not always regular, and the width varies as well. The degree of irregularity of the contour denotes the quality of the engraving and also shows that the tool used for polishing must have been rather uneven — or, in other words, that this was no mechanical operation and required great skill. In groups of engravings treating the same subject there are figures of which the contours are not polished but pecked out. Both techniques were employed simultaneously, for unfinished figures show that engravings with polished contours were first pecked out. This technique of preparatory roughening is still used today by stone-masons, who before setting about polishing marble or granite chip it with a hammer to obtain small indentations and give their polishing tools or machines a better grip. On the prehistoric engravings the pecked lines consist of rows of small conical holes, generally not connected with one another but separated by fairly small spaces. As a rule it can be said that where these holes are closer together this makes for greater regularity and beauty of form. In some engravings the whole area within the outline, or part of it, is also pecked out and polished.

The techniques of polishing and pecking were employed in several epochs by artists following different styles, but it is easy to establish that the older works are superior and that a gradual decline in quality occurred; the most recent engravings show signs of rough chipping and are no more than mediocre as works of art.

According to some authors the reason for the greater perfection of the oldest engravings is that the artists of that epoch were more skilled in working stone; technical quality would thus act as a criterion of a work's antiquity.

No tool has as yet been found which could provide an explanation of the technique employed at the time in pecking, and more particularly in polishing. The finest engravings are to be found on sandstone rock, which is undoubtedly more easily worked than harder types of stone, although *Tools* quartz and granite are also found bearing engravings. Striking with a hard pointed stone can produce small indentations in the rock, but not so deep, and — more especially — not so regular, as is the case with the old engravings. One pointed stone must therefore have been used as a chisel and another one as a hammer. This hypothesis is borne out by the fact that striking tools of a Neolithic type are frequently to be found close to some engravings, whereas this spot cannot have been used as a depôt. This is, however, not always the case; not a single Stone Age tool, for instance, was found near the large assemblages of old engravings in the Wadi Djèrat in the Tassili.

The polishing of the groove is an even greater puzzle, for it is difficult to imagine what kind of tool can have served this purpose. Some grooves with a V-shaped cross-section suggest that the tool used may have been the cutting edge of a Neolithic axe, with the aid of damp sand. But the grooves in which the cross-section is levelled off in the shape of a U, as is the case with the finest engravings, cannot have been produced with any of the stone implements known to us. Had stone axes been used, to make either V- or U-shaped grooves, specimens of them with appropriate traces of wear would inevitably have been found close to the sites of the engravings. But this is not so. Possibly the artist used a pointed stick of very hard wood and damp sand to polish the grooves after pecking them. But in these questions we have to resort to hypotheses, since no tools have been found which could help to determine the date.

Patina Another criterion for establishing the antiquity of the Saharan engravings is their patina. It has been ascertained that with some engravings the colour of the contours is identical with that of the rock worked, whereas with others they are lighter, and indeed are found in a whole range of shades.

In the Sahara all rock is covered with a layer which is always darker than the rock itself; this also applies in the case of the different kinds of sandstone, the natural colour of which is white. This forms a protective layer and is called desert patina. According to geologists it could only be formed in a hot and humid climate, its development being due to an amassing of oxides: iron oxide, manganese dioxide, and various carbon dioxides, which dissolve in the rain-water that soaks into the rock and are brought back to the surface by capillary action, insolation and evaporation. If one chips a rock in the Sahara, the cut will have the original light colour of the rock, while the adjacent parts of the surface will be darker; from this it follows that the more recent an engraving the lighter the patina, and *vice versa*. Thus on a rock covered with engravings it is possible to

Elephant. Engraving with polished lines. The elaborate ear, with the folds shown, stands out as though in relief. *Bubalus* or pastoralist period. Bardai. *Height approx. 7–8 in.*

distinguish with certainty between the early works and those of a later date, and to arrange them all chronologically. But the reservation must be made that this method is not applicable in every instance, for there are various factors that can lead to erroneous conclusions. For patina does not always form evenly. First the position of the rock in relation to the sun has to be taken into account, since those parts exposed to its rays are more liable to oxidization. Secondly, patina is formed with varying rapidity and produces different shades of colour according to the geological structure of the rock and its oxide content. Thus on many engravings depicting camels the patina is as dark as on others representing elephants; but as we know that the camel was introduced into the Sahara at the beginning of the Christian era, the engravings can only be relatively recent, whereas those of elephants are Neolithic. This method must therefore be applied with caution where we are not dealing with engravings on the same rock or stone slab. Nevertheless, examination of the patina, supplemented and controlled by other methods, is an invaluable means of establishing the age of a work.

Further guidance is provided by the species of animals represented. Here the criterion is whether they are still to be found in the Sahara or not.

EXTINCT ANIMAL SPECIES The earliest discoverers of animal pictures in southern Oran and the Sahara were struck by figures of extinct species such as elephants, rhinoceroses, cattle, etc., and concluded that these were early engravings which testified to a subsequent change in the climate.

The explorer Gerhard Rohlfs, however, who was well acquainted with the western Sahara and saw a number of the engravings, attached no significance to these figures of elephants, cattle, etc., for, as he said, "these pictures are in just the same category as the primitive reproductions of steamships that I have seen at Tafilalet and Tuat; they were drawn by pilgrims who had returned from Mecca to give their fellow-countrymen an idea what a ship looked like."

Gerhard Rohlfs has had followers, some of whom hold that the engravings are the work of travellers who had seen elephants and rhinoceroses in

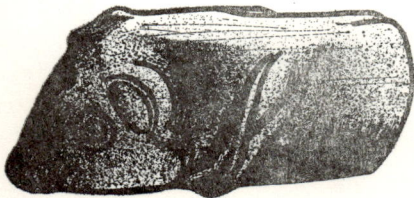

Fig. 37 — Stone sculpture. Recumbent ox. Tarzerouc, Hoggar

108

the Sudan or chariots in the Roman towns of North Africa. This view is superficial, to say the least, and will not be shared by anyone who has seen the Saharan engravings and studied them *in situ*. It will not stand up to serious examination, especially since it takes no account of the large number of rock pictures of this kind that have now been recorded, which if this theory were true would presuppose an equally large number of travellers with the talent of relating their adventures in artistic form; it also overlooks the fact that prehistoric tools have been found close to the sites of many engravings.

In actual fact the species of fauna portrayed in the rock pictures is of the greatest importance, in that it enables us to identify the major epochs in Saharan engraving and painting. In southern Oran, the Tassili and the Fezzan, for example, there is one species of animal that is represented particularly frequently. This is the prehistoric or Cape buffalo *(bubalus antiquus)*, a species now extinct but known from fossil finds. An engraving of a *bubalus* is in itself testimony of antiquity and cannot be interpreted as it has been by Rohlfs.

Together with this prehistoric buffalo, executed in the same technique and covered with the same patina, we can see elephants, rhinoceroses, large oxen with stout horns, wild asses, lions, panthers, ostriches and rams, which may perhaps be domesticated.

In the Wadi Djèrat in the Tassili we come across almost the same species of fauna, but rams are entirely absent and cattle are depicted very frequently.

As evidence of a later period we find many renderings of domesticated oxen, very different as regards technique, patina and style. The elephant, rhinoceros, ostrich and lion are still represented, but the prehistoric buffalo has disappeared. In comparison with the engravings of the preceding period there is a marked and unmistakable change: the great wealth of cattle is particularly striking, and can be regarded as evidence that these animals were reared on a large scale.

Later still the domesticated horse appears, at first as a draught animal before a cart and then mounted. The ox, where it does occur, is no longer prominent; the elephant is only rarely represented, and the rhinoceros, hippopotamus and equine antelope have disappeared altogether. And when the camel finally appears on the scene we only find it in the company of species now found in the Sahara (or in adjoining regions inhabited by nomadic peoples), such as the moufflon, addax, oryx, gazelle and ostrich. The absence of all pachydermata is proof that the climate had changed and that the Sahara now became a desert.

Change of climate

Alongside figures of animals we also find human beings, whose weapons and armour help to determine the date of the pictures.

In the engravings belonging to the *bubalus* period humans are depicted armed with boomerangs, axes — the Neolithic form of which can clearly be seen — and (less frequently) bows.

In the period when cattle were represented the chief weapon was the bow, whereas boomerangs and javelins occur only here and there.

With the introduction of the domesticated horse we see men armed solely with lances and round shields, which survive until after the appearance of the camel — although round shields only disappear gradually, making way for swords and fire-arms.

Ox. Probably a domesticated animal, for it has an ornament round its neck. The human figure standing before it is holding a curved object, possibly a palm-branch. The lines of the engraving are polished smooth. The superposed engravings are stippled; the figure of which only part is depicted here represents a small camel from a later period. *Bubalus* period. Wadi Djèrat, Tassili. *Length of the animal 5 ft. 3 in.*

In conclusion it must be mentioned that the style varies greatly from one stage to the next. As has already been pointed out, the older engravings are technically and artistically more accomplished, and we can clearly trace a steady decline in rock art.

The oldest engravings in which the *bubalus,* elephant, rhinoceros and *Naturalistic style* hippopotamus are represented are remarkably naturalistic; the elaborate care given to detail reflects a highly-developed sense of observation and admirable knowledge of the animal depicted. No doubt hunting was the main occupation of those who were able to produce engravings of this quality; the chase, the ambush, and the setting of traps heightened their sense of observation, as it did with the rock painters in the Franco-Cantabrian caves.

The engravings of this period are not equal in quality. Some of them are the work of great artists, but others are by beginners or men of lesser talents. In addition to naturalistic figures there are others schematically drawn which may have been produced by genuine artists with creative imagination or by incapable dilettantes. There is an exception to every rule, and in all the schools of art in the Sahara and in every period we find works which are of differing styles.

In each stage of stylistic development there is a distinct tendency to represent objects in certain dimensions. Thus in the oldest engravings animals and humans are frequently rendered life-size, sometimes even larger than life. In the Wadi Djèrat there are rhinoceroses as much as 26 ft. 6 in. long, humans over 11 ft. tall, and a group of giraffes of which the tallest measures 23 ft. and covers an area of 98 square yards. But in this case, too, there is no hard and fast rule, and within the same group one may find, in the Wadi Djèrat as well as in southern Oran, small-scale works with dimensions varying between 1 ft. 6 in. and 3 ft.

There are different reasons for these variations in size. They are derived *Variations in size* either from the artist's individual conception or his inability to render the subject on a large scale; another reason may be the gradual decline in the rock art of these regions. Undoubtedly these engravings were produced during the course of countless centuries, and each of the periods which has the same style and subject-matter may have lasted for several millennia — so that even a similarity in the patina does not permit conclusions to be drawn with regard to chronological sequence.

In the group of figures of domesticated cattle the style appears less naturalistic than in the preceding period, and the attention to detail is less marked. Not infrequently one finds legs without hooves, or feet that are incomplete. One may observe a certain stiffness in the rendering of

Heads of pelicans. Birds are depicted relatively seldom in the rock art of the Sahara. *Bubalus period. Wadi Djèrat, Tassili. Height 1 ft. 7¾ in.*

Twisted perspective form, a certain conventionalism reminiscent of children's drawings; thus, for example, ears are placed above the body, making them look like the wings of butterflies, or the horns of oxen are rendered in twisted perspective, i.e. full face, whereas the body is drawn in profile. In general they are represented on a smaller scale than in the preceding stage, and range from 2 ft. to 3 ft. 6 in.; but these are average measurements, and both larger and smaller figures can be found.

With the appearance of the horse a new style develops, related to a special technique, making it easy to distinguish this group of engravings from the others. Many figures are represented in a naturalistic style, which is

not inferior in quality but manifests a certain uniformity in the case of horses rendered 'at the flying gallop'. These pictures are on a smaller scale, with the sides generally measuring between 10 and 20 in. in length; there are also some exceptions, and human beings in particular are occasionally more than 3 ft. tall. The figures have no contour lines but the entire surface is pecked and frequently polished as well.

When chariots are replaced by mounted horsemen the style forfeits some of its quality and the human body is rendered in a most conventional manner; by two isosceles triangles placed one upon the other and joined by their vertices. This has been called the double triangle style; either the entire surface is pecked and polished, or alternatively the lines only are pecked out.

The appearance of the camel seems to mark the beginning of a period of decadence in engraving; if some of the pictures are at first not devoid of a certain quality, most of them manifest a rapid decline towards schematization and come to resemble children's drawings.

This summary of the various factors that make it possible to classify the engravings into various groups applies particularly to the central Sahara, where almost all types of engraving can be found; but there are also local styles and techniques which, though still coming within the general framework, deserve special consideration.

The first attempt at classification was made by the geologist G. B. M. Flamand, who studied the engravings of southern Oran and published a standard work on them which is still today fundamental for any systematic treatment of this most complex subject.[3]

The ethnologist Frobenius also studied the question of the engravings in southern Oran and the Fezzan, but his works opened up no fresh approaches as regards the classification or chronological sequence of the various stages.[4] The interpretation which he gave, in terms of the psychology of the different peoples, was greatly weakened by the fact that he failed to appreciate the differences between the groups of engravings; his disregard for their relative antiquity deprived his final conclusions of all real value: he was, as it were, attempting to juggle with two packs of cards at once.

A more reliable work was written by Professor Th. Monod (of the Museum of Natural History in Paris), who spent 18 months at the Adrar Ahnet, a spur of the Hoggar. He made an inventory of the engravings in this region and as a result of his studies evolved a classification which, like that of Flamand, was based upon the criteria set out in the preceding pages.

CLASSIFICATION

The work of these experts, supplemented by later studies, made it possible to define four different stages:

    I. BUBALUS OR HUNTER PERIOD
   II. PASTORALIST PERIOD
  III. PERIOD OF WARRIORS WITH CHARIOTS AND HORSEMEN, OR HORSE PERIOD
  IV. CAMEL PERIOD

Crouching lion, apparently lying in wait, about to spring. The patina of the lines is not so dark as in earlier engravings. It may date from an intermediary epoch between the *bubalus* and pastoralist periods. Wadi Djèrat, Tassili. *Length 1 ft. 9¾ in.*

114

The most important characteristics of these stages may now be outlined.

I. BUBALUS OR HUNTER PERIOD. The presence of the *bubalus* in the engravings of this stage is an essential criterion, since the *bubalus* belongs to a species that is now extinct. The designation 'hunter period' implies that hunting formed the main means of livelihood during this period, since all the animals represented (elephants, rhinoceroses, hippopotamuses, giraffes, large antelopes and ostriches) belong to the category of wild fauna.

The ram is also represented in rock pictures of this period, but it is not yet possible to say conclusively whether this is a wild species or one that had been domesticated. In southern Oran figures of oxen have now been discovered as well; in the engravings in the Wadi Djèrat this animal appears simultaneously with elephants, rhinoceroses, etc., although there are many indications that it was already at this time a domestic animal. It might perhaps be preferable in future to call this merely 'the *bubalus* period' in order to avoid the confusion and generalizations that result from a classification based upon the characteristic feature of human activity in a given period.

Apart from the fauna represented, considered in detail above, the main distinguishing characteristics of this period are: 1. naturalistic style; 2. contour formed either by a polished groove with a V-shaped or levelled-off U-shaped cross-section, or alternatively by regular pecking out of holes not connected with one another; 3. dark patina; 4. large scale, but found together with engravings of average size; 5. men shown armed with clubs, boomerangs, axes or bows, but never with javelins.

II. PASTORALIST PERIOD. 1. The fauna are the same as in the preceding period, with the exception of the *bubalus*, which is no longer to be found; 2. the style becomes semi-naturalistic, but one also comes across schematic figures, probably of later date; 3. the contour is represented either by polished lines with a levelled-off U-shaped cross-section (rarely V-shaped), or by regular pecking out of disconnected holes; the technique, however, is inferior to that of the preceding period, and the polished grooves are neither so deep nor so regular; 4. the patina is dark, generally a little lighter than that of the rock, but sometimes of identical colour; 5. the engravings are of average size and (with a few exceptions) vary between 1 ft. 6 in. and 4 ft. in length; 6. the human figures are armed with bows.

III. HORSE PERIOD. This is divided into three sub-periods:

A. Chariot sub-period. 1. The large pachydermata have disappeared — apart from the elephant, which is only occasionally depicted; domesticated cattle still appear; moufflons and tame dogs occur very frequently. The

Bubalus or hunter period

Pastoralist period

Horse period

equine antelope has likewise disappeared. 2. The style, at first still semi-naturalistic, becomes conventionalized. The older chariots are exquisitely drawn and have only one shaft; the chariot horses are almost always depicted in profile, but some are viewed from above with the animals standing back to back. Several chariots drawn by oxen have also been recorded. In the more recent engravings chariots are represented schematically, very often only by the wheels and shaft; some have several shafts and may have served useful non-military purposes. The men represented together with these chariots are schematized in the double triangle figure already mentioned. 3. As far as technique is concerned, the whole surface is pecked, with the holes close together and for the most part overlapping one another, and then polished. 4. The patina has a dark chamois colour. 5. The engravings are small-sized, the sides varying in length between 10 and 20 in.; but there are also some human figures measuring more than 3 ft. in height. 6. The weapons are very different from those in the preceding periods: javelins and round shields appear, but there are still some bows to be seen. In combination with chariots of later date men are shown with a knife dangling from their forearm, which in shape resembles the dagger carried by the Tuareg.

B. Horseman sub-period. The chariot is superseded by the mounted rider, although there are still a few schematically drawn chariots in this period. 1. There is no noticeable change in the fauna. 2. The style is semi-naturalistic in the case of the animals but schematic in the case of the human beings, who are represented in the form of double triangles. 3. The technique consists of fine pecking, with the holes usually overlapping one another, but less elaborately executed than in the chariot sub-period; the inner surface is rarely polished. 4. The patina is chamois-coloured. 5. The engravings are small-sized, varying between 10 and 20 in. But there are also local schools where the engravings measure as much as 3 ft. or more and the style is almost schematic — as, for instance, at Tit in the Hoggar. 6. The men are armed with a javelin, round shield and a knife dangling from their forearm; but several bows have also been found. The type of weapon, moreover, varies from area to area, and three zones can be clearly distinguished: Mauritania, the central Sahara and the Tibesti area. Plumes, which previously appeared here and there together with chariots, now form a decorative head-dress worn by all warriors. In the central Sahara Libyco-Berber written characters now also appear; these were introduced by the horsemen.

C. Horse and camel sub-period. This is the period in which the camel appears, but the horse is still in use as well.

FIG. 46

PLATE P. 126

FIG. 36

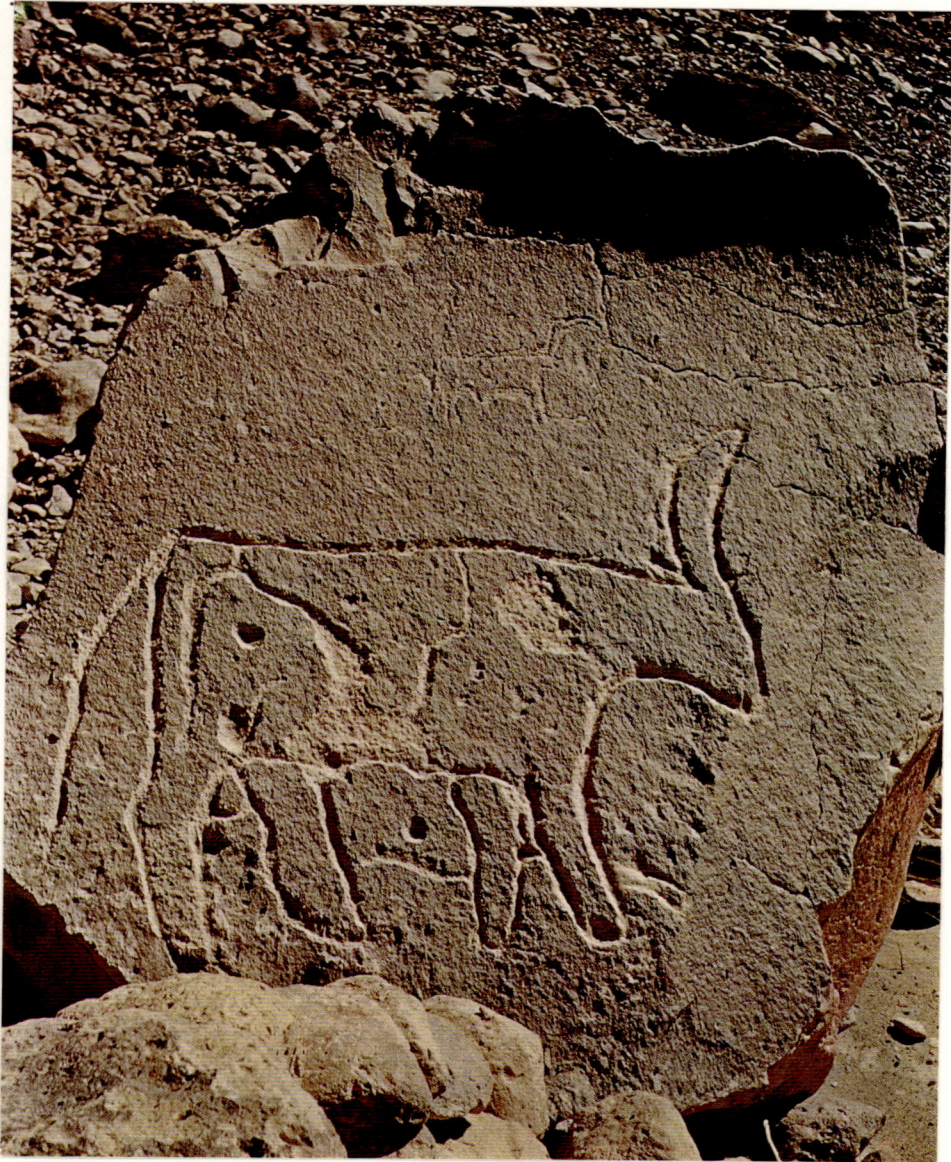

Ox with thick horns pointing forwards. The lines are very deeply incised. The style is mediocre. Late pastoralist period. The smaller figure superposed upon the larger one dates from the same period. Bardai. *Height from foreleg to tip of horns approx. 2 ft. 3 in.*

1. There are no changes as regards the species of fauna represented, but figures of cattle become ever rarer. 2. The semi-naturalistic style becomes decadent, but a few fine figures are still to be found. 3. The technique employed consists of fine pecking (which is, however, cruder than in the preceding period), frequently covering the entire inner surface of the figure; the surface is rarely polished. 4. The patina is chamois-coloured. 5. The engravings are small, varying between 7 and 16 in. 6. The weapons are the same as before, and the warriors still wear plumed head-dress.

Camel period IV. CAMEL PERIOD. This is the most recent period, which is still in progress, for the present-day population of the Sahara continues to practise the arts of rock engraving and painting.

1. The fauna comprise only those animals still extant in the Sahara and adjacent areas to the south: the antelope, oryx, addax, gazelle, moufflon, ostrich, zebu and goat; the horse occurs rarely (in Mauritania, however, more frequently than elsewhere) and is now depicted with a stirrup saddle of the Arab type. Figures of giraffes are still to be found in the southern districts of the Aïr and the Adrar des Iforas, where this animal was extant until only a few years ago. 2. The schematic style is on a par with that of children's drawings; human figures in the form of double triangles become rare and are superseded by linear forms. 3. The technique consists in roughly pecking out the entire figure. 4. The patina is very light, almost white. 5. The engravings are on a very small scale, varying between about 6 and 8 in. 6. In the older engravings of this period almost the only weapon found is the javelin, which is still in use today, but here and there one also comes across swords, such as are worn by the Tuareg, as well as fire-arms.

PAINTINGS The classification given above was worked out on the basis of a study of engravings, before the discovery of the numerous rock paintings; if these had been taken into account this would doubtless have influenced the general principles of our theory.

Rock paintings are not found everywhere. In contrast to engravings, which occur wherever there are rocks capable of taking them, paintings are only located in places protected from inclement weather, owing to the perishable nature of the materials used. As in all other parts of the world, the sites containing rock paintings are either in caves or beneath overhanging rocks. In the Sahara there are no real caves, but only overhanging or hollowed-out rocks, which are found solely in areas with a specific mineralogical structure, especially in sandstone massifs. Some paintings have also been identified in the granite of the Hoggar, but this is exceptional, whereas they occur in thousands in the Silurian and Ordovician sandstone formations in the Tassili-n-Ajjer.

The first rock paintings of any importance were discovered on the Ennedi plateau and the Djebel Ouénat, i.e. south and east of the Tibesti massif. These were soon followed by further discoveries, at first in the Tassili, then in the Hoggar, and finally in Mauritania and the Tibesti. Most of these paintings could be classified according to the major categories of rock art as established on the basis of the engravings; judging by the species of animals portrayed, they fell into the cattle period, chariot and horseman period, and camel period. But in 1956 and 1957 new discoveries were made in the Tassili that surpassed in number, quality and variety everything found hitherto. During an expedition lasting 16 months more than 10,000 pictures were registered and photographed to scale in their natural colours. On a number of these frescoes one may identify several strata or superposed paintings. One of them has no less than 16 such layers and makes it possible to establish the chronological sequence of the various styles and periods. The analysis of this important find is still in progress and far from complete, but we are already able to distinguish between some 30 different styles, i.e. far more than have hitherto been identified in the engravings. More than half of them can be classified into the three major epochs of cattle, horses and camels, but the rest cannot simply be attributed to the so-called *bubalus* period. Many of the paintings have numerous features in common with this period and may belong to it; but the majority of them seem to originate from a long intermediate epoch between the *bubalus* and pastoralist periods. From a stylistic point of view these paintings display characteristics of negro art (symbolism and highly-developed animism); and several representations of typical negro masks lend support to the view that these paintings are the work of negroes.

Fig. 39 — Rock engraving. Aouilalam, Adrar des Iforas

Ox with long horns. Wide, deeply incised lines. Schematic decadent style. Late pastoralist period. Bardai. *Height from hoof to dorsal line approx. 2 ft. 9 in.*

In this most unusual complex of rock paintings, in which the human face is uniformly portrayed in a symbolist style, round and featureless (resembling somewhat the hooded inhabitants of Mars in Jules Verne's tale!) and later takes on the features of animistic masks, it seems as though we are confronted with the earliest works of negro art — indeed, one is tempted to say, with its origin. We thus have completely new elements that are later to lead to a modification of the present 4-stage classification of the Saharan rock engravings and paintings.

The discovery of the rock art of the Sahara, with its figures of animal species that have since vanished from this region, has shown conclusively that this area, today the largest desert on the earth's surface, was once inhabited, and that in the course of its long history it has afforded shelter to peoples having the most varied modes of existence.

THE SAHARA
IN PREHISTORY

The presence of prehistoric man is, moreover, confirmed by numerous finds of Stone Age implements and other traces of human habitation, particularly kitchen refuse, in which one often discovers bones of extinct animals depicted in the rock pictures. With the aid of these implements, which are scattered throughout the area, we are now in a position to give an outline sketch of prehistoric civilization in the Sahara.

We are familiar with the history of the gradual development of Stone Age implements in Europe; we know that in the beginning these were crudely worked pebble tools or flake tools which later displayed increasing refinement as new knowledge was acquired, new needs developed, techniques were perfected, and the general conditions of life improved. Axes, scrapers and blades, which at first were produced merely from roughly hewn flakes, gradually became objects of more elaborate and accurate workmanship, and simultaneously decreased in weight. The final products of this experimentation were the polished axes and smooth flint arrow-heads that were later slavishly copied by the incipient metal industry. The first group of these tools is Palaeolithic, the second Neolithic. This chronological division, introduced with Europe in mind, eventually had to be adopted in other parts of the world, and particularly in Africa, for it has been ascertained that in this continent industry developed on the same lines, and the same types of implement were produced, as in Europe — some small details excepted. Each of these two regions is in fact an extension of the other, and even today we do not know in which of them the human race first appeared — although Africa has in recent years furnished evidence suggesting that it was one of the cradles of mankind. However that may be, in the past the Sahara could boast of a population as large as, if not larger than, any other region in the eastern

Tools

hemisphere. Its density was greatest in the Lower Palaeolithic, at the time of the Chelles-Acheul industries; the typical products of that era, heavy pieces crudely chipped on both sides and referred to as hand axes, are found in all areas: in the ergs (deserts of sand dunes), regs (deserts strewn with pebbles), at the outlets of valleys in the mountain massifs, and in the coastal areas. These objects are for the most part widely scattered about, but in isolated cases they were also found at hearths together with remains of bones, among them those of prehistoric elephants, large hippopotamuses, prehistoric buffaloes, a zebra that cannot definitely be identified, and several fish of the Silurian period, as well as species that are now largely extinct.

The much older and far more primitive pebble-tool industry exists in the Sahara as well as in South Africa, where it has been discovered in recent years; it represents the first fumbling effort by man to produce implements.

In Africa, as on our own continent, the people of this epoch lived from hunting and fishing, and probably also gathered certain kinds of red berries and herbs.

Race What race did they belong to? The question still remains open, for no Palaeolithic human skeleton has as yet been found together with implements from this period. But they probably belonged to the race that inhabited North Africa and which we have recently come to call the race of Atlanthropos of Palikao.

The Levalloisian-Mousterian industries, which in Europe were superseded by those of the Chelles-Acheul culture, were likewise indigenous to the Sahara, but were more localized, particularly in the northern region; they have, however, left fewer traces, an indication that the area was now less densely populated than before. The Upper Palaeolithic, which corresponds to the Ice Age and reindeer hunter culture in Europe, is represented in North Africa by clearly identifiable local industries, but these do not appear in the Sahara. There is a gap here, the causes of which are still unknown; but it seems that the conditions of life, which had been so favourable in the Lower Palaeolithic, deteriorated in the subsequent period, as is indicated by the low density of population in the Mousterian.

Change of climate Did the Sahara go through a phase of desiccation on some previous occasion? This is not impossible, as seems to be suggested by the existence of fossil dunes, ascribed by geologists to the final stages of the Palaeolithic. Suddenly the scene changes completely! Once again masses of people stream into the whole region between the Atlas range and the Niger; mountains and valleys are resettled by numerous tribes. This is the

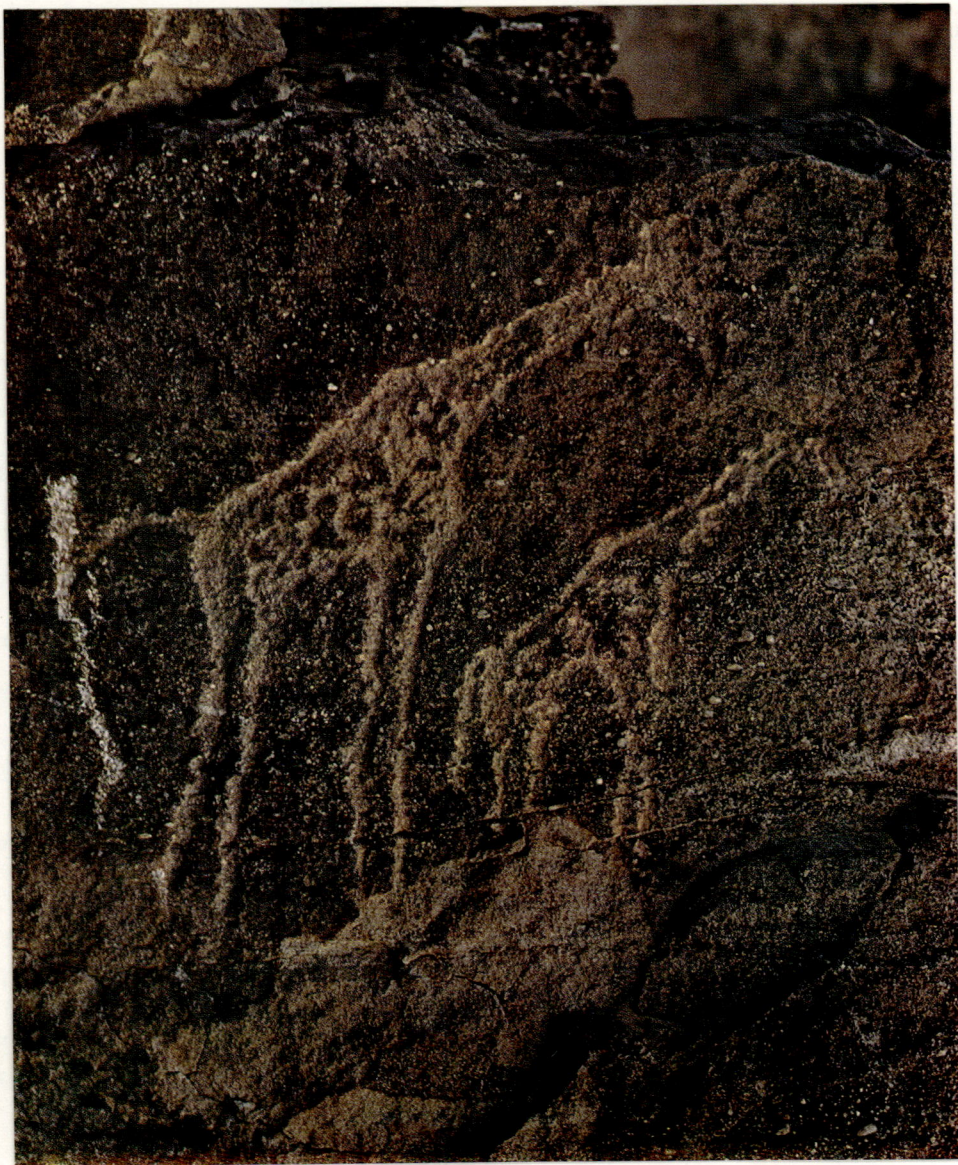

Giraffes. Wide, crudely incised lines. Mediocre style. Late pastoralist period. El Greiribat. *Height of taller giraffe approx. 1 ft. 10 in.*

Fig. 40 — Stone sculpture. Recumbent wether. Wadi Amazzar, Tassili

beginning of the Neolithic epoch with its polished axes, flint arrow-heads and various types of potsherds. Thousands of finds in all regions of the Sahara bear witness to this period; they are of the most assorted shapes and sizes, indicating that numerous waves of migration took place and that the modes of life of the various tribes were very different. The valleys were, of course, the most densely populated parts, for they were at the same time the trade routes. Ancient settlements of fishermen have been identified in the south of the Hoggar, in the Tanezrouft and Ténéré; here vast quantities of fish-bones and mussel-shells were found. As is still the case today on the banks of the Niger, the menfolk fished in the deep water and hunted hippopotamuses, whilst at low water the women-folk gathered mussels.

Agriculture Several skeletons recovered from strata of this period show that the fishermen of the Sahara were negroes. In other areas axes with an arched blade at right angles to the handle seem to have served as hoes, suggesting that the soil was tilled on the low-lying land and areas subject to flooding by the rivers. The rivers, incidentally, seem to have been deep, at least during several months of the year, for otherwise they could not have held such an abundance of fish — nor, in particular, of hippopotamuses and crocodiles. Remains of these animals are frequently to be found in the kitchen refuse left behind by humans on terraces situated high above the floor of the valley, which apparently served them as places of refuge when the water began to rise. Herbs began to play an ever greater part in the diet; this is evidenced by the abundant finds of grindstones, crucibles and pestles made of stone, as well as the large number of potsherds.

Hunting Hunting, too, was practised on a large scale, with the bow as the most common weapon. Arrow-heads are to be found in the ground everywhere: in the valleys and ergs (deserts of sand dunes) as well as in the mountains, where the hunters had a wealth of game available.

Cattle-raising Cattle-raising appears to have been held in high esteem by some tribes;

although excavations have until recently been unable to provide us with much information on this subject, some light is thrown upon it by the evidence of the rock pictures.

It is possible to follow with a fair amount of accuracy the receding of the water in the rivers, i.e. the beginning of desiccation. One can note the formation of numerous lakes, indicating that the water could no longer discharge and was held back in the low-lying land. Furthermore, there are traces of settlement on the banks of the rivers, indicating that the people were no longer forced to take refuge from the floods on the terraces, but descended into the valley to be closer to the receding water. In deposits of the Late Neolithic aquatic fauna are completely absent. Gradually the desert began to spread, and man was compelled to withdraw either to the humid lowlands, where oases were formed, or into the mountainous regions, where there were, and still are today, springs and water-holes — natural basins that are fairly plentifully and regularly filled and refilled with rain-water.

From our study of prehistoric deposits we can attempt to determine the age of the engravings and paintings of the Sahara.

AGE OF SAHARAN ROCK PICTURES

Many authors, influenced partly by the work done on the Spanish paintings and partly by the extinct species of animals depicted in the old engravings, were at first inclined to ascribe the large-sized engravings of the *bubalus* period in southern Oran to the Upper Palaeolithic. It is particularly difficult to determine the age of the rock pictures since, in contrast to the finds of implements, they do not occur in archaeological strata. In Europe, in the Franco-Cantabrian area, sacral or profane implements, as well as plaques of ivory or limestone bearing engravings, were found in archaeological strata which corresponded to the representations on the walls of the caves; and by comparing them it was possible to establish the antiquity of the rock pictures. But the archaeologist in the Sahara has nothing of this sort to assist him.

Implements discovered in the proximity of the sites can help to determine the age of the pictures, although it is impossible to prove that the man who produced an implement discovered at the foot of an engraved or painted rock must also have been the creator of the work concerned. At the sites in southern Oran, which could be examined most thoroughly owing to their ease of access, most of the tools discovered at the foot of the murals were Neolithic, and no older pieces were found, even in the general proximity of the works. In the light of this fact the hypothesis that these engravings belonged to the Palaeolithic had to be abandoned, and instead they were ascribed to the Neolithic. These were the conclusions

Archer. The inner surface of the figure is chipped. The three feathers on the head resemble those on Libyan warriors in Egyptian figures. The clothing consists of a bell-shaped tunic, fastened at the waist and hanging half-way down the thigh. The bow was very rare in this period. Horse period. Wadi Djèrat, Tassili. *Height 1 ft. 5¹/₃ in.*

reached after several months of study on the spot by Professor Vaufrey of the Anthropo-Palaeontological Institute in Paris.

But Abbé Breuil, the internationally acknowledged authority on prehistoric art, was inclined to place them at a slightly earlier date, although he did not support the thesis that these works should be ascribed to the Palaeolithic; instead, he put their origin at a time of transition from the Palaeolithic to the Neolithic.

The observations of Professor Vaufrey are incontestably correct in so far as they concern the general occurrence of Neolithic implements, but the complete absence of pottery and the rarity of arrow-heads and polished axes suggest a very early Neolithic.

This question again became acute recently, after a fresh examination of the engravings in the Tassili, particularly of the famous sites in the Wadi Djèrat, where more than 4000 engravings were registered, originating from different epochs and distributed over a length of more than 18 miles. With each complex of engravings of the *bubalus* period situated near a terrace, crudely worked flakes were found bearing an obvious affinity to those of the Levalloisian-Mousterian. There are unfortunately only a few typical specimens which, judging from a cursory examination, may belong to a very primitive Neolithic; but it is still too early to draw final conclusions. In any case, these 'knocked off' flakes, even if they originate from the Palaeolithic, show that these engravings are prehistoric; they can be ascribed at least to a very early phase of the Neolithic following closely upon the Palaeolithic; here one may agree with the view of Abbé Breuil.

It should be mentioned in this connection that the Levalloisian-Mousterian industries, which in Europe belong to the Middle Palaeolithic, were able to survive in the Sahara up to the beginning of the Neolithic. If pieces of the crude tool used in this industry have been found below engravings of the *bubalus* period, and identified as Mousterian in origin, this would not make the engravings older but would indicate that those who produced them were Palaeolithic men; from an anthropological point of view they would thus be distinct from the Neolithic peoples who suddenly poured into the Sahara, about whose movements we still know so little.

If one takes as a basis the chronology that applies in Egypt and North Africa, early Neolithic would date back to approx. 7000 B.C.; the engravings of the *bubalus* period would thus have originated at this time — with a margin of 2000 years either way, since this period must have been very lengthy.

*Sites in the
Wadi Djèrat*

The paintings in 'round-headed style' seem to follow immediately after the *bubalus* engravings, if indeed they are not contemporaneous with them. Here the student is confronted with the same difficulties as before. In view of the fact that the walls on which they appear frequently also bear more recent figures of cattle and horses, it is impossible to ascribe the tools found at the base of the rock to the creators of these works.

In any case, wherever a site is stylistically pure and free from alien influence, the tools found on the ground nearby are crude axes formed by large flakes, the workmanship of which is reminiscent of those found in the Campignian culture in Europe. Never do we find any pottery, grindstones or pestles, whereas these items occur very frequently with the paintings of the cattle period. They may thus be considered early Neolithic, although the reservation must be made that it is not yet certain whether those who painted the pictures in round-headed style also produced these tools.

Pastoralist civilization

We are better informed about the pastoralist period, for tools and household implements are to be found in great abundance in the rock-shelters which contain their remarkable works of art. Below the overhanging rocks where they dwelt the ground is strewn with potsherds, grindstones, crucibles, pestles, polished stone axes, and flint arrow-heads. Quite frequently remains of ashes are found; these are not always located at the same spot, which suggests that the sites were not permanently inhabited — as is only to be expected with nomadic pastoralists constantly in search of new pasture-grounds. This refuse, which at times is as much as 2 ft. thick, has yielded ample material for study, particularly pieces of bone, which are no doubt remains of meals; they are mainly bones of cattle, but there are also some from goats and sheep, for these two animal species were likewise domesticated. The bones of cattle found in great quantities are, so to speak, the visiting cards left behind them by these pastoralists which make it possible to identify other débris. The finds buried under the ashes are mainly potsherds, arrow-heads, grindstones, crucibles and axes similar to those found on the surface, but there are also pendants of schist, armlets of the same material, ostrich egg-shell necklaces, awls, hollowed-out bones engraved with geometric designs, and furthermore a number of small accurately-shaped round discs of sandstone; the use to which these latter were put remains a mystery, but they may have served as amulets worn by animals. We are thus well informed about the material aspect of this pastoral civilization. Remains of charcoal have also been found in the deposits and have been subjected to radio-carbon analysis. Two tests made on samples taken from different sites showed the dates of origin as 3550 B.C. and 2450 B.C. Systematic excavation and more tests would probably yield dates even further apart. The pastoralist period presumably lasted for several millennia. The date of its commencement can be put at 4000 B.C., and its termination may coincide with the appearance of horsemen around 1200 B.C.

For the chariot period we have other sources of information: firstly, the chronicles of the Egyptian architectural monuments, and secondly writings of authors of antiquity, such as Herodotus and Strabo. We are now no longer in the prehistoric era but at the beginning of recorded history.

Chariot period

The domesticated horse was only introduced into Africa at a very late stage, by the Hyksos on their conquest of Egypt, about 1550 B.C. But the chariots drawn on rock walls in the Sahara are more recent and originate from the time of a second invasion, that of the 'people of the sea'. These came from Crete to Cyrenaica, allied themselves with the Libyans settled in that area, and launched an attack upon Egypt. This makes it possible to interpret this style, in which horses and other animals are rendered 'at the flying gallop', the human figures have exaggerated slender bodies, and are armed with javelins and round shields: all these elements also occur in Cretan or Mycenaean art. The association of this artistic style, and the weapons represented in it, with the invasion of the 'people of the sea' lends this hypothesis a very high degree of probability. It should, however, not be inferred that Cretans were also responsible for these pictures, although we know that the invaders, who landed with their families and their chariots, were driven back and compelled to withdraw into the territory of their Libyan allies. The influx of population into such a narrow strip of land as Cyrenaica probably led to emigration to more southerly areas which were less densely populated (and if anything wealthier), and to interbreeding between different tribes. It was through contact with the 'people of the sea' that the Libyans acquired the most characteristic features of their art; thus the rocks of the Tassili attest to the sudden efflorescence of a new school devoid of any

Invasion by the 'people of the sea'

Fig. 41 — War chariot. A fine illustration of 'flying at a gallop'

Fresco. In the centre two lions devouring an ox; a jackal appears to be waiting for the remains of the lions' meal. There are also other figures of cattle, warriors armed with javelins and round shields, Libyco-Berber characters (*left*), a moufflon and several camels of more recent date than the lions and cattle. Horse period to Libyco-Berber period. Wadi Djèrat, Tassili. *Total length of fresco approx. 8 ft. 3 in.*

connection with the preceding pastoralist school. Particularly astonishing is the wide diffusion of works in this style, which are not only to be found in the Tassili and Hoggar, but also cross the borders of the desert region of Tanezrouft (where there are five figures of chariots 'at the flying gallop' at the spring of Ti-m-Missao), and reach the Adrar des Iforas, and almost reach the Niger.

Fig. 41

There can be no doubt that the arrival of the 'people of the sea' in Cyrenaica had decisive consequences for the history of the Sahara, and that the introduction of war chariots gave the Libyans great military superiority, enabling them to spread their power rapidly to the middle reaches of the Niger. Ten centuries before the birth of Christ war chariots crossed the Sahara, and white men who had hitherto occupied only the most northerly regions of Africa penetrated into the heart of the Dark Continent.

In the 5th century B.C. the Greek historian Herodotus recorded that the Sahara was inhabited by Libyans and described the customs of particular tribes such as the Nasamones, a tribe from Augila, the Asbystae, Macae, Lotophagi and others living in the coastal districts, and the Garamantes, Atarantes and Atlantes in the interior of the country. The war chariot was familiar to most of these peoples; Herodotus records that the Asbystae womenfolk were skilled at driving them and that the Garamantes in the Fezzan hunted down the Troglodytes with chariots drawn by four horses. The Troglodytes were no doubt the inhabitants of the Tibesti, that is to say Teda or Tibbu. The Atarantes and Atlantes lived in the Tassili or the Hoggar. The chariot continued to exist for a relatively long time and was still in use among the Libyans who served in Hannibal's army. We do not know when it disappeared from the Sahara, but it certainly was still current in the period of the decline of engravings depicting horses. But it should not be concluded that it was still in use at the time when the camel came on the scene, for there is no evidence that this is so.

Herodotus

The riding of horses was apparently not known to the Libyans before the time of Herodotus in the 5th century B.C., for he makes no reference to this. But the oldest known equestrian figures in the Sahara are in the 'flying gallop' style, the same style as that of the chariots. The use of horses as mounts therefore seems to have already been introduced to the Libyans earlier, but not to have met with immediate general acceptance. One interesting point of detail may be noted here: these earliest Libyan horsemen led beside them a second horse, i.e. a near horse to replace their mount if it were killed in battle.

It is reasonable to assume that the chariot was only superseded by mounted riders after the time of Herodotus. But horses are also represented in the Sahara at a later epoch, long after the introduction of the camel into that region. Its disappearance was doubtless due to the increasing desiccation. Strabo, who died in 21 A.D., records that the desert peoples travelled on horseback but as a precaution took with them a bag of water, which they tied under the belly of their steed.

Opinions are greatly divided with regard to the time when the domesticated camel was introduced into the Sahara. Some authors give a very early date, others a very recent one. The written records appear to support the view that this occurred relatively recently: the camel is first mentioned in an account of the battle of Tapsus, in which the Romans took from King Juba 22 of these animals as booty. From this time onwards the camel becomes indigenous throughout North Africa.

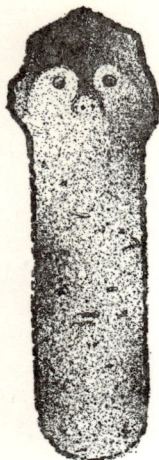

CHRONOLOGICAL COINCIDENCE OF ENGRAVING AND PAINTING

Examination of rock engravings and paintings shows that the camel was never represented in the early periods and makes its first appearance together with a horse. This strongly supports the argument that it was introduced at a late juncture. Today the camel is the only animal capable of traversing the Sahara under its own power. Its introduction (apparently from the Arabian peninsula) and diffusion were doubtless a consequence of the desiccation of the Sahara.

All this gives an idea of the chronological framework in which the rock engravings and paintings of the Sahara are set.

Two modes of expression

The fact that both rock engravings as well as paintings appear in the Sahara intimates that both these modes of artistic expression were in use simultaneously and that painters and engravers existed at the same time. We do indeed know of epochs in which both techniques were employed side by side, but this was not always the case. It is worth examining this question more closely, for it is of importance if we are to understand what kind of peoples lived in the Sahara in early times and the migrations that took place in this area.

From the *bubalus* period we only know of engravings, and as yet no paintings have been discovered that were produced at this time. All we can say is that some *bubalus* engravings are superimposed by paintings — as, for example, at Kef Bou-Bekeur near Tiaret in southern Oran.

Research now being carried out in the Tassili may perhaps eventually lead to analogies being established between the paintings in the round-headed style and the *bubalus* engravings, but there is as yet no evidence of this.

The cattle period surpasses all others in wealth of artistic works; the engravings and paintings from this period may be numbered in thousands. One might almost think that these works all originate from the same era and were produced by the same tribes according to their various whims and circumstances. In his study *Rock Drawings* H. A. Winkler advanced the thesis in regard to Kargour Thal in the Djebel Ouénat that the paintings were the work of women and the engravings of men. But this is unlikely, for if that were so paintings and engravings would have had to appear simultaneously in one zone, which is far from being the case. In this connection an important discovery has been made in the Tassili, the area of the Sahara containing the largest complex of paintings of the cattle period. In this zone, which boasts of more than 10,000 painted figures, there are practically no engravings dating from the same period, although rock faces suitable for this purpose are to be found there in abundance. From this significant fact it may be inferred that the painters and engravers of the cattle period were not necessarily members of the same community and that there must have been groups of painters and groups of engravers existing independently of one another.

If there are nevertheless some sites where engravings and paintings are to be found side by side, these are rare exceptions. The heterogeneous character of these two techniques is evidenced not only by the geographical distribution of these works but also by the ideas that inspired them. Thus, for example, human beings are frequently portrayed in paintings, but rarely appear in engravings. The paintings are always scenic compositions, whereas in the case of engravings objects are almost always represented singly.

Representation of human beings

It is difficult to explain these contrasts except by the existence of two groups of people of different origin, one of whom introduced cattle-raising to the other; this would suggest that as the pastoralists advanced into the central Sahara they came across inhabitants of that area not yet familiar with cattle.

But as far as the chariot, horse and camel periods are concerned it may be taken for granted that a chronological correlation existed between paintings and engravings.

The distribution of the various genres of rock pictures must be considered with reference to the work of each individual period.

DISTRIBUTION OF ROCK PICTURES

The *bubalus* period only boasts of engravings, the majority of which are

Bubalus period

large, although there are also some of average or even very small size. Three centres of art are known in this period: southern Oran, the Tassili and the Fezzan. Some engravings from this period may also exist in the Hoggar, the Tibesti and in southern Morocco, but no conclusive evidence of this is as yet available. However this may be, such a pattern of distribution is most curious, for the various centres are separated from one another by vast areas in which *bubalus* artists have left no trace of their

Warriors, mounted on horses and camels, and armed with javelins and round shields. The horses carry saddles with back supports (so-called Arab saddles), an indication that these figures date from the period after the hegira (Mohammed's flight from Mecca). Wadi Djèrat, Tassili. *Maximum height of figures 9¾ in.*

activity; this implies that they were probably not members of the same tribe, even though the techniques applied are the same and the styles are akin to each other. This seems to be corroborated by the fact that the subjects treated in these engravings are not the same, from which it follows that their religious conceptions must also have been different. In southern Oran human figures are frequently rendered in an attitude of supplication and in combination with animals, such as, for example, the *bubalus*, the ram (shown with a disc between its horns) and the lion; these figures apparently had some religious significance. Neither in the Tassili nor in the Fezzan is this motif to be encountered. The ram with a disc is also absent, whereas the ox with symbols on its horns appears quite often; a few exceptions apart, it is not, however, depicted in combination with human figures. In the Tassili spiral-like ornaments are often found in combination with animals. This motif may have had some symbolic or religious character; its significance remains a mystery. In southern Oran and in the Fezzan, incidentally, spirals are not known. In the Tassili, on the other hand, there are a large number of figures connected by a line drawn from the genitals of one to the genitals of the other, of such a grossly indecent character that one has qualms in presenting them to the reader. Scenes in this genre also appear in the Fezzan, but are, however, completely absent in southern Oran. All these rather marked diversities confirm the fact that only a very slight affinity existed between the three groups of artists.

We do not know who produced these fine engravings, and their distribution, as we have just seen, is of no assistance in answering this question. But the discovery of an engraved plaquette in a Capsian layer in southern Tunisia, bearing a figure drawn in a style reminiscent of the figures in southern Oran, permits the conclusion that this art originated in the Capsian civilization that sprang up on the plateau land of western Algeria and Tunisia, among men related in type to Cro-Magnon man.

Cro-Magnon man belongs to the white race, so that these engravings were the product of white men. This assumption is by no means so surprising as it may appear, for some of the figures portrayed in the engravings of southern Oran have a profile which, though imperfectly executed, can be identified as European rather than negroid. The same applies to the figures of humans in the Tassili, the majority of whom have European profiles. Some of them possess negroid features, but this is not necessarily significant, for many human beings in these pictures are portrayed with ape-like animal heads. Yet these animal heads provide no evidence of the existence of animistic cults as practised by the modern Bushman.

White race

Nor should one forget the role played by certain animals in Egyptian culture.

Period of 'round-headed men'

The paintings of the so-called 'round-headed men' are later in date than the engravings of the *bubalus* period and are doubtless the work of peoples of different origin. This singular school is, so far as we know at present, confined to the eastern part of the Tassili-n-Ajjer, i.e. to the region of the Sahara in which there are the largest number of overhanging or hollowed-out rocks. These paintings, though small to start with, gradually increase in size and finally attain extraordinarily large dimensions; with their figures of human beings measuring more than 16 ft. in height and of cattle and other animals in natural proportions, these are among the largest prehistoric paintings anywhere on earth. In order to produce such works sufficiently extensive rock surfaces were required such as are only to be found in the Tassili; it may even have been the case that the extra-large protected rock walls of the Tassili gave the painters the idea of working on a large scale. The absence of similar hollowed-out rocks in adjacent areas accounts for the marked localization of this school, but we cannot simply conclude from this that the tribes to which these artists belonged were not settled in other regions as well. These paintings, as already mentioned, constitute the earliest elements of negro art hitherto known, which again is evidence of the fact that the Sahara, its northern districts included, was once inhabited by coloured people.

This negro art must have lasted for several millennia; during the last phase of its development it shows a marked tendency towards ornamentation, a feature that can be seen very distinctly in the 'White Lady' of Auanrhet. This is one of the finest works and portrays the goddess of an agrarian cult, possibly of Isis. At the end of this most advanced stage one can find traces of foreign Egyptian influence: the human figures are more fluent and elegant in style, and wear head-dress resembling that worn by the Egyptians. In the Tassili this unexpected contact between negro and Egyptian art has given us such impressive works as the portrait of a woman, no doubt a high-ranking personage, whom we have christened 'Antinea' and whose pure Greek profile make her seem a strange and inexplicable phenomenon in this negro setting.

Where did these coloured peoples spring from? The fact that this genre of painting is confined to the Tassili and is absent from other areas prevents us as yet from putting forward hypotheses as to their origin and the routes they took on their migrations. All that can be said with certainty is that they are related to the negro peoples of present-day West Africa.

Masked woman, wearing ornaments above the knees, anklets and armlets. She is clad only in a girdle, the ends of which hang down to her knees. The curved object that she is holding in her hands cannot be identified; it may be a bowl. Period of 'round-headed men'. Sefar, Tassili. *Height approx. 2 ft. 3 in.*

Fig. 43 — *Stone sculpture. Recumbent mammal (wether?). Silet, Hoggar*

Pastoralist period

Works of art originating from this period are spread over a particularly wide area. They are to be found in all the mountain massifs, as well as in the hilly country west of the Nile, in southern Oran, southern Morocco, Rio de Oro and Mauritania. From this it can be inferred that at some given point in history the whole Sahara was inhabited by pastoralists whose economy was based upon cattle and to a lesser extent upon sheep PLATE P. 120 and goats. The cattle was of two species: firstly the *bos africanus*, an ox PLATE P. 117 with long horns; and secondly the *bos brachyceros*, an ox with stout horns. The sheep seem to have belonged to a species with a fat tail, the Berber sheep and not the *ovis longipes* depicted in the engravings of southern Oran and still reared today by the shepherds of the Sudanese steppe and the Sahara; it was an *ovis longipes* which incarnated the Libyan deity Amon, later adopted by the Egyptians.

It has been held that cattle were domesticated in the Sahara. This is very unlikely, and the most recent research suggests that the wave of pastoralists that streamed into the Sahara came from the adjacent Upper Nile region. The paintings appear to be older than the engravings; their most important centres of distribution are the Tassili and Tefedest massifs, parts of the Hoggar. There are also some in the Ennedi and in Mauritania, but these are more recent products, indicating that the immigrants did not reach these areas until much later. It may not be mere chance that the main centres of painting are situated in the east, on the borders of these massifs; from this it can be inferred that the cattle-

Origin of the pastoralists

raisers came from the east. At first they must have arrived in the Tibesti, then have moved on to the Tassili and Hoggar, and finally have reached the Djebel Ouénat. It may also be mentioned that paintings of cattle do not occur in the Aïr and Adrar des Iforas massifs on the border of the steppe, and that the engravings discovered in the Adrar des Iforas belong to a school centred in the Hoggar.

These facts refute the hypothesis advanced by Rhotert, a follower of Frobenius, according to whom the pastoralists advanced into the interior of the Sahara by way of the Sudanese steppe after conquering the Aïr

138

and Adrar des Iforas massifs. In fact they came through the valleys and over the massifs of the central Sahara, for in this area there were at that time suitable pasture-grounds which made a more southerly route unnecessary. Everything points to the fact that the Sahara was still covered by patches of grassland and that the pastoralists painted the animals which dwelt around them, such as rhinoceroses, elephants, giraffes and even hippopotamuses. The latter appear in pictures representing hunters in a boat, indicating that in that epoch the vegetation was very luxuriant and the rivers deep enough for these animals to live in them.

These pastoralists, especially the painters among them, were artists of note. Their art, contrary to that of their negro predecessors, is devoid of any symbolism or animistic influence; with their astonishingly keen sense of observation, they were able to create one of the finest schools of naturalistic art. Figures rendered singly are rare, whereas composite figures, in which humans occupy a prominent place, occur frequently. Strict attention is paid to perspective, to an extent that is nowhere found in Palaeolithic Franco-Cantabrian art; indeed, the pictures often give the impression of photographs, which shows that these pastoralists had great talent in composition.

COMPOSITE FIGURES

They also produced works of sculpture. A dozen stone figures, representing animals or humans, have so far been discovered. None of them are very large (the tallest measures some 10½ in.); they were carved from hard rock, granite or limestone, and are polished smooth. Their proportions are lost in the mass, giving them a certain ungainliness without, however, diminishing their genuine artistic expressiveness. Among them are figures of cattle, with and without horns, rendered in a crouching position; with one gazelle and one ram the head only is reproduced. The human figures are of two types: some have owls' heads, and others have twin heads, recalling the two-faced Janus of ancient Rome. Most of the sculptures were found in the central Sahara (in the Hoggar and Tassili), the ram's head near Tuat. The significance of these stone figures is not known; they may possibly have been idols. Some of them were found by the Tuareg and put to use in their fertility rites.

FIG. 44

FIG. 45

In the painted human figures, which are sometimes life-size, the profiles reveal different racial characteristics. Some of them are European and others negroid, but the majority have long straight hair and copper-coloured skin, and apparently represent an intermediate type similar to the modern Ethiopians. It seems probable that during the pastoralist epoch people of several races lived in the Sahara at the same time; some, the negroes, may have been slaves of the others. Slavery was a common

RACES

institution among all primitive pastoralists; they had a patriarchal society of a highly military character, and
once their flocks reached a certain
size, they were forced to keep slaves
to look after them and perform other
menial tasks. Judging by the paintings from the Tassili the pastoralists
of the Sahara were already slave-
owners.

In their headgear, clothing and most
typical physical characteristics the
human figures of the pastoral period
resemble the Fula (Peuhl), a tribe
inhabiting the Sudanese steppe at
the present day. They are also pastoralists and are said to have introduced cattle-raising to West Africa.
They are not negroes, for their skin
is copper-coloured, their hair is long
and not curled, and they are endowed with fine features; from an anthropological point of view they belong to the Ethiopian race. Various hypotheses have been advanced about
their origin and the route whereby
they finally migrated to the Sudanese
steppe. According to their own
legends they came to Futa Jallon
in the 8th century; from here they
started out on their last migration
east of the Senegal, which brought
them to the Chad region. Previously
they are said to have settled in
Mauritania, where their ancestors
were known by the name of Bafours.
A people so numerous as our pastoralists of the Sahara, who left such
prolific evidence of their existence,
cannot simply have disappeared

Herd of cattle. In the foreground one of the animals is being sacrificed. Pastoralist period. Jabbaren, Tassili. *Length 10 ft.*

Masked male and female dancers. Only the men wear masks and dance ornaments on their arms and thighs. The same ornaments are worn by the 'White Lady' of Auanrhet, which belongs to the same school. The figure on the left is holding a wind instrument apparently made of horn. Period of 'round-headed men', with Egyptian influence. Sefar, Tassili. *Length 2 ft. 10¼ in.*

without trace. Probably they were driven from the central Sahara by other invading tribes and forced to move further to the west, where the rock pictures they left behind them are indeed of more recent date. Moreover, they were compelled to look for better pasture-grounds owing to the desiccation of the Sahara, for which they and their animals were to a certain extent responsible. It is by no means a mere coincidence that the Fula (Peuhl) today inhabit the entire grass steppe of the Sudan, and it is very likely that they are the direct descendants of our Saharan pastoralists. The paintings and engravings which they left behind them are signposts along the route of their migration.

War chariots
FIGS. 41, 46

The war chariots belong to two different styles: 'flying gallop' and schematized. The former is incontestably the older. It is found only in the central Sahara, the Tassili-n-Ajjer, and the Tassili of Ti-m-Missao. These chariots are thought to have been drawn from memory by people who had attended circuses in the Roman style in North Africa. A similar explanation has been given for the animal engravings of the *bubalus* and pastoralist periods: elephants, rhinoceroses, hippopotamuses and giraffes, which the artists may have seen when participating in caravans or campaigns in the Sudan. This thesis fails to take into account the large number of figures, as well as their distribution and antiquity, which in the case of the engravings is proved by the patination and in the case of the paintings by the resistance of the ochre colours. Surprising though it may seem, these chariots were used in the Sahara, just as the *bubalus*, elephant, rhinoceros and other animals were also once denizens of this area.

The fact that the chariots 'at the flying gallop' are limited to the central Sahara shows the original location of the warrior peoples who used them. These were the tribes referred to by the ancients as Garamantes. The fact that several of these paintings were discovered near the spring of Ti-m-Missao, in the centre of the Tanezrouft, half-way between the Hoggar massif and the Adrar des Iforas, proves that the chariot peoples advanced far on their journeys of exploration and penetrated as far as the Adrar des Iforas, where an engraving of a chariot was discovered at the oasis of Arli. The southern latitude of these engravings suggests that these peoples even reached the Niger in the area of Gao.

Any remaining doubts as to the use of chariots in the Sahara may be dispelled by the fact that they appear in hunting as well as in battle

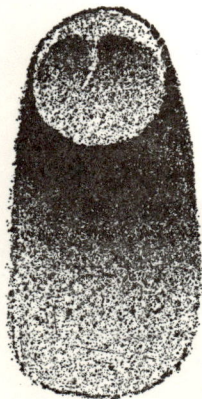

Fig. 44 — Idol with head of owl. Tabelbalet

142

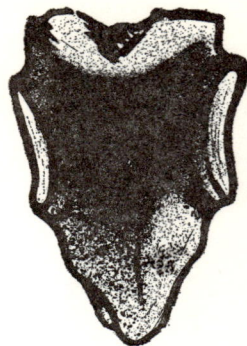

Fig. 45 — Stone sculpture. Head of ram, viewed from the front. Tamentit, Tuat

Expansion of the white race

scenes and that there are also representations of ox-drawn chariots with two shafts which apparently served the purpose of carrying loads. In addition to this the authors of antiquity make frequent reference to the use of chariots among the Garamantes, and the chronicles of the 16th Egyptian dynasty mention this in connection with the Libyans. Thus these chariots and the accompanying human figures in the double triangle style are evidence of the penetration of the white race into the Sahara and their expansion to the south along the mountain massifs. The schematized chariots, mainly depicted in engravings, are, as has already been mentioned, of an early date and belong to the equestrian period. These are much more widely diffused, for they are to be found not only in the central Sahara but also in the Fezzan, Mauritania, southern Morocco, southern Oran and north of the Tibesti. Soon after it first appeared in the central Sahara this vehicle must have conquered a vast area and been adopted by neighbouring tribes. In many pictures two or more shafts are depicted; these are apparently carts.

Riding, which is the next stage after chariots, is only a modification in the use to which horses are put; and the horsemen are represented in the same style and carrying the same weapons.

The area in which these equestrian figures are found is the same as that of chariots 'at the flying gallop', but the pictures are more numerous, indicating that this mountainous area was more densely populated. In this epoch the old Libyco-Berber written characters appear, frequently combined with equestrian scenes. The horseman equipped with javelin and round shield, a decorative plume upon his head, and finally with a knife dangling from his forearm, is not seen beyond the mountains of the Sahara but only as far as the Aïr and the Sudanese plain between the Adrar des Iforas and the Aïr. This corresponds roughly to the territory inhabited nowadays by the Tuareg.

It was only much later that the horse appears to have been introduced into the west, that is to say into Mauritania, and to have been adopted by the population of that region; these people also differed from the others in regard to their weapons, since they carried spears and did not have a knife dangling from their arm. Furthermore, it seems that with the advance of the Arabs the use of horses became general, an assumption

The 'White Lady' or 'Horned Goddess'. This fresco, a splendid work of art, is painted beneath a small overhanging rock at a site that cannot have served as human habitation. The stippling on the body, shoulders, breasts and legs probably represents tattooing. The loin-cloth and dance confirmed by the appearance of the saddle with a support for the back. In the east, in the direction of the Tibesti and Ennedi regions, the horse remained unknown for a long time and is rarely represented; early Libyco-Berber inscriptions are also rare. The horse may not have reached this area from the north or the central Sahara, but from Darfur; here, too, its use became general only after the advent of the Arabs.

Camel period

We have already mentioned that the relatively recent introduction of the camel can be proved by the evidence of rock pictures. Engravings and paintings of camels are to be found throughout the Sahara. The simultaneous appearance of written characters, the occasional association with the horse, and the differences in weapons and harness make it possible to classify these representations chronologically.

Thus it can be concluded that the camel came from the north-east, for most of the oldest representations are to be found in the central Sahara, i.e. in the Tassili and Hoggar. From this area it conquered the south and west. More characteristic are the pictures in the Tibesti showing riders with a knife dangling from their arm, as is common among the Tibbu of the present day. The legends of these peoples also relate that the camel came from the east. The harness consisted of a primitive wooden saddle similar to that still used today by the Moors of the western Sahara; the side-saddle did not come into use until later, and its origin is unknown. The camel is nowadays found throughout the Sahara and it may justly be said that all life in the desert depends upon it — in so far as conditions have not already been revolutionized by motor transport. Thus we see that the engravings and paintings of the Sahara are veritable historical chronicles which enable one to reconstruct in broad outline the past of the peoples who lived in this area.

The existence of rock pictures in the Franco-Cantabrian region and eastern Spain, as well as in South Africa, has given rise to the idea that

AFFINITIES WITH ROCK ART OF EUROPE AND S. AFRICA

ornaments, arm and knee bands, and the cuffs and tassels worn round the wrists and ankles consist of plaited fibres or thin leather straps. The horns on the head appear to be supporting a cornfield, from which seeds of corn are falling. This may be the goddess of an agrarian cult, a predecessor or copy of the goddess Isis, who was credited by the Egyptians with the invention of agriculture. The small figures painted in red ochre appear to be covered by the 'White Lady', but in reality they have been painted over this figure; the impression of transparency is due to the fact that the ochre would not adhere to the white pigment and faded. The 'White Lady' dates from the period of 'round-headed men', with Egyptian influence; the figures painted in red ochre date from the pastoralist period. Auanrhet, Tassili. *Height 4 ft. 1 in.*

Fig. 46 — Engravings of schematized chariots. Haut In Daladj, Hoggar

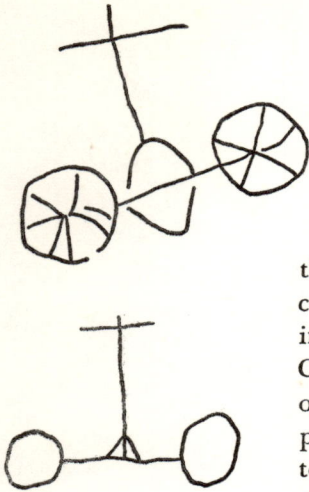

the engravings and paintings of the Sahara, occupying as they do a central position between these two regions, could be the connecting link in a large civilization of prehistoric artists spread over the two continents. Certain resemblances between the paintings of eastern Spain and those of the Bushmen have led some authors to speak of an affinity and to draw parallels which at first sight appear convincing. This theory was very tempting, but lacked any serious scientific foundation, especially from the chronological point of view. The decisive factor here is the age of the works concerned: is it really in order to attempt to establish an affinity in style between works separated from each other by as much as ten millennia or longer? Moreover, the rock pictures of the Sahara are so numerous that it is easy to find among them human or animal figures that bear a striking resemblance to those found in Spain or South Africa. The mistake has been to select examples quite arbitrarily and to neglect the broader issues which, had they been considered, would have changed the picture completely.

It is true that these three art regions do have one thing in common — the naturalistic character of the works; but even if there are some affinities between particular styles, this does not prove that they can be traced back to a common origin.

The antiquity of the eastern Spanish paintings is disputed, and the same applies to those of South Africa. Breuil used to hold the view that the art of eastern Spain, which is so very different from that of the Franco-Cantabrian area, belongs to the final phase of the Palaeolithic or at the latest to the Mesolithic. Spanish archaeologists nowadays plead for a later date, i.e. the Neolithic. According to Breuil the appearance of the bow is evidence of an African contribution to the eastern Spanish school, but in a purely technical, not in an artistic sense; and for a long time he believed that the influences which gave rise to the art of the Saharan pastoralists were transmitted in the reverse direction. But since the great discoveries made in the Tassili this world-renowned authority on prehistory has become more reserved in his opinion on this issue.

When one examines the matter more closely, one finds that the oldest engravings of the *bubalus* period in southern Oran have no demonstrable affinities with the engraved or painted rock pictures of Europe. Not only do these monumental figures only display very vague stylistic affinities with the art of the Franco-Cantabrian area, but it appears that religious conceptions played a part in the choice of these motifs of human figures in association with animals. How could it be otherwise when the two complexes of rock pictures are separated from each other by some 12 to 15 millennia? Can one imagine an artistic tradition being handed down over such a long period of time? In any case such a transmission could not have taken place through the intermediacy of the eastern Spanish painters, for their style has absolutely nothing in common with that of the *bubalus* period. We are therefore of the opinion that the great *bubalus* engravings owe nothing to European art, and that the analogies to be found in the engravings are probably only accidental. *Stylistic affinities*

The oldest paintings of the Sahara, those of the round-headed period, are purely negroid in style. It is beyond question that no affinity exists between them and European rock paintings, either in the Franco-Cantabrian area or in eastern Spain. The art of which they are the expression is even more independent than that of the *bubalus* period engravings; it is inspired by specific religious conceptions and manifests such originality of form that it must be regarded as an indigenous creation and the source from which negro art sprang.

The art of the pastoralists can at the most be compared with that of eastern Spain. In both groups human beings are frequently represented in action and the themes are the same: scenes of battle, hunting and daily life. In both cases it is profane art, to all appearances devoid of any religious conceptions. At first sight some relationship seems possible, but a more thorough examination shows that the art of the Saharan pastoralists was far more highly-developed and considerably less conventional. What then are the affinities between this art and that of other regions and periods? *Profane art*

Until recently the antiquity of the cattle period paintings in the Sahara was still uncertain, although they were believed to be products of the Neolithic epoch. But the latest discoveries in the Tassili have brought two reliable clues: the first of these is the age of two layers of deposit dating from the cattle period which have been subjected to radio-carbon analysis. The pieces of charcoal found in these layers, consisting mainly of kitchen refuse in the form of bones of cattle, date from the years 3550 and 2450 B.C. As already mentioned, these are only average figures, from which it may be inferred that the first pastoralists came to the

Sahara about 4500 B.C. The second clue is to be found in the paintings of the Tassili, where river barques are shown very similar in construction to the barques of the Nile found in Egyptian pictures, particularly in the rock drawings of the Upper Nile. They are classical Nile barques with the state insignia on the prow. Boats of this kind certainly did not originate in the Sahara, and the state insignia suggest Egyptian influence. If this is so, the pastoralists would have come from the Upper Nile area. This argument is reinforced by the human type represented and the remarks above concerning the origin of the Fula (Peuhl) tribe.

Nile barque

The painters of the cattle period thus did not come from Spain, driving before them their *bos africanus* and *bos brachyceros* (which some scholars believe to be of Asiatic origin). We now have to consider the question

Shepherd with a long rope, to which lariats are fastened on at equal intervals. At the end of the rope is a stake, which was driven into the ground. In the Sudan shepherds still today use this method of tethering calves. Pastoralist period. Sefar, Tassili. *Height of figure 4¾ in.*

whether the eastern Spanish paintings are really so old as they are alleged to be and whether they do not contain elements of African origin, as several Spanish archaeologists hold. This daring hypothesis must of course be treated with caution, and the whole problem will remain unsolved so long as the age of the eastern Spanish paintings is not reliably established.

As further evidence of affinity between the eastern Spanish paintings and those of the Sahara, it has been pointed out that articles of clothing similar to the bell-shaped skirts worn by the 'Dancing Women' of Cogul also occur in the Tassili; however, in the Tassili this skirt does not appear during the cattle period, but belongs to the horse period, which began after the 12th century under the influence of Cretan art. This impulse from the eastern Mediterranean therefore rules out the possibility that the paintings were introduced from Spain, and the gap in time is an additional argument against the thesis of a direct link between Spain and the Sahara.

The question of the relationship to the South African paintings is equally far from solution. As in the case of the eastern Spanish paintings, their antiquity is still in dispute, especially as some of them appear to be older, while others are doubtless later in date; the latter are the work of Bushmen who still engaged in painting less than a century ago. Apart from the 'White Lady' of Brandberg, an exceptional case, all the human figures in the South African paintings have negroid and Bushman features. From the stylistic standpoint they are unrelated to the works of the Saharan 'round-headed men', but greatly resemble those of the pastoralists. As evidence of their religious and magic character Frobenius has pointed to the occurrence of plants with a religious significance, which is an important factor distinguishing the South African paintings from those of other centres of rock art, both in Europe and the Sahara. It has been held that the Saharan and South African paintings both originated from one and the same artistic centre, which thus gave rise to two schools. Such a centre has as yet to be discovered and one asks oneself whether it ever existed.

In fact there is no denying that rock art is primarily a Eurafrican phenomenon. Possibly similar causes may have produced similar results on groups of people who were particularly susceptible to a certain aestheticism of form and colour, for did they not also (apart from minor differences) use similar stone implements? This would also explain the existence of various zones of rock art, with the schools arising locally and developing independently of one another.

A certain affinity has been established between the engravings and paint-ings of the Sahara and those of pre-dynastic Egyptian art — particularly in the case of the southern Oran engravings, where the figure of the ram with the disc bears a startling resemblance to the ram-god Amon. This was, as we know, a Libyan deity, venerated in particular at the oasis of Siouah; later this cult was adopted by the Egyptians. Were the rams of southern Oran ancestors of this deity, or was the reverse the case? Moreover, in the engravings of the *bubalus* period in the Wadi Djèrat a large number of human figures with animal heads have been identified reminiscent of the animal cults of ancient Egypt. In this case, too, the question arises which of the two centres influenced the other. But even though the antiquity of the *bubalus* period engravings in the Tassili cannot be established with absolute certainty, there is no doubt that these works do not date from historic times but, in the view of most experts, from a relatively early Neolithic. The oldest documents of pre-dynastic art, on the other hand, originate from a time which does not go back beyond the El Amrah culture. These are not rock pictures but figures painted on clay vessels or incised on schist or ivory plaques; they are all in a geometric style which bears no resemblance to our large-scale naturalistic engravings. Some authors, such as Pétrie, consider that El Amrah art was influenced by Libyan elements.

*Chronological
differences*

The semi-naturalistic style does not appear in Egypt before the El-Gerzeh period, and these figures resemble those of the cattle period engravings in the Sahara. The engravings discovered by the archaeologist Winkler in the Wadi Hammamat in Upper Egypt and ascribed by him to 'ancient inhabitants of the Nile' belong to this period. These early documents of Egyptian art are mediocre in quality and far removed from the perfec-tion attained in the cattle period engravings in southern Oran and the Sahara. The fauna depicted do not comprise any archaic species, and the *bubalus* is conspicuous by its absence. In Egypt there are no engravings with polished lines such as are to be found in the Wadi Djèrat and in the In-Habeter (Fezzan); nor are there any figures of elephants, rhinoc-

Fig. 47 — Goddesses with birds' heads. Egyp-tian influence. Jabbaren. $9^1/_3 \times 14^1/_2$ in.

'Antinea'. A woman kneeling in ritual posture. The arms and breasts are painted. The head-dress suggests that this is an eminent personage; in front a motif can be identified reminiscent of the Egyptian *pschent,* a royal symbol. The human figure painted on the head-dress at a later stage dates from the pastoralist period, the small figure on the right from the period of 'round-headed men'. Post-pastoralist period, with Egyptian influence. Jabbaren, Tassili. *Height 6 ft. ¾ in.*

eroses, hippopotamuses, giraffes, ostriches, etc. Among the works that are most accomplished in point of technique, which must also be regarded as the oldest, is the striking picture of an elephant with ears drawn above the body like the outstretched wings of a butterfly. But this curious style is also known in the Sahara, particularly in the Hoggar, Fezzan and Tibesti. The dating is fairly clear, for it was repeatedly found superposed upon figures of domesticated cattle, and must therefore be ascribed to the pastoralist period. This style is thus of great value to us as evidence that the *bubalus* period art of the Sahara is older than that of pre-dynastic Egypt.

And when we recall the rams with discs of southern Oran and the human figures with animal heads in the Tassili and Fezzan, we feel justified in concluding that it was the Saharan artist of the *bubalus* period who was responsible for giving birth to Egyptian art.

---

[1] Aissala has been analysed by Barth. The engravings of this site were recorded by the author in 1934 and published in 1949. Cf. *Investigaciones arqueologicas en El Sahara Central y centro méridional, Cuadernos de Historia Primitiva*, No. 1—2, Madrid, 1949.

[2] The author has examined personally the Hoggar, Tassili-n-Ajjer, Aïr, Kaouar, French Sudan, southern Morocco and southern Oran.

[3] *Les Pierres Ecrites*, Paris, 1921.

[4] *Die Felsbilder Fezzans*, Leipzig, 1937.

THE ROCK ART OF SOUTH AFRICA

BY

ERIK HOLM

When Europeans reached the southern tip of the African continent on their first voyages of discovery they found there peoples with three entirely distinct means of livelihood: nomadic pastoralists, primitive agriculturalists who engaged in a certain amount of cattle-raising, and hunters or food-gatherers pure and simple. These three modes of existence may be regarded as phases in human evolution: it was as though in this part of the world the different means of livelihood had not yet superseded one another.

The Hottentots and Bantu, who were pastoralists and agriculturalists, belonged to the Late Stone Age, those in the third group to the Early Stone Age. These hunters and food-gatherers had no metals or domesticated animals; they lived solely from what they could obtain by hunting, fishing or gathering natural products. To make weapons, implements, clothing and ornaments they had only the rock about them and the bones, sinews, hides and feathers of the game they killed. They also had vessels made from ostrich egg-shells in which to store the most vital commodity of all, water.

These dwarfish people (the hunters and food-gatherers) had an infantile skull formation, graceful but powerful bodies, and remarkably small hands and feet; but they possessed keen senses and adapted themselves readily to their natural environment. They knew the habits of the animals and the effects of various herbs upon man and beast; and they could interpret the meaning of all the celestial phenomena for their most vital needs with far greater skill than might be expected of a mere 'savage'. In particular they had a highly-developed instinctive sixth sense — a faculty absent in modern civilized man, whose instincts have become increasingly atrophied, but which it is not surprising to find in a people living in complete harmony with nature. This instinctive sixth sense often manifests itself in a manner which is little short of miraculous. Most striking of all is their ability to reproduce what their natural talents enable them to perceive. It is astonishing to find an old Bushman telling his European master that, for instance, he can sense on the side of his

Sixth sense

body the approach of a herd of springboks on the far side of the hill, because the animals' dark stripes are transmitted to his own person. He may also explain that he can foretell the killing of game because he experiences a distinct sensation, as he walks along, of the blood of the animal he is going to carry home dripping on his heels.

A people with such intensity of feeling and perception can scarcely be expected to possess powers of imaginative speculation. But this is the criterion which ethnologists are fond of applying when assessing the intelligence of a primitive race. They are surprised to find that these people are unable to count beyond ten, the number of their fingers. But this shortcoming is counterbalanced by a practical wisdom that is hardly to be met with among Europeans. Thus a minister once condescendingly asked a very old Bushman how old he was, thinking that he would hardly be able to count the score of his years, and was dumbfounded to receive the reply: "as old as my keenest disappointments and as young as my boldest dreams."

It was only to be expected that Europeans who three centuries ago came across these curious people should have come into continual conflict with their way of life, their ideas and their incalculable pattern of behaviour. These 'savages' were in their eyes incomprehensible prattlers and idlers, even thieves and vagabonds, who could neither be employed in any kind of service nor be entrusted with the least responsibility. On hunting expeditions, however, they were of course indefatigable and indispensable.

Artistic talents But the most astonishing fact about these prehistoric people was that they possessed a rich art of their own, a boundless passion for relating the most subtle tales, and a love of music, dancing, and ornamentation on their implements and their own persons. But all these manifestations of cultural awareness would have been inconceivable if they had not had distinct philosophy of life and an ancient system of religious beliefs. In Europe and in other parts of the world where the only evidence of this primitive food-gatherer culture is in the form of stone tools, it was assigned to the Upper Palaeolithic, i.e. to the last phase of the Old Stone Age. It is to these hunters that we are indebted for the rock paintings of Africa.

At the southern tip of this ancient continent the prehistoric pattern of existence has been preserved unspoilt right up to the present day. Here it was possible for students of prehistory to talk to the men who created rock pictures, to get to know their way of life, watch their dances, learn their language and record their myths, legends and religious beliefs; these *Myths* could even be studied in relation to the expression given them in rock

'Encircled' rhinoceros. Very advanced silhouette style, with 'stopping out' of inner surface. Fragment of diabase from a hill with pictures. Western Transvaal, site not known. *Transvaal Museum, Pretoria. Half actual size.*

paintings. Thus a most complete and vivid idea was obtained of a vitally important stage of culture, of which all trace seemed to have vanished until, in our own day, signs of it were rediscovered in unbelievably impressive, mysterious — but mute — pictures in dark caves. This prehistoric art was, however, already known in South Africa for almost three centuries, although no one suspected its connection with European prehistory. In actual fact even today hardly anything is known about the deeper meaning of European cave art. It is simply taken for granted as perfect, grandiose and mysterious. Since we have no documentary evidence of the religious beliefs that motivated it, we approach it in the manner of someone who sets out to study Christian art without knowing anything about Christian doctrine. The interpretation given of cave art owes everything to the personal imagination of the observer. Surely it ought to be possible to attain a better understanding of the significance of this art by studying that of South Africa?

Prehistory in the living present

Whereas prehistorians in Europe are necessarily concerned only with events that occurred many thousands of years ago, in South Africa we have the paradoxical situation that the study of prehistory is synonymous with the investigation of the living present. It is this that makes it so stimulating to deal with this rock art: one can hope to obtain results which not merely concern the present day but also the remotest past of mankind — in Europe as well as Africa. This presents a challenge to our whole outlook on history.

Characteristically enough, although we know that this art was practised until recent times (and is even practised still today), we know very little about its date of origin. Some early travellers gave accounts of the men who painted the cave pictures and described their equipment. They are said to have carried with them, hanging from their belts, ten different kinds of paint in the same number of receptacles, shaped like antelope horns.

The Stone Age artist is alive today

A warden in one of the game reserves, whose duties include the protection of the last surviving Bushmen in the Kalahari desert, was fortunate enough to be able to persuade one of them to demonstrate the technique of engraving on stone. With the aid of a sharp stone tool, using his right and left hands alternately, the Bushman pecked out an episode involving a lion, an ostrich and a human being, adding on top of them, in the form of a circle, a number of antelopes. Whilst doing this he hummed and sang to himself, giving expression to his pleasure in what he was creating by repeated exclamations and peals of laughter. It is quite likely that he was following some legend with which we are unfortunately unfamiliar. It may be added in passing that the warden played a joke on some prehistorians by showing them this work and asking them their opinion as to its date. They gave evasive replies and finally cautioned him against "unlawfully removing a prehistoric work!"

The problem of dating

Most of the European scholars who have studied this art naturally emphasize its Palaeolithic character, since they are used to dealing with Palaeolithic works at home and recognize the same traits in South African rock art. Scholars from South Africa, on the other hand, tend to ascribe the works to an extremely late date. No doubt subjective factors play a certain part on both sides: the European is accustomed to the fact that from the Renaissance onwards Europe has exerted a cultural influence upon the rest of the world, and subconsciously he assumes that the primitive artists 'colonized' Africa from Europe in a similar manner. The prevailing idea among South Africans, the descendants of recent immigrants, is that theirs is a young country which they themselves, so to speak, have discovered and brought under cultivation. They find it difficult to imagine that mere dwarfish creatures, whom they have come to know in a primitive state, should be able to look back upon such a long cultural tradition, and that they should even have had some part in creating the earliest paintings, including those in Europe. And yet this culture is very old indeed!

In South Africa, as in Europe, prehistorians have discovered the most important finds along the banks of the rivers, which attracted the earliest inhabitants — mainly on account of the water, as one would expect, but also because of the pebble-stones, which they used to make tools. Here, embedded in heaps of broken stones on the terraces along the banks,

Distribution of rock art in South Africa

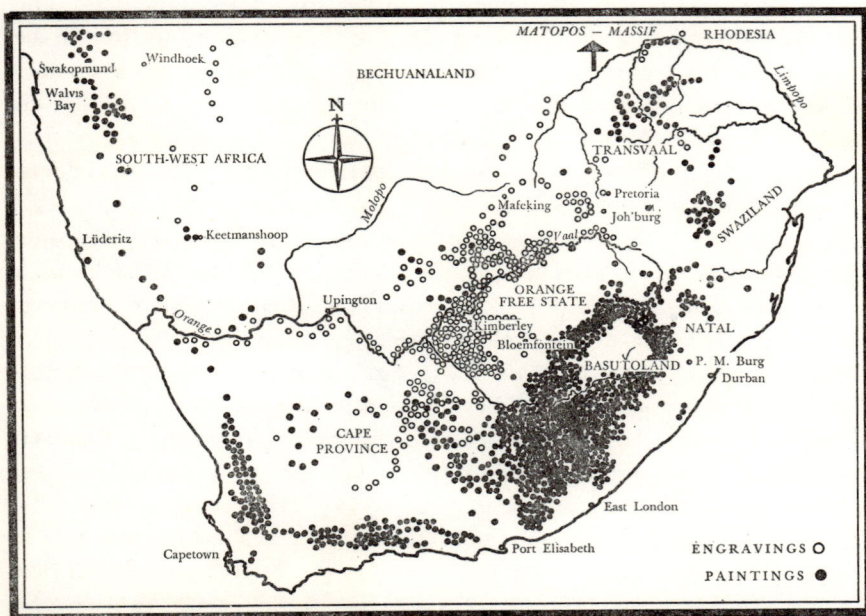

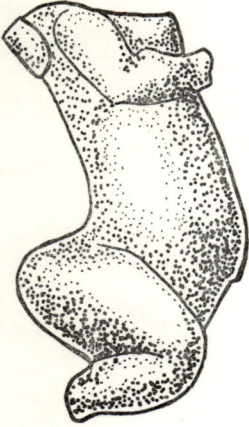

together with the fossilized bones of the animals they killed, there have been preserved stone artefacts which were produced out of medium-sized pebble-stones over the course of many thousands of years. The different types of tool and the technological modifications that occurred in the utilization of the material — as well as the geological evidence, from the alterations in the flow of the river — make it possible to determine the date of these prehistoric implements.

Unless these old stone artefacts had been discovered, and the astonishing fact ascertained that they are sometimes identical with those found in Europe, no one would ever have thought that human settlement in this remote subcontinent dated so far back in time. But every year further evidence is accumulated to show that this region was settled by man at a very early stage — if not actually earlier than any other area. It soon emerged from careful comparisons of the oldest artefacts with those found in Europe, as well as in other parts of Africa, that — contrary to the original supposition that the impulse came from Europe — there took place here a homogeneous independent development, rooted in its own beginnings and not at all dependent upon European influences. The necessity therefore arose for a separate scheme of classification to be worked out for South Africa, governed by the alternation between arid and humid periods, as distinct from the alternation between mild periods and Ice Ages in Europe.

Periodization

But by and large there is a certain coincidence in the morphological development. For this reason, as is the case in Europe, the Stone Age is divided into three stages; but the periods do not coincide. In South Africa only the earliest phases are classed in the first stage, the 'Old Stone Age', which corresponds roughly to the hand-axe or so-called Chelles-Acheul culture in Europe. It is known as 'Stellenbosch'.

The next phase is the 'Middle Stone Age', in which there appear new blade artefacts produced by a Levalloisian technique, in some way akin to the Mousterian in Europe, but showing greater refinement. Between the earliest phase and the Middle Stone Age are the Fauresmith facies and a stage of culture running parallel and known as the Sangoan. The 'Late Stone Age' in South Africa would thus correspond roughly to the Upper Palaeolithic in Europe, i.e. the stage in which European art first appears. In South Africa this Late Stone Age in fact continues up to the present day. The European Mesolithic and Neolithic can only be traced in minor details, such as, for example, the decreasing size of tools and a few polished artefacts. We are therefore primarily concerned with a Palaeolithic stage (according to the European classification).

It is of particular importance to note that no interruptions took place in this evolution, that the thread was never broken, and that each new phase developed out of elements of the preceding one. This indicates an undisturbed organic growth, in particular extending up to the decisive culminating stage of the Middle Stone Age, the Magosian, a homogeneous culture diffused over the entire continent, in which the art of the south is born. Apart from this single, though important point, not nearly so much information for the history of art is derived from the study of tools as happened to be the case in Europe. Attempts to associate the development of art with that of artefacts, as in Europe, have led nowhere, and so far as South Africa is concerned it is necessary to follow a completely different line — one that will be set out here for the first time.

Uninterrupted evolution

What we have in mind may perhaps best be indicated by reference to the study of tools. From the start there appear certain types of tool with a specific shape: either a leaf-shaped 'pick' or a sort of 'spearhead', a beak-shaped 'scraper' or a 'disc'. But it is quite impossible to determine what practical purpose these types were designed to serve. They have therefore with reason been termed artefacts, a designation which throws light upon their most striking characteristic: they are fashioned almost like small works of sculpture. This technique represents an effort to give expression to an impulse to model plastically. It is thus difficult to avoid the impression that these oldest 'works of sculpture' were really attempts to fashion very simple idols, or alternatively abstractions of some kind. This need not rule out a practical purpose, such as a weapon; for in his undifferentiated state man does not distinguish between 'abstract' and 'practical' spheres. Even in our own eyes a weapon means more than simply a 'lethal instrument'. For this reason we ought not to find it impossible to understand the Bushman who believes that an arrow-head of glittering crystal is made of the substance of the stars, and who, as he sharpens it, addresses to it the prayer: "may I hit my mark, for you never miss yours and are quite unerring!"

Art and artefacts

This example should really suffice to show that not even artefacts can be fully explained by a purely technological approach, particularly at a time when a mania for technology seems to prevail over all spiritual matters. How then should such an approach be capable of disclosing the secrets of human customs and attitudes? It is equally inadequate to try to comprehend the spirit of a new-born form of art by reference merely to external needs, to *culture matérielle*. But this is the domain into which the study of artefacts falls, and it is on this that the study of Stone Age art in Europe has been based.

In Europe this occurred under strangely contradictory auspices: in the very caves in which excavations had been carried out for decades in an eager search for artefacts (as supposedly the sole evidence of prehistoric civilization), prehistoric art was discovered — by a child! And this materialistic outlook was so deep-rooted that scholars were at first loath to admit that there was a spiritual aspect to Stone Age man, let alone that he was capable of creating works of art.

'Magic' When this great mural art had finally found recognition, and 'sketches' for the pictures were discovered as well as artefacts, it was doubtless to be expected that these artefacts should be regarded as the first stage in classifying this art. But here again undue significance was attached to the utilitarian aspect in approaching this question of artistic expression, which is after all a purely spiritual matter. The inevitable consequence

Detail of a quagga in engraving and pecking technique, on diabase. Maretjiesfontein, western Transvaal. Various periods. *Author's collection, Pretoria University. Slightly less than actual size.*

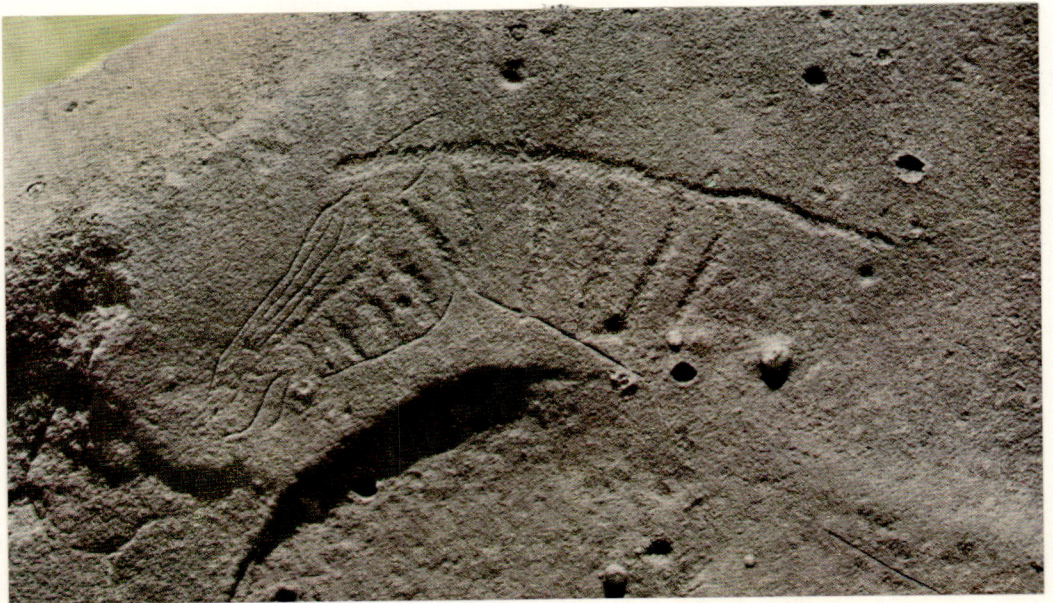

was that the concept of 'magic' was employed as an adequate means of explaining the 'purpose' of this prehistoric art. It was thought that in all 'primitive' cultures a specific belief had prevailed, in the light of which it was possible to explain the holes made by missiles and the 'arrows' added subsequently: the hunter was supposed to have painted figures of game on the cave wall to assist him in making a kill. In this way art was considered to have had the same 'purpose' as the manufacture of weapons: both merely served to provide man with food!

In South Africa, fortunately enough, conditions were not so simple as all that, and it was therefore necessary to search for different principles in trying to understand rock art.

Among the most important works are the engravings cut in the rocks found on exposed hill-tops situated over an extensive area in the interior of the country. At these sites tools could not remain preserved in strata undisturbed by time, as was the case in deep caves, but are found scattered about the surface, the earliest ones next to those of very recent origin. The archaeological picture thus resembles the ethnological one, as though in Africa successive periods had not superseded or overlaid one another — although the passage of time is clearly evident from the terraces formed by the rivers. Such formation of terraces was, of course, not possible on a rocky hill-top. *Engravings*

A similar situation prevails with the other important pictures found in rock galleries in the mountain massifs where paintings have been preserved. Most of these sites are open caves (galleries) with sloping rock floors on which it was no more feasible than it was on hill-tops for cultures to be deposited in an undisturbed and stratified form. But even in the case of those few sites where deposits are to be found the question arises — and rightly so — whether it is at all permissible to regard these rock-shelters as habitations, or whether they should not rather be considered primarily as places of worship; and whether secular life, of which relics have been found, can tell us anything about the 'meaning of art'. *Rock galleries*

When all the evidence is considered it must be assumed that these were places of secret initiation, access to which was prohibited to those not concerned in the rites. (It was for this reason that in Europe places of worship were located in the interior of dark caves!). It was only once people had begun to lose their awe of these sacred spots and the mysteries associated with them, and these localities were perhaps used merely as places of refuge, that the whole picture changed. But this change must have come about as a result of some extraneous influence, such as invasion by some new tribe who competed with the hunters for the means of subsist- *Initiation* ence. In this case the bulk of the secular refuse can only date from a period in which the sites had lost their original ritual significance. In South Africa there was no need to seek shelter in caves from the cold, and caves were not frequented until this region was invaded from the north by pastoralists, and later by primitive agriculturalists. Thus excavation at these sites would almost certainly give us an erroneous picture; the evidence of tools from the last phase would suggest that this art was of very recent origin. According to some scholars who have sought to apply undiscerningly European methods of excavation and investigation to paintings in the Drakensberg, they date only from the 17th century, when the indigenous peoples were driven back into these inaccessible mountain fastnesses by Bantu tribes migrating to the south.

But can such a situation of utmost distress have been at all suited to artistic representation of an almost Elysian peaceful existence, as suggested by the thousands of magnificent animal pictures preserved in these caves? Is it conceivable that the hunter peoples, themselves now hunted, persecuted and fearing for their lives, should have only developed their art at a moment of the gravest emergency? Only the last pictures originate from a period of such calamity; and they clearly reveal in the choice of subject the change that had taken place. For now these paintings depict battle scenes between the dwarfish hunters and their gigantic negro adversaries, who are shown carrying shields. Instead of peaceful hunting there is cattle-stealing, and the sacred places become refuges for rogues proudly vaunting their villainous exploits. These stirring little placard-like pictures merely illustrate the decline, the complete disintegration — as Breuil put it succinctly, 'the total mobilization' — of an ancient hunter culture. They tell us as little about the real character of these peoples as do excavations.

AREA OF HABITATION

Only one positive fact emerges from what has just been stated: in their utter despair these primitive hunters endeavoured to remain in their ancient area of habitation, sanctified by the existence of hundreds of sacred places. In the course of this struggle their whole character underwent a complete change: instead of men used to leisure and contemplation, endowed with a rich mythology, who cultivated hunting as a fine skill and regarded art as the supreme purpose of existence, they became vagabonds, rendered treacherous by their inferiority, who carried off as booty the invaders' cattle and waylaid them with poisoned arrows.

Thus in these pictures we can follow the tragic fate of one of the most interesting peoples on earth — a tragedy all the more unfortunate because it was inevitable. It might be objected at this point that the diffusion of

Above, monochrome red cow antelopes; below, elands running towards the right; below, and on the left, small red human beings and animals. Sandstone gallery in the National Park, Drakensberg Mts.

this rock art — the paintings in inaccessible mountains and the engravings on the edge of the Kalahari desert — in itself clearly indicates that this race of artists was dying out. This common opinion has probably been suggested by the presence nowadays in this area of peoples with other modes of existence: pastoralists and primitive agriculturalists. But one has to bear in mind that the hunters actually preferred this kind of country because it was easier to find game there.

In the case of the semi-desert country (such as the areas on the edge of the Kalahari have been from times immemorial) the twofold advantage is immediately obvious: the primitive hunters not only preyed upon wild animals, but were themselves sometimes the prey of these ferocious beasts.

What chance would a dwarfish man stand against these creatures in an impenetrable thicket or in tropical jungle — quite apart from the existence there of disease-carrying mosquitoes, against which he could not even protect himself by fire, his main safeguard against wild animals. An almost arid region with occasional water-holes was for him the ideal hunting-ground; at these few places the game was easily caught, for at some point thirst would drive the animals to the water-holes, where they could easily be ambushed. The hunter also has excellent opportunities along tracks through the mountain passes, particularly at the foot of steep precipices. A map showing the various rock picture sites, of which more than 2000 have so far been discovered, will serve to demonstrate how extensively diffused they were. It can be taken for granted that the hunters had the whole country to choose from when selecting their hunting-grounds. But they had very important reasons for confining themselves to certain specific regions. For their cult and the art connected with it they needed suitable sites, and these were to be found only where there were either protected walls for paintings or suitable rock surfaces for the execution of engravings (Map. p. 157).

REGIONAL DISTRIBUTION The following regions can be distinguished:

1. the granite caves of the north, extending from the north of South-West Africa right across the subcontinent to Rhodesia and the northern Transvaal;

2. the sandstone galleries, forming a semi-circle around the entire remaining southern part of the subcontinent; (here the paintings appear exclusively in their natural setting);

3. the interior of the country, where the smooth vulcanic tufa, particularly in the form of diabase, provided a tempting surface for engravings. This phenomenon is of special significance because it shows that to the primitive hunter artistic considerations seemed just as important as economic ones when choosing a suitable hunting-ground. It was one of the essential necessities of life for him to be able to express his ideas in the form of rites and art; without this he could not exist. Thus the impression of the primitive peoples gained by the Europeans on their arrival in the country, although based on their own observations, was an erroneous one; to obtain a proper picture, it would have been necessary to visualize them in their original state.

Significance of the sites In general rock art is envisaged even today as a more or less mechanical pastime, simply as a means of whiling away the time by decorating one's natural habitation. Although these Bushmen were sometimes met with in the open, leading an almost animal-like existence in primitive nests

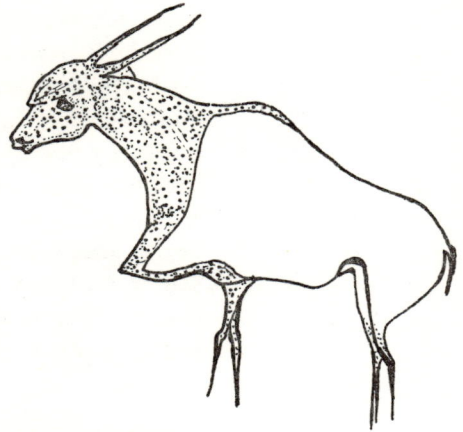

made of grass, they had for the most part already fled into their mountain fastnesses. This led to the belief that the caves containing paintings were their regular habitations, which like ordinary tasteful civilized people they had decorated with nice little pictures depicting their daily environment and occupation. But originally, as has already been mentioned, the hunters used these caves neither as dwelling- nor as hiding-places, but for their devotions, since they credited them with mysterious magic powers; their remoteness and seclusion gave them a natural aura of sanctity. This is readily apparent if one thinks of the low hills bearing pictures in the interior of the country, which assuredly could not afford the least shelter against an enemy, and not even against inclement weather. The fact that these hill-tops, as well as cave walls, are literally covered with the most magnificent pictures, elevates them to the status of primitive natural sanctuaries; they are thus among the oldest sacred places of mankind.

From the start Europeans studied the Bushmen and their art from the standpoint of social pathology; and this approach, like that of the archaeologist, made it difficult for them to obtain a correct idea of the fundamental principles by which their art was governed. Thus doubt could be expressed as to whether such an inferior primitive people could have been responsible for the majestic ancient pictures which can be identified in strata and are older than the neglected ones of the last phase. Serious scholars who recognized that these pictures were of greater antiquity were reluctant to abandon the view that they could have been produced only by some extinct race. But hitherto it has not been possible to discover anywhere a find which could substantiate the claim that a connection existed between this art and forerunners of the Bushmen.

The various racial types with Neanderthal characteristics must be ruled out, for the reason that even in Europe no artistic achievements can be ascribed to them. Boskop man, frequently put forward in this

Racial type

165

connection, cannot be excluded, but with his much greater cranial capacity he displays unmistakable Bushmanoid characteristics. In this connection the hypothesis was advanced that the dwarfishness of the present-day Bushmen represents a sort of infantile involution. In the caves on the south coast of Cape Province, where many interments took place, this burning question seemed to have been solved, since it was ascertained here that over the head and the upper part of the body of the deceased a stone slab was placed, the lower side of which sometimes bore paintings in the same colours as the murals. But these interred men had in the main San or Bushman features — although some scholars have established that the producers of a modified form of microlithic artefact (known as 'Wilton facies') had Cro-Magnon characteristics. These men were not buried in

'Cloud' elephant, with rain pouring from its body. Silhouette style. Mount St. Paul massif, near Harrismith, Orange Free State. *One-third actual size.*

the manner described above, but had interred with them elaborately executed implements which pointed to the manufacture of paint.

Excavations in Southern Rhodesia, South-West Africa and the Drakensberg range yielded indications of a correlation between a particular type of tool and the paintings of the caves concerned; but the existence of such a link was accepted by some scholars and rejected by others according to their personal opinions, so that no final conclusions can be drawn from these finds.

But in this connection an analysis of the psychological make-up and the traditions of the last pure Bushmen have yielded most astonishing revelations which are of fundamental importance for the whole of prehistoric art. Although these traditions have already been known for a century, strangely enough the results of these studies were not utilized as one would have expected.

In the last century the British authorities in Cape Province were forced to treat these uprooted primitive hunters as convicts. The German philologist Wilhelm Bleek succeeded in obtaining from them by kindness and much painstaking effort a wealth of fables and tales which, taken in conjunction with their cults and rites, have made it possible to reconstruct a primeval mythology which throws light upon the earliest art of mankind.

Each work gives us a glimpse of a world of ideas and beliefs of the deepest significance!

Thus the Bushmen appear as the true upholders and heirs of a *Weltanschauung* which inspired all the earliest rock art in Europe and Africa. In the light of this common spiritual foundation, relatively little importance need be attached to the many technical and stylistic diversities that exist within this single zone of primitive rock art. We shall now attempt, so far as is possible, to elucidate the position as far as South Africa is concerned.

In attempting to establish the *Weltanschauung* of the Bushmen on the basis of these profound and often obscure fables, one must begin by considering their metabolic approach: that basically there is no difference between matter and spirit.

The fables, like the pictures, deal mainly with animals. But it is clearly apparent that these represent more exalted concepts.

Just as the arrow-head can be a certain star, the powers of which are immanent in it, so also animals can symbolize other celestial bodies, as they have done since the earliest times in the constellations as we know them. At the same time these animals are also human beings, and each

MYTHOLOGY

Weltanschauung

167

fable begins with the preamble: such-and-such an animal was formerly a man, who belonged to the first tribe of men on earth.

In the primitive state there was apparently no differentiation, and no special significance was attached to the individual living being or material object: a man can be a stone, just as a stone can become a picture, a spirit; everything can take place in heaven as well as on earth.

The finest picture of this unity of all existence is given in the fable of the origin of the Milky Way:

A girl threw glowing ashes from the evening camp-fire — which was an offence — up into heaven to enable the distant hunters to find their way home in the darkness. These ashes form, as it were, a link between the terrestrial and celestial path.

The celestial luminaries wander about on earth unrecognized in human and animal guise, and each slain animal may contain some secret of the cosmos within itself.

Mantis   In particular, the mysterious 'praying mantis', which even the Greeks still associated with *mantis*, or soothsayer, is associated with an exalted divine miracle-working force. He is even believed to be the creator and guardian of life; he has his favourite animals, especially the eland, cow antelope and gemsbok, which he protects, in which he becomes incarnate, and which can then embody the stars, the sun or the moon.

For the cardinal belief is that a living creature can be transformed into a higher being: even Mantis, the Creator, submits to death in order to reveal himself in fresh glory as a celestial body. The sun, the moon and every living thing is naturally subject to this eternal cycle of death and re-birth. In one of the principal fables, for example, Mantis is transformed into a cow antelope, who feigns death because it wants man to dismember it and deliver it from life. But soon the severed limbs slip from the hands of the terror-stricken men, and with the first rays of the sun are joined together once again. And now this being soars up to heaven in its true essence and circles the earth with a dancing step. It is now no longer animal, insect or man, although still recognizable as such, but a being comprehending the Universe, representing totality and the source of life, the very day-star. In South African art this Protean being is portrayed with exactitude in its various manifestations; but it is also to be found in the so-called 'magician' in the French cave of Les Trois Frères, and this in turn is the prototype of many later cosmic gods and demons, which speed across the sky like the day-star, with a dancing step.

Dualism   Another important factor is the dualistic principle immanent in the whole of creation. The Bushman considers everything that is plump, weak and

Two polychrome giraffes, surrounded by human figures carrying loads and a 'tent', over an area densely covered with small painted human and animal figures in several layers. A little higher, taller men with javelins; on the right, a recumbent figure. Above, a white demon wearing a mask. Detail from the granite cave of Silozwane, in the Matopos. *Large figures almost actual size.*

small to be female. Thus the full moon can only be female — but it also has an infantile neuter phase and even a male one. But in accordance with the idea of metabolism the moon can also be a girl or an animal, in which case rudimentary legs indicate growth. When full the moon represents a mature woman, or, more especially, that magnificent great animal, the eland.

The new moon can be symbolized by a feather thrown into the air, the wish-bone of a blue crane, or the horns of various animals.

From these, or from the blood-stained feathers of a slain ostrich, a shoe thrown into the air, a piece of hide cut into ever smaller pieces, the praying mantis causes the moon to rise again, slowly and well-guarded, from the waters of a lake. Each time this is preceded by death; yet the sun

FIG. 48
restores everything to new life; so also does the moon, in its various guises, behind which shines forth the image of an attractive and well-groomed woman.

In the narrow cave of Sireuil in the Dordogne is a small picture of a little girl with rudimentary arms and legs stretching herself and 'blossoming out'. This and other early French pictures have their exact counterpart in South Africa — as, for example, in the eland from Vryburg in the Transvaal Museum. Here, too, the animal's legs are still rudimentary, corresponding to the waxing moon, although the head is not only fully-grown but shines in the bright rays of the sun.

FIG. 49

What might otherwise be regarded as a badly-executed or unfinished figure, or even as one worked in two different techniques, is in fact clearly a well-thought-out illustration of a profound and beautiful mythological concept. And it is only from this mythological aspect that we can understand the significance of the various motifs, and how it is that, although seemingly remote from each other, they yet have the same meaning. Many more examples could be adduced from South and North Africa,

Fig. 50 — Large painting representing a rain myth. From Philipp Cave, near Ameib, Erongo Mts., South-West Africa. After H. Breuil

as well as the Franco-Cantabrian area, to show how underlying mythological concepts, as well as Bushman fables, have been illustrated in rock art. Everywhere this art is based entirely upon mythology.

This uniformity was not thwarted by the fact that the fauna in the north differed from that in the south, or that climatic and material conditions varied: for example, in Europe there were no antelopes in primeval mythology, but their place was taken by other appropriate animals. There is a beautiful fable (rather similar to our tale of Little Red Riding Hood!) which Bleek's daughter Dorothea has made known from her father's notes:

Mantis (the praying mantis), which must be imagined as male, fatherly, even avuncular, like a wise old hunter, fetches for his little sister, the young springbok, some wild bees' honey from a hole in the ground which has been dug for this purpose. After being asked repeatedly whether it still liked the honey, the little springbok suddenly stopped answering. Instead a fearful trumpeting resounded from above. When Mantis crawled out of the hole to see what had happened, he discovered that a herd of elephants had approached stealthily, abducted the child and exchanged for it a baby elephant. Enraged, Mantis kills the ungainly baby and goes to look for the little springbok. Eventually he espies its red body as it frisks about nimbly and merrily in a broad valley, among the slow-moving elephants, and he rejoices at the sight. But when he approaches, the elephant swallows up the little springbok, and when Mantis tries to climb into its mouth threatens to spit at him. Then Mantis quickly slips into its navel, wraps up the child, and lacerates the elephant's intestines. The other elephants come to its aid with sticks and spears; but instead of coming out at the navel as they expect, Mantis emerges from the elephant's trunk, carrying the baby springbok, and stabs the monster to death.

Legend of the rain

It is not too far-fetched to recognize in this tale the mythological description of a thunderstorm. The nimble springbok with its red stripes represents sheet-lightning, Mantis lightning, and the gigantic elephant the cloud, rent asunder by Mantis.

Pictures that clearly illustrate and substantiate this interpretation are to be found in all the regions of Stone Age art.

In the plate on p. 166 there is a silhouette figure from Mount St. Paul in the Drakensberg range, showing an enormous misshapen elephant, which may be identified as a cloud, emitting streams of rain. The rendering in pure silhouette form is simply explained: the gigantic and shapeless form of a cloud is here illustrated by the massive towering figure of the elephant. From its extremities, which are sketchily indicated — and even from its unfinished trunk — there are fine brush-strokes suggesting rain.

From the opposite end of the country, from Philipp Cave, near Ameib in the northern part of South-West Africa, comes Fig. 50, depicting an elephant in white with a red springbok 'in its belly'. Breuil has rightly pointed to the close stylistic affinities with the oldest European figures, the elephants of Baume-Latrone (Gard department, France), where the curious distorted perspective of the head corresponds absolutely to that at Philipp Cave. The same nebulous manner of representation clearly suggests the cloud-like quality of the mythological elephant. It is not surprising, therefore, that in all the European mammoth figures, with their inordinately long 'hair', which sometimes shoots out arbitrarily

Eland, in three colours, with small figures venerating it. Roof painting in the gallery near Herenveen, east of Chrissie-Maars, Drakensberg Mts. *Width 1 ft. 3¾ in.*

from the body in straight lines, and generally even covers their legs completely, conjures up the idea of a great rain-cloud moving along silently.

There is even what might almost be called a literal illustration of the motif in the tale mentioned above engraved on a bone from the floor of the cave of La Madeleine in the Dordogne (Fig. 51). One can see quite clearly the insect entering into the gigantic animal's navel, the animal stumbling and being strangely transformed, curious objects pouring forth from its ear, 'horns' growing out of its head, its trunks disintegrating, lightning striking before its eyes, and (NB!) rain even beginning to pour forth from its tusks. It surely cannot be thought that these vertical lines simply indicate hair.

'In the belly' one can identify a bison calf, a substitute for the little springbok. The foreshortening of the latter figure is typical of the symbolic manner of representation; this is found very frequently in rock pictures. This fact alone shows that abstract ideas are a basic element in the mythological outlook of primitive man.

In North Africa, too, where the art is apparently so different, the same mythical subject-matter has frequently survived: in the Djebel Bes Seba (Algeria) there are elephants festooned with clouds (Fig. 52), and between them is the slender spirit-like springbok. In Ain Gudeja, near Asla, the cow elephant can even be seen 'swallowing up' this small animal (Fig. 53). Thus, as this example (which could be supplemented by many others) shows, the mythical element is to be found wherever rock art occurs. What has been said here makes it necessary for us to revise our conceptions about the 'purpose' of rock art: it will no longer suffice to assume that the portrayal of an animal figure was simply motivated by utilitarian ideas, even 'magic' ones. The animals are not thought of as game; in South Africa, for example, the springbok — the most popular quarry among Bushmen even today — is very rarely depicted, and if so then always bearing a distinct relationship to the myth mentioned: it is represented as a young animal nimbly leaping or playing about. It ought perhaps to be emphasized once again that all animals are characterized from a mythological standpoint.

Nor does there seem to be any basis for the view that the animal figures are 'totems', i.e. that a specific animal may be the idol of a particular tribe or clan. The eland, the favourite animal of the sun (Mantis) is to be found throughout the whole vast realm of South African rock art, in all phases, and in drawings as well as paintings (in the latter case it is almost the only subject treated in the mountain galleries). This can only point to

'Totem'

Below, old remains of animals in outline; blurred monochrome silhouettes; on the left, head of a kudu cow in good condition. In the centre, line-drawing of a zebra. Above these, smaller figures in red and a demon holding javelins or switches. Right-hand wall of granite cave of Nswatugi, Matopos, Southern Rhodesia. *Length of zebra approx. 13¾ in.*

the fact that the eland had a hierarchical significance in a system of beliefs common to all primitive hunters. From their mythology it is clear that it was an embodiment of the moon, which plays a vital role in their life. Of all natural phenomena it was the moon that was venerated most, and this magnificent great animal, the favourite creature of the giver and taker of life, occupied a special place in the heart of the primitive hunter. In other regions and ages the ox took the place of the eland as the symbol of the moon.

Cosmic symbols The primeval form of this cosmic symbol is to be found in the myth of the 'killing' and 'resurrecting' of the evening-star by the sun. This is connected with the sacrificial slaughter of animals, which can also be interpreted in the sense that only the creator of all things, the day-star itself, can take away again this animal's life.

Leo Frobenius studied carefully among the Pygmies of Central Africa the rites connected with this all-embracing belief in the everlastingness of the cosmos. These correspond with their myths, for at the first ray of dawn the Pygmies drew a picture of the animal they were going to kill, as though at the moment of sunrise this act created the animal and through its image placed it under the sun's spell; on the morrow, after it had been killed, it would then rise again, in a higher sense — after performance of the rite of covering the picture with the dead animal's blood and hair. It is thus not, as has been thought, a question of securing a substitute when no game was caught, but of the animal returning to the 'Father' who is the preserver of all life. The animal figures therefore represent immortalizations or deifications and, as it were, enter into the heavens as eternal stars.

Another point that is often overlooked is that once the rites have been *Rites* performed and sacrifice made, there is no further desire on the part of these primitive hunters to preserve the animal figure. If it is not destroyed, they fear that this might adversely affect their fertility. It is for this reason that the pictures are placed in subterranean refuges, caves and other secluded places. Or at least signs of destruction have to be made on the picture, so that the animal should no longer 'walk about'. Thus we have here yet another clear indication of belief in transcendentalism, in an after-life of the soul.

We will now turn to consider some examples. EXAMPLES

In the Matopos, a massif of granite cones south of Bulawayo in Southern Rhodesia, we find magnificent caves as large as cathedrals, which form deep semi-circular recesses in the glittering blue rock. The beautiful view which they afford over a splendid landscape of acacias suggests that this must have been a veritable paradise for hunters. On the walls in the interior of these caves we find this paradise most artistically represented in exquisite pictures, with a profusion of wild animals. The modern observer, who can no longer appreciate the mythology here represented, is content with this superficial visual experience. He hardly expects more from these animal figures, with their unusual colouring and consummate draughtsmanship, portrayed in animated movement. The cool of the vaulted cave, the trickling of a rivulet nearby, the softly shimmering twilight: what could have a greater emotional appeal? And yet all this conveys nothing of the motives that brought the primitive hunter to these caves.

Fig. 51 — Rain myth, as in Fig. 50, on ivory. La Madeleine, Dordogne

For him the great mystery lay in the rock itself: it was the rock, he believed, that could transform this 'chamber of the dead' into a vaulted heaven. To the walls of this glittering blue chamber he entrusted his ideas of the cosmos: with bold strokes he embellished them with his conception of the universal and the eternal, in the same way as the girl cast the spark from earth up to the stars in heaven.

Nswatugi   The plate on p. 185 depicts a fairly large section from the wall of the cave at Nswatugi. One can almost sense the vaulting of the cave in the curved bodies of the animals, which seem to be running along the 'horizon' — rather small reddish-brown silhouettes above an indecipherable jumble of countless superimposed paintings in dark and lighter layers, similar to those found in the engravings below the 'magician' at Les Trois Frères (France). There are so many paintings on this lower part of the light granite wall at Nswatugi that it is completely obscured by them; it is in vain that one seeks to make out the bodies of the animals, which appear to merge into one another. Between all these figures, each of which is a perfect drawing in its own right, is a mass of animated human silhouettes, red and dark-coloured, and accurately portrayed — a teeming mass of bodies.

PLATE P. 187   But upwards into the blue vault there stretch two great giraffe figures. Depicted in exactly the same solemn attitude, these fine slender animals stride along, dominating the whole vault (cf. plate on front cover of slip-case). Below them, at an angle, is a third giraffe, which also stands out from the mass of other animals; the galloping motif, accentuated more than in real life, conveys a greater impression of movement.

176

At first sight one can identify three different versions of one and the same motif. The giraffe in the centre (depicted on the front of the slip-case) is portrayed in a more rigid manner, with less attention to detail, almost like a simple archaic silhouette. The dorsal line is overlaid by another, somewhat darker colour, thus accentuating the head and legs. The spots are less conspicuous than on the giraffe painted a little higher up the wall; striding along in step, this animal is smaller, but represented plastically with classic poise. In both pictures the modelling and colour effect is produced by the use of only two colours, the lighter areas being left untouched when the second coat of paint is applied.

The third picture, the most recent, has more than classical repose and stateliness. The animal is depicted galloping along, with its tail swinging; its legs are raised slightly higher than in the case of the other two animals. The general effect is enhanced by a new vision of colour, which makes the body appear vivid and bright, almost luminous. This picture shows greater maturity; the rigid, composed and static character of the other pictures is here relieved and relaxed. This is particularly apparent when one compares it with the monochrome silhouettes of small animals upon which the giraffe picture, with its white ground, is superposed. A sense of distinction and elegance is evoked by modelling with finely-ground pigment. It is not the neat bichrome spots on the body that set the tone, but the delicately shaded modelling. When compared with other styles, it appears as though these three specimens on one wall represent three definite phases of development; and indeed, this gradual evolution suggests that each period may have lasted for a considerable length of time. But it is impossible to estimate for how long, undisturbed in this secluded location, the infinite mass of indecipherable pictures below the three main figures continued to accumulate. Perhaps they bear some relation to the three giraffes? But this question is not what mainly interests us at the moment.

What we are chiefly concerned with is the striking phenomenon that, despite their different dates of origin, the three versions of the giraffe motif correspond in such a striking way. This parallelism must have some significance. It would be easy to attribute it to emulation, and to say that the older picture must have served as the model. But we have to consider that the later versions are superior to the prototype and therefore could also have brought innovations in the way of motifs. We must thus reckon rather with a sanctioned version of an 'essential' motif, as is to be found later with pictorial representations in temples and churches, where the model is laid down and defined by specific religious conceptions.

177

Rhinoceros, on western side of a rock; on the eastern side there is a lion. Below, an older small rhinoceros with dark patina. Summit of hill at Leeufontein, western Transvaal. *Length of main animal approx. 2 ft. 6 in.*

<table>
<tr><td>*Constellation*</td><td>What the basic idea in this case was may perhaps be discovered from information furnished by the Tati Bushmen, who identify the constellation of the Southern Cross as a giraffe. Taking this constellation as the body, and the surrounding stars as the legs and head, the figure of a giraffe striding along can be reconstructed — just as has been done since time immemorial with many constellations in the northern sky, which have been interpreted as animals. The image of the giraffe was evolved by primitive man from the idea of the cosmos evoked in his mind by the cave, and from the transcendental meaning of the religious mysteries which were revealed to him there.</td></tr>
</table>

One technical archaeological point should not be overlooked in this connection, since it has a bearing on the age of these pictures, i.e. the phase of development from which they originated. Both in the cave at Nswatugi and at Bambata nearby cultural deposits were found which positively invited excavation. At Bambata, in a mine of cultural information almost 20 ft. deep, there were found, in addition to weapons, blade artefacts, mostly older and dating from the African Middle Stone Age, which pointed to great antiquity. The tendency was to regard these cultural deposits, which were rightly taken as belonging to an early period, as coinciding in time with the predominantly monochrome paintings in the cave at Bambata. However, it has also been held that pictures from this very early period could scarcely have been preserved owing to the constant flaking of the rock wall.

But on closer examination it clearly emerges that on these principal animal figures some parts of the paintings have been destroyed. This can be explained with relative ease: the figures must have been damaged and defaced deliberately, for the missiles or blows which caused the damage were aimed at the animals' heads! In the case of all three animals it is only the head that has been damaged. On the other hand, it is precisely where the superposed paintings form a compact layer that no flaking took place. If weathering left its mark anywhere at all, then it did so on these layers bearing many superposed paintings, for these are doubtless of the greatest antiquity.

Ritual destruction

In the case of our 'constellations' we are therefore faced with ritual destruction, an act which should not be considered divorced from its cosmic significance. If we recall to mind the blurring of pictures in the cult of primitive hunters (or the myth of Mantis, who, in the guise of a cow antelope, desires to be put to death), we see that this is a reflection of 'cosmic death and rebirth', the idea of the regeneration of the universe. It is in any case not a matter of killing the animal in effigy with the aim of procuring game, but a sacral safeguarding of one's own vitality against influences from the beyond; and this very fact indicates that these animal figures symbolized supernatural forces.

Regeneration of the universe

It is therefore not surprising to find that damage was not done to every picture — for instance, most of the smaller pictures at Nswatugi were spared. We are sufficiently familiar with the psychology of primitive hunters to realize that we are not *only* dealing with pictures of transcendental import.

With his mundane eye, so to speak, the hunter accurately observes the animals' proportions, and so is able to capture their likenesses with brush and crayon with the same skill that he shows in shooting them with his arrows. He strives to obtain verisimilitude, to come closer to their true essence — as he conceives it; and this is far from being equated with mere terrestrial existence. His 'naturalism' is wholly remote from this world: in the most animated figure in the group of giraffes, the one on the right at the bottom, on the horizon, no attempt has been made even to show its spots; this served to emphasize all the more its vitality, its essence. We shall come back to this picture again in due course.

The giraffe in engravings If we now consider the giraffe figures in other media of South African rock art, in the engravings in the interior of the country, we again find very different stages of development. In point of style our 'classical' bichrome version corresponds completely with the fine engraving in the Transvaal Museum at Pretoria. Both the colours of the tufa, the purple-brown colour of the thin oxidized coat and the light blue of the core, were utilized to obtain in two layers something approaching the same bichrome effect as is found in the 'classical' version.

Also with a completely different engraving technique, pecking out with a pointed stone tool, the contours are neatly incised and the spots in the animal's coat 'stopped out'. The head is conceived as a single unit of colour, and the hind legs, which are 'in the shadow', are executed in a darker colour. 'Stopping out' the surface also serves to convey the visual impression of overlapping, and thus to produce a certain modelling effect in the area of the eye. As in the 'classical' version, this long-lined animal with its great neck is rendered in the same superb attitude of static repose.

Morphological experience The motif must, however, be explained by a completely different morphological experience: the stone stands erect like a dolmen, and the animal figure is accommodated to it. This stone offers such an inducement to plastic modelling that the animal's mouth even extends round the edge of the stone. Instead of being transferred on to a large surface curving inwards, like the sky, the figure bends outwards around the curvature of the stone and strains upwards with its long neck as though cast up into the air. But the underlying genetic basis is still the same: in one case it is the vaulting, in the other the shape of the stone which seems to form a link between earth and heaven, in the same way as the glowing ashes which the girl threw up into the sky to form the Milky Way.

In so far as this idea was suggested by the location of the stone, rising up on the summit of a small hill, the artist's conception reaches out beyond the limits of this world. Both versions, despite their differences, therefore have the same purpose. This is the decisive point: it is no mundane vision that gives this artist his inspiration. One might suppose that the upraised head indicates browsing on a tree-top, but there is no evidence in rock art for such an interpretation. The motif is profounder, and must be

Giraffe on upright diabase cone. The outline and the spots on the animal's skin are pecked out.
Western Transvaal. *Transvaal Museum, Pretoria. Height of animal approx. 2 ft. 3 in.*

interpreted in terms of the transcendental emotions that underlie the whole of this art.

That it is indeed an essential feature of rock art that the living picture should step forth from the stone, so to speak, may be illustrated by another engraving, from the top of a hill bearing pictures near Leeufontein in western Transvaal. Here the rough-edged surface suggests the armoured hide of a rhinoceros, this resemblance being still further enhanced by the sharp ridge of the rock. In this instance, too, the body of this great pachyderm is only pecked out in outline, with the ribs barely being indicated, in order to accentuate the two-dimensional effect. As in the case of the giraffe, the head is executed in detail, and thus given special prominence. This figure is also depicted with deeply incised horns (but on the other hand with a raised tail) and extends around the edges of the stone.

PLATE P. 178
Suggestion

On one of the lateral planes there appears the figure of a lion, in the shadow and scarcely visible; and below the stomach of the rhinoceros is a very archaic small animal, with a dark patination, which can be identified as another rhinoceros. On the large rhinoceros the outline seems to have been retouched in some parts at a later date, which may indicate the significance of this hill-top picture.

As is shown by the points that correspond, the rhinoceros picture also originates from a classical period of art; it is vigorously rendered on a large scale and represents a vital mythological concept. The rhinoceros must no doubt have held a high position in the animal hierarchy; on every hill that bears pictures it is rendered in a prominent place, usually on the largest and tallest stone, next to the figure of the lion. And here we come to a new rule of this art, which shows that the animal figures stood in the closest relationship to the emphasis laid in the rites on the cosmos: the figure of the lion is the first to be struck by the rays of the morning sun, thus showing (as Frobenius already discovered in North Africa) that the radiant lion is related to the day-star. The fearsome dark rhinoceros, on the other hand, must personify night, when the monster is especially unpredictable and dangerous: its image on the hill-top faces west, i.e. towards the setting sun.

Cosmic significance

The full effect of this picture can only be appreciated when the moon is rising, and its horns shine like the 'horns' of the new moon over the horizon. It is in this effective manner that these pictures give expession to the most profound mythological concepts! The demon of night and darkness — from which the 'horns' of the waxing moon stand out, bringing consolation to the onlooker — is an impressive mythological symbol. (To it a crude humorous touch has sometimes, as here, been added: the tail is raised for excretion!). The dark demonic side in the imagination of primitive man was also represented pictorially in the figure of the angry and violent rhinoceros. These rhinoceros pictures are often invested with a fearsome majesty, as, for instance, when the animal is depicted in the act of frenzied attack.

The interpretation given here of the sinister character of the rhinoceros is confirmed in a remarkable manner by the well-known figure in one of the lower mouths of the cave of Lascaux in the south of France, which has been the object of a good deal of misleading comment. This painting, situated in a secluded spot, represents an analogy of a Bushman fable that has several versions and treats the theme of total darkness: contrary to the sacred order of the cosmos, the moon (in this case a bison instead of an eland) has been killed, not by the sun, which alone would be her right, but by the rhinoceros — and, moreover, before daybreak. Out of revenge Mantis pierces the spleen of the dead animal, bringing darkness upon the world. It falls both upon the murderer and upon the God of Light, but the latter causes the new moon to spring like a bird from a feather thrown up into the air.

In the picture at Lascaux the rhinoceros, the cause of this evil, is sprinkled with black drops of bile at it flees away. This theme is frequently met with in South African engravings, thus furnishing further evidence of the fact that the whole of Eurafrican rock art has a common mythological foundation.

Fall of darkness

Fig. 52 — Rain myth, as in Fig. 50, from Djebel Bes Seba, Saharan Atlas. After H. Obermaier and L. Frobenius

It is only after one has elucidated these mysterious affinities, with the aid of living oral tradition, that one can appreciate the full spiritual subtlety of such a beautiful gem as the picture of the rhinoceros on a purple

PLATE P. 155 fragment of diabase from western Transvaal (now in the Transvaal Museum). This animal seems to be hampered in its movements; apparently blinded, it stamps about and sniffs the ground. This has been interpreted as though it were drinking at a water-hole, but the crudely chipped circle which seems to hold it captive means something more than a mere pool of water. The natural vesicles in the rock above the animal's head suggest, as in the examples just mentioned, the source of darkness from

Mythological which the bile spurts forth, enshrouding the universe in darkness. As *explanation* with the picture at Lascaux, drops of black fluid can clearly be seen spurting forth from one of these vesicles, forming a circle around the animal.

In contrast to the technique hitherto applied, the entire contour line of the rhinoceros is pecked out in a dark silhouette. This example illustrates once again how misleading it can be to classify works of art merely from a technical point of view, without giving any consideration to their deeper meaning. Seen in isolation, this monochrome silhouette might be thought to represent an early stage of evolution; but in fact we are dealing here with a more advanced, animated and fluent style than that of the large static rhinoceros at Leeufontein; since in point of subject-matter it probably corresponds rather to the small and apparently older picture under its belly, these two silhouettes are related to one another.

In the plate on p. 155, however, we have a work in which the inner surface is 'stopped out' to form narrow ridges and which, taken as a whole, shows a high degree of psychological empathy. The dark silhouette is explained by the nature of the theme, which is darkness — as at Lascaux, pigment is sprayed by means of a blow-pipe on to certain parts only of the rhinoceros and the bison's belly. The impression evoked is as though the guilty demon has been caught fast in his own snares and struck with blindness.

These figures therefore express an ethic which is very far removed from the conventional idea that they served as a utilitarian means of obtaining prey through magic. To attribute such a purpose to rock art shows the lack of imagination characteristic of the modern world.

MOTIVATION This latter remark automatically raises the question of the motivation underlying South African rock art.

In discussing engravings we have mentioned cases where the artist's imagination was easily stimulated by slight similarities of form and structure, and even by natural vesicles in the rock, which sufficed to

184

evoke a certain image in his mind — just as the granite cave at Nswatugi inspired him with a vision of the cosmos. But these stimuli, which led to the creation of 'cosmomorphic' pictures filled with emotional intensity, were merely external; the real motivations lay deeper. The artist's mind was overflowing with these images, as it were, and in the rock before him, in the perfect vaulting of the cave, he found the revelation of his earth-bound perceptions. Thus the pictures of these animals, which he 'sought with his spirit', so to speak, are filled with intrinsic significance. With his lively instinctive sense, he was ever on the look-out for manifestations of his mythological beliefs. At the same time he kept an alert eye upon the terrestrial world, for the heavens appeared to him to abound in figures suggestive of the splendour and beauty of the animal kingdom.

Below, innumerable superposed paintings in various colours and sizes; above, a number of kudus, over which towers a group of giraffes and zebras. Between these and the uppermost group of giraffes (reproduced on front of slip-case) are scattered small human beings in dark red. Main part of rear wall at Nswatugi, Matopos, Southern Rhodesia.

It might almost be considered miraculous that these animal pictures, for all their mythological significance, are nevertheless so naturalistic and down-to-earth. But could we really expect it to have been otherwise? The man who kills an animal for his own subsistence is most likely to feel a sense of awe when beholding its striking beauty; how much more must this animal have meant to him when he thought it a divine being! Nevertheless, the decisive factor is still the part played by each animal in the great drama of cosmic change.

Drama of cosmic change

The esoteric ethical value with which each individual animal was endowed by virtue of its place in a higher world was made clear to the young hunters when they were being initiated into mysteries. There can be no doubt that these pictures also played a part in the propaedeutics of religious beliefs. This is evident from the mere fact of their relation to mythology and the naive way in which information is imparted in the form of fables. Moreover, we know of actual examples of propaedeutic exemplars and precepts taught to young Bushmen. These often contain straightforward explanations of the reasons why certain animals have a particular character in mythology. "Don't you see that the head of the cow antelope resembles Mantis? That is why he loves this animal." This, we are told, is how their fathers taught them the meaning of these fables.

Animal parable

The plate on p. 189 may serve as an instructive example of the way in which the Bushmen interpreted their mythological identification of an animal (cow antelope) with an insect (praying mantis) and at the same time also with the sun. In Fig. 49 we have a similar representation of the myth about the moon and the eland. The same disproportion between illuminated head and sketchy body is also met with here. But where the eland was a static reposed figure, in this case the cow antelope is depicted in motion — like the hastening sun; it is regarded as the swiftest animal, and it is probably for this reason that it is related to the sun. The 'resemblance' to the mantis is not merely based on its curved horns, resembling the posture of the raptorial limbs of this insect, but also on the fact that when the antelope gallops its forelegs are bent, thus forming another curve.

It might be thought that the body has been crudely touched up by some amateur and that it is much more recent. But the very fact that only two legs are rendered shows that it dates from a particularly early phase, as is also apparently indicated by the twisted perspective of the horns. This mode of representation thus had an esoteric motivation: it was designed to convey a mythological idea to the initiate — as is clear from the remark made by the young Bushman quoted above.

Giraffe and quagga without spots or stripes, over a jumble of smaller animals painted in a darker colour. Detail from rear wall (Plate p. 185) of the granite cave at Nswatugi, Matopos, Southern Rhodesia. *Height of giraffe 3 ft. 3 in.*

But at the root lies the idea of the sun regenerating itself, in that, according to the myth, as its first rays appear over the horizon the severed limbs of the animal are again joined to its head of their own accord. As in all ancient cultures in which these deified animal figures were worshipped, we have images of these gods (idols). The believer was no less close to the person of the deity where the latter was represented in animal form. Thus the history of this art comes into its own only when it is seen as an attempt to grapple with sublime religious ideas, with a spirituality and transcendentalism that cannot seem to anyone today so very strange and remote, since behind these animal figures there stands, invisible, man himself with his ideas of the supernatural.

Man is a humble creature, inferior in rank to his fellow-animals; in them the enigma of life is manifested in such a pure and simple way that he need only comprehend this to recognize that he is a human being. This is how it is explained in the fables: in animals one can see human beings; they are merely the various masks donned by men; for man is a perpetual initiate, ever marvelling at his own existence; were he to divorce himself from his animal masks, he would merely be a wretched creature, driven from the beneficent universe.

In this primeval age the world, of which man with all his human faculties formed a part, was still whole and undifferentiated; later man could only revert to this primeval unity orgiastically, or — much later — emotionally and romantically.

Modern man approaches this art from a purely historical point of view. In general he attempts to find his bearings in it by expecting it to provide confirmation of his own theories of evolution.

There is indeed no better opportunity to free oneself from the restrictive fetters of modern intellectualism than by endeavouring to comprehend South African art.

Art is unhistorical This art is not only ageless, but in the narrower sense is unhistorical. If we do not recognize this fact we are continually in danger of falling into error or at least of overlooking essential points. For most of us this art can tell us little about ourselves. The second approach towards 'classifying' this art, the topographical and geographical one, also leads to continual disappointments, since it adheres in equal measure to superficialities, such as ethnographical and geographical boundaries.

We have hitherto deliberately made no distinction between two different categories of rock art which scholars maintain should be treated separately, not only because their essential characteristics are different, but also because they were produced by completely different cultures and are, moreover, not contemporaneous — not to mention the deeply-rooted prejudice that all art in South Africa must be much more recent than that of Europe! Instead of going into this controversy in detail, we shall adhere to that never-failing source, mythology, which throws adequate light on the subject. What is really important, in our view, is to comprehend art from the standpoint of its spiritual content, its matrix — particularly when, as in this instance, we have the unique opportunity of learning about it from the living tradition of the people who produced it.

Significance for history of art In the plate on p. 160 we have a fine engraving of a quagga — a sub-species of zebra that became extinct only a short while ago — on a fragment of diabase in which particles of molten quartz are still to be seen. Because of its significance for the history of art this rock, together with some other pieces, was taken by the author from its site in the western Transvaal to the collection at Pretoria University. The original is not much larger than this reproduction. And yet a great deal may be deduced from it about the history of South African art.

PLATE P. 160

At first sight it looks as though we have here nothing more than a preliminary sketch executed in a fine engraving technique, with part of it in pecking technique. This is a delusion. First we notice that a natural crack in the rock, not far in front of the quagga's mouth, gave the original suggestion of a horse's mouth, just as similar natural details have been utilized on other occasions by rock artists in Europe as well as in Africa. In the first version this natural line was probably simply continued to

Cow antelope running. The entire head is executed in silhouette, but part of the stunted body is only represented in outline; this is connected with ideas of the cosmos. Maretjiesfontein, western Transvaal. *Length approx. 9¾ in.*

produce the prototype of the present head. The additional lines which must once have existed seem to have fallen victim long ago to weathering, despite the hardness of the rock.

Suggestion of pictures

This earliest outline of the head was probably bounded at the lower jaw by a slight ridge in the rock, so that it stood out in relief. This would correspond to the plastic conception of our large rhinoceros, for example. The head was thus larger and of a heavier type than the present elegant head of the quagga. Perhaps this was even a rendering of a more heavily-built species of horse, of which there are many varieties among those long ago extinct. In any case this head was superseded by another, still just visible, of which the nose commences approximately half-way between the old crack and the most recent head. The line runs roughly parallel to the present profile and ¾ in. from it; but it was adapted still more exactly to the original profile and had a greater curvature, resembling that of the *equus capensis* and other old species of horse in South Africa. In the second engraving one can also still easily pick out in its proper place the ear turned towards the front.

Even the present outline of the quagga's head and neck, which is the first to have the inner surface filled in, is not the next version, but is clearly a more vigorous retouching. The lines are more deeply incised and more defined than those of the rest of the body, of which in our plate we can only see the lines of the back, chest and belly, running diag-

Phases

onally. We accordingly have a sequence of four versions executed in the engraving technique, between each of which there was an interval long enough for the engraving to become completely invisible in the hard rock. And since this phase (which, as the most simple outline drawing, corresponds to the Aurignacian in Europe) nevertheless was preserved in some places — as it was in this instance — this enables us to realize how durable such engravings are.

But this was not yet the end of the evolution of this quagga picture; much later the engraving was retouched in the new pecking technique. From the lighter patination it can be distinctly seen that a considerable length of time must have elapsed between the touched-up engraved lines and the pecked-out grooves, which still have a bluish shimmer about them.

Engraving and line engraving

The evolution illustrated here is by no means a special case, but can be substantiated everywhere. The art of line engraving passes through various stages: first the simplest outlines with only one foreleg and hind leg shown; then a crude representation, gradually coming closer to nature and to true perspective; then complete mastery of the art of filling in the inner surface and portraying movement; finally, with the pecking technique, the addition of colour and the development of the artistic vision of a real painter.

The final product of our unfinished small quagga figure would take us approximately to the 'stage' of the large rhinoceros and the giraffe discussed above. But how are we to date this stage? Two stages already existed; and one must rule out any question of a sketch, or of any influence upon these two stages by the artist who did the pecking. Perhaps each stage was separated from the other by centuries, and probably even by millennia.

As a result of this examination of its genesis it can be established that

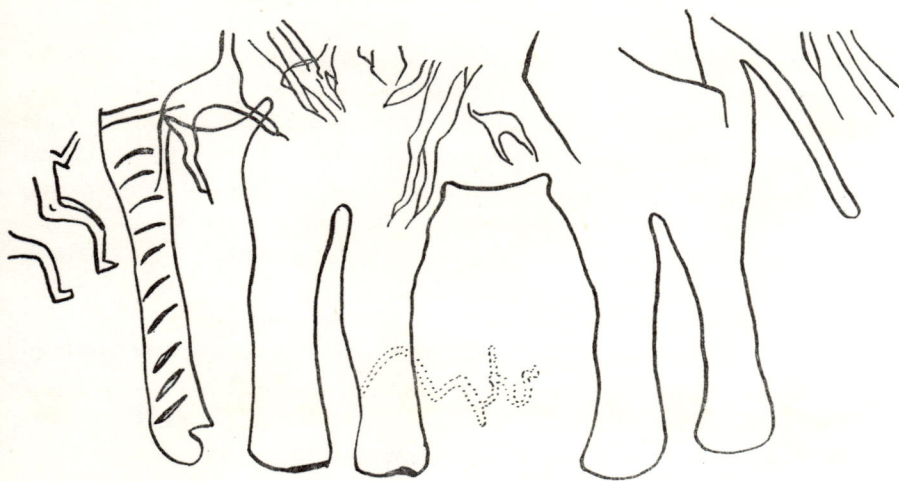

Fig. 53 — Rain myth, as in Fig. 50, from Mt. Ain Gudeja, North Africa. After H. Obermaier and L. Frobenius

South African rock art spurns any kind of historicism. It is, like mythology, ageless; a picture commenced thousands of years ago can be taken a stage further by artists in our own day. An effort could, it is true, be made to take technique as a criterion, and to establish (in this case, at any rate) that the pure form of line engraving represents an older stage. It is, however, certain that, once pecking came to play a dominant part, it ceased to be employed as the sole means of representing the entire outline of the figures. On the other hand, there is no evidence that pecking did not appear already at the time of line engraving; indeed, everything points to the fact that it is at least just as old, or even older.

Technique as criterion

In Europe, as throughout the whole of Africa, we find broad grooves as outlines already from the very beginnings of rock art. They originated with drawings made with the finger in sand or clay and are the primeval form whereby a simple rite performed at an open hunting-ground was represented on stone. As Leo Frobenius established in the case of the *Primitive cult* Pygmies, this primitive cult has survived right up to the present day. Our works of art are thus deliberate acts of immortalization, which derive their origin directly from a ritual act, from a technical point of view as well.

What is the source of this fine art of engraving, of which the origins, in South Africa as elsewhere, go back to the remotest past? Engraving is in essence illustrative, and the fact that in Europe it was at first applied to small movable objects, such as tablets and bones, and only *Propaedeutics* later to walls, seems to point to its use in propaedeutics, i.e. in the expounding of myths. The same applies, of course, to South Africa, although we do not find here any movable objects decorated in this way; instead we occasionally come across miniature drawings incised upon largish or smallish stones conveniently located on exposed hills bearing pictures. In many places there are hundreds of these drawings, frequently superposed upon one another, and at the older sites they are sometimes not pecked.

In their origin the broad-grooved outlines must derive from actual cults, whereas the fine engravings must derive from the instruction given to those being initiated into mysteries. In the course of time the two forms will have been blended, or even have superseded one another, as is the case with our quagga picture. In Europe, too, the same combination of engraving with painting occurred, so that the two techniques have thus constantly fertilized each other. Painting may have exerted an influence upon the abundant pecking out of the surface, so that a colour effect was obtained; but such a colour effect could also easily have been produced simply by working the stone.

Colour For corroboration of this opinion, we may consider the eland in the plate on p. 193, which has a magnificent colour effect. In this engraving, which is in the very important collection in the Transvaal Museum, one can distinctly see the colouring of the rock: the core is bright blue and the layer formed by oxidization a brownish purple. The animal, which is of splendid physique, is modelled with the utmost sensitivity, even the 'texture' of its coat being beautifully brought out; it is not incised deeply into the blue core but is only cut through the dark surface layer as far as the core, thereby obtaining a silvery tone of colour. Particularly exquisite,

Eland buck on diabase, in combined engraving and pecking technique, with the inner surface 'stopped out'. Western Transvaal. *Transvaal Museum, Pretoria. Length of animal approx. 1 ft. 3¾ in.*

both as a painting and as an engraving, is the light pecking in stripes to indicate the mane; even the hair on the forehead is depicted (this is an exceptional feature) by means of delicate engraving. In this respect this work reaches an acme of perfection in the art of engraving. But certain signs point to the existence of an early prototype, or at any rate to a stage when this art had not yet been completely mastered: the horns are rendered in twisted perspective, as in the plate on p. 189; that is to say, the horn which in foreshortening is normally visible *in front of* the other is in this case behind it. The same applies to the forelegs: the one further away in perspective appears to be longer than the one closer to the observer.

This last point must, however, be treated with caution. We have already referred at the beginning to the fact that in mythology the growth of the animal embodying the moon is suggested by the fact that the legs often still appear to be stunted, and the plate on p. 172 shows the same phenomenon as can be seen in Fig. 48. It has even been established that as a rule the legs of almost all the eland figures in the Drakensberg region appear too short, and this has even been regarded as a stylistic feature distinguishing this whole group of works!

In any case the elaborate care with which the coat of this animal is treated is often clearly explained in propaedeutic tradition. The legend of the creation of the elands — by the sun (Mantis) out of a shoe placed in the water — emphasizes the point that Mantis anoints the coat of his little favourite with liquid honey to give it a beautiful sheen. What the artist particularly sought to accentuate by his unusually elaborate execution was the analogy of the silvery moon waxing to fulness; and no image can convey this so beautifully as that of this exquisite animal, with its velvety coat of honey, quietly browsing.

Rock galleries When we go on to consider the paintings of the Drakensberg rock galleries, in which elands are the prevailing theme, we have here veritable masterpieces of composition in colour, inspired by real poetic imagination. When the moon rises the hunter gives expression to his joy by ritual dancing and singing, which go on all night long; no celestial body is so close to his heart as the moon; to women it is a mysterious goddess, to men it is an auspicious sign of clear nights for hunting — this recalls the part played by Artemis in Greek mythology.

The Bushmen of the mountain caves had a most revealing myth, handed down by Orpen, which shows the transcendental significance these pictures possessed. The following tale is told about one of their deities: "Quanciqutschaa killed an eland, cleansed himself and his spouse, and ordered her to grind some canna. And he sprinkled the ground with the powder, and all the elands he had killed rose up, and some came with javelins sticking in their bodies which had come from those who wanted to kill him. And he pulled out the javelins, a whole sheaf of them, and they stayed with him; it was a place surrounded by hills and deep ravines. . ."

This is a distinct reference to one of the typical mountain picture galleries. In the lighter sandstone of the mountain massifs which, where it is suspended beneath firmer rock strata, weathers and falls down as large boulders, galleries were formed that were protected by a kind of projecting roof. The artists here found a wall which provided a tempting surface for painting, in colours that became ever brighter in the course of time. A popular solution of the problem is a frieze extending along the rock ceiling. Could there have been anything closer to the hunter artist's heart than to paint in the form of animated figures the cosmic myths in which he believed, and the joy he felt at the earthly incarnations of the celestial bodies?

The plate on p. 163 shows, in addition to smallish red animals and small human figures which correspond to them in colour, size, and lively vigour, a file of reddish-white elands darting along, and also, a little higher up, some cow antelopes — the fastest animals on earth, which in mythology embody the sun (Mantis). In this composition we thus find again the same pattern of cosmic imagery as in the Rhodesian cave: inferior men and animals are related — indeed, are interchangeable — as required by the metabolic conception of life; great celestial luminaries rise into the supernatural sphere, lending enhanced significance, colour and grandeur.

In such galleries dances and rites were often performed far below this frieze, but in the lower galleries they were frequently performed opposite it. Among the animal figures paintings of men were added, dancing and leaping wildly to express their unbounded joy at being alive and at the promise of abundant game which each new moon denoted. In each case he gives figurative shape to his emotions by the *Emotion* performance of a solemn rite, by dancing, or by the joyous pursuit of animals which do not even appear commonly as prey; for he is here giving expression to his inner tension. And plump women are also frequently portrayed to denote the same feeling of exuberance at the blessings of life.

Sometimes hymns of praise to the gifts bestowed upon man by the moon are characterized by a greater stateliness and sense of repose, as when elands are shown congregating in large groups (cf. Plate on p. 197). Inexhaustible is the hunters' joy when contemplating the impressive size and ample proportions of these magnificent animals, with their bodies glittering like gold; the artist represents them resting, browsing, seen from all angles, and even daringly foreshortened; it is as though he is inviting the sun, the source of all fertility, to accept with pleasure the sacrifice offered to him.

Such idyllic animal scenes suggest an Elysian existence in the midst of nature — an impression enhanced when, after examining these pictures, we come across one of the herds of these fine animals in their natural surroundings in the Drakensberg reserve.

But closer study of the picture soon reveals motifs of undeniable mythological import. First of all we may point to the motif of recumbent animals, particularly the cow at the bottom on the left-hand side, which is being approached in a playful manner by an ox. There is a striking parallel with the famous pair of reindeer from the cave of Font-de-Gaume in the Dordogne. The fact that this picture represents the mythological concept of the male animal rousing and cherishing the female moon is distinctly emphasized by the stunted legs of the female reindeer.

But the connections with ritual dances go much deeper still. A young Bushman girl is isolated at the time of her first menstruation and initiated by an old woman into the mysteries of womanhood. When she is once again permitted to show herself to her fellow-tribesmen a dance of elands is performed in her honour. Two fairly old men disguise themselves as bull elands, and the girl lies down in the middle of a circle of married women, who dance around her and encourage the 'bulls' by exposing their buttocks and making provocative gestures. In this way the girl is given an illustration not only of the mystical relationship that henceforth will exist between her and the moon, but of the whole myth of the fertilization of the moon by the sun.

It lies beyond our scope here to discuss whether the famous figures of the cow bisons depicted on the cave roof at Altamira are connected with this ritual dance, as we believe to be the case; but we must certainly make the point that a connection exists with our foreshortened rendering of the cow eland. There is no explanation whatsoever for the introduction of foreshortening other than as an indication of this principal motif in the dance of elands performed in honour of young women. And this leads us once again to warn against laying down a preconceived 'evolution' for art! Foreshortening is not an achievement reached only at a certain stage of development, as one may be inclined to think. If a motif with a profounder meaning is to be represented in visual form, some artistic means will always be found of doing this, as is shown here already in prehistoric art. This again seems to show what a decisive influence mythology and ritual had upon this art.

When one surveys these delightful pictures of elands, executed in such varied techniques and colouring, and spread over so vast an area, one asks oneself the question whether this diffusion can be solely responsible for these very considerable differences in style, and whether they were not produced by some chronological development, even at the same locality. If one looks beyond the boundaries of the Union of South Africa to Rhodesia and further north, eland figures no longer take up the almost exclusive position in the caves which they occupy throughout the South African subcontinent, and again the question arises as to the connections between these different regions, and the stage of artistic development to which each figure belongs.

In the case of the engraving shown on p. 193, one would be inclined, despite the 'unique' southern engraving technique, to think of European parallels from the flourishing Magdalenian period; in the case of the fleeing elands shown on p. 163 (especially if one includes the small red male figures) Spanish Levantine art comes more readily to mind. The larger composition on p. 197 is reminiscent of the roof at Altamira, and not merely on account of its motif. On the other hand, the elegant sketch-like character of the little picture from the eastern Transvaal (Plate on p. 172) brings to mind Mediterranean rock art, such as that of Levanzo.

But it is impossible to divide up this compact group of southern paintings and to assume that any influences could have been felt in particular

Group of elands resting. Above, on the left, an animal in a faded dark colour; all the others are bichrome. Bold postures and foreshortening. Near Bethlehem in the Drakensberg Mts., eastern Orange Free State. *Length of individual animals approx. 13¾ in.*

The first part of this legend is probably Bushman in origin; the second part indicates the transition from hunting to cattle-raising, with the emergence of a tabu as regards horses, and probably horse-meat as well. This process, important from the point of view of cultural history, is represented in many North African rock pictures, in which we can note renderings of the sun in its manifestation as an ox. (As is well known, and need not be elucidated further here, the Egyptian cow goddess Hathor belongs to the same tradition).

In any case this legend provides a clue to the divorce of the Hottentot pastoralists (with their admixture of elements of Hamitic and North African culture) from the Bushman hunters, who are in some respects related to them.

Let us now consider briefly whether our figure of the zebra without any stripes is in keeping with this legend, and whether this is an allusion to a mythical primitive state — as in the case of the giraffe 'without any spots'. For it is quite possible that the legend was inspired by the fact that the quagga, a kindred species, which was a more favoured subject in rock art (and for this reason must also have had a higher mythological rank) only possessed stripes on the front part of its body and was almost completely brown on its hind quarters, like the whole of this figure on the cave wall. At first we are struck by the fact that the animals appear so close together and are almost entangled with one another. The brightness of the picture has already been stressed above. The fact that both figures are the work of the same artist indicates that they belong to a single group, that of renderings of a subject referred to in Hottentot legend as 'riding'. This could also suggest fertilization; for this is probably the deeper meaning of the connection between the sun and the moon represented as a bull. What then would be the significance of the giraffe in this connection?

FIG. 50

Let us now go back to the picture of the elephant at Philipp Cave: the head of a giraffe has been painted over the belly of a cow elephant, as though penetrating into it and trying to reach the little springbok inside. Might it be possible that in this case the giraffe, too, is an embodiment of Mantis? This is suggested by the explanation given to Bleek by a wise old Bushman: "Don't you see that Mantis looks like a female antelope? This is why he loves this animal." It was in this way that former generations must have explained to young initiates the relationship between Mantis and the antelope.

Assimilation   In the case of the cow antelope this 'resemblance' is based on the curvature of the horns, which corresponds exactly to the posture of the raptorial limbs of the praying mantis, just as 'consanguinity' was also suggested, to

Two isolated kudu cows, painted over small blurred figures of earlier date. Destruction by missiles. Left-hand side of rear wall, Nswatugi, Southern Rhodesia. *Length of animal approx. 1 ft. 4 in.*

a keenly observant eye, by the way in which both the insect and the animal have their heads turned sideways. The term 'sympathetic magic' has been coined to denote the drawing of parallels in this way by primitive peoples between things which according to our conceptions are completely unrelated. But (so far as the Bushman is concerned, at any rate) this overlooks one fundamental fact: the metabolism of a pantheistic *Weltanschauung*, according to which insect, animal and man are seen as consisting of identical 'substance' and as identical manifestations of a supernatural Creator.

Anyone who considers the giraffe from this point of view will be quick to see the parallel, particularly if one observes this animal whilst it is drinking: in this posture its forelegs are bent, the rest of the body is held erect, and when it looks at something it turns its diminutive head sharply to one side; this suggests most convincingly that there could be some intrinsic relationship between the giraffe and the praying mantis. Since Mantis embodies the sun, its metabolic animal figure, the giraffe, may be regarded as substantiating further our interpretation of this legend.

This also provides a ready explanation of the way in which both the giraffe and the accompanying zebra are represented. The zebra is shown at the moment before it puts the sun on its back and is 'scorched' by its rays. Indeed, this even explains why this group was painted at this particular spot 'on the horizon', below the large giraffes: in order to put the sun on its back, the zebra must have found it close to the ground, i.e. on

Spiritual aspects

the horizon. The punishment inflicted on the zebra is the natural consequence of its presumption in failing to recognize that the giraffe is a superior creature. The same idea is expressed very well in the myth of the cow antelope being dismembered by the young girls: after the failure of their attempt to dismember a spiritual being, they do not simply go home in disappointment, but are stricken with terror, and on their return home are taught a stern lesson by their father.

Such an admonition may not be entirely out of place with regard to students of rock art: before one draws conclusions about 'style', it is advisable to become familiar with the higher purpose by which the artist was motivated. If we wish to understand the spiritual character of this art, we must beware of approaching it with our concepts of evolution. There is no inconsistency between the giraffe represented as the sun and as a star, for the eland, too, can be a constellation. Perhaps this twofold meaning may actually explain the duplication of the figures in the cave at Nswatugi, and enable us to understand more clearly their comprehensive cosmic-terrestrial structure.

The Bushman as teacher

The blending of legendary motifs through the contact between the pastoralists and the older hunters can be followed in rock art. Although the pictures in the Drakensberg show this art in its death-throes, even the Bantu recognized the maxim: "the Bushman was our teacher"!

Protohistorical elements

In Rhodesia there seems to have been an assimilation with other protohistorical cultures. In the painted caves of this group extraneous influences can be clearly identified.

A taller type of man appears; there are traces of new cults; men are portrayed in action; and they carry javelins and heavy loads upon their heads — as do immigrants or nomads. New types of dwelling spring up, and these, too, are depicted. In the south we even find occasional renderings of herds of cattle. In some localities the caves contain granaries, like small huts, built of clay and sticks. These huts are even painted on the walls, indicating cultivation of the soil and rites associated with it. The whole north-eastern part of the country long inhabited by hunters comes to be dominated by the mines constructed there; mysterious stone buildings (Zimbabwe) tower up massively on the slopes of the granite hills. Tin, copper and gold, and even iron (!) are smelted on rocky perches and in caves, as though in the great cauldrons of primitive alchemists. And all this is shrouded in mysterious protohistorical darkness.

The plate on p. 169 may illustrate this, the final battle for survival fought by the ancient hunter culture. This is part of a wall in the impressive cave at Silozwane, situated high up on a mountain side, and reached by a precipitous climb over bare granite rocks. The whole vault right up to its roof is dominated by naked human figures, larger than life, painted in dark red and yellow. From them there emanates a distinct aura of solemnity, as in a sepulchral vault, and the animals of the hunters seem crushed and cramped. On the lower section is a jumble of little sacred pictures, the work of many millennia, which has been painted over with a dark colour. Across it stretch gigantic snakes, extending almost round the whole circumference of the cave. A new era has dawned, and the ancient sacred chamber is now in the hands of a new race of men. The animals representing stars, the giraffes, are overrun by large human figures.

One senses the atmosphere of a later era, a time of ancestor worship, ritual sacrifice and sacral kingship.

The delightful and graceful little pictures of kudu from Nswatugi, in the ancient granite district of the Matopos, reproduced on p. 201, are two final gems, in which the vanished world of the hunters is depicted in very light colours on the glittering blue vault of the cave. As though able to sense the impending calamity, the timid animals part company and prick their ears. Never before has the almost divine purity and beauty of the animal kingdom been painted with such tranquil calm, and at the same time with such emotional depth.

The shadows of animals and men from bygone ages hover about their golden bodies. Here the most recent and accomplished stage of hunter art has been reached, expressive of serenity and profound spiritual feeling.

It has been suggested that the damage done to them resulted from the vandalism of European big-game hunters, who were tempted to aim their fire-arms at paintings of animals that were so true to life. This sounds like a joke in bad taste. It is more probable that, as in other prehistoric caves, the picture was destroyed in the course of some ancient ritual.

THE ROCK ART OF AUSTRALIA

BY

ANDREAS LOMMEL

The best point at which to begin the study of Australian rock art is with the so-called *wondjina* figures of north-western Australia.

The *wondjina* paintings are to be found beneath overhanging rocks affording protection against the tropical rains. Such rock surfaces frequently occur on the large isolated stones that rise from the flat tableland; these are often mushroom-shaped, i.e. on a comparatively narrow base the rock extends outwards on all sides, so that all the pictures beneath the overhang are protected from the rain. Occasionally painted rocks are also found on ridges which can only be reached by a difficult climb. Still others are situated in deep ravines or in rock crevices running parallel to a ravine; the latter are particularly hard to find. Unless one is accompanied by a native familiar with the district, one can easily spend days searching the sides of a ravine only about two to three miles long before one finds the painting. Other pictures, by contrast, are visible from afar; already when one is half a mile away one can see that the rock is painted, and as one rides up closer one can gradually make out the figures.

The *wondjina* figures are anthropomorphous representations, generally PLATE P. 207 ungainly and often crudely worked. Sometimes, however, they have a certain primitive ingenuity, and very often the natural protuberances and recesses of the rock are utilized to give the effect of relief. A *wondjina* is usually rendered in a recumbent posture. The face is enclosed within a broad horseshoe-shaped band in red or yellow ochre. Only the eyes and nose are depicted, not the mouth. There are several explanations from mythology for the absence of the mouth, but since they do not agree one feels inclined to call all of them in question. The body of the *wondjina* is generally painted in shades of white and filled in with vertical stripes; the arms and legs are sharply defined; the hands and feet are in most cases very rudimentary; and the feet are often rendered in such a way as to show the sole, i.e. instead of the foot we have a footprint. This is not really surprising if one considers the important part played by tracking in the lives of these hunters, and if one bears in mind that throughout Australia footprints are often depicted in lieu of the creatures who made them. The *wondjinas* wear on the chest a longish object which may denote either the heart or the breastbone, but this explanation is not convincing. The sex of the figures is only very rarely indicated, but despite this the aborigines are mostly very certain in stating whether a *wondjinas* is male or female.[1]

Next to the *wondjina* figures, above them and on the top of them, smaller *wondjina* figures are often painted, or merely suggested by their heads. These are 'children of the *wondjinas*' or the souls of men who have developed out of this *wondjina*. There are also numerous representations of animals such as kangaroos, fish, birds, dingo dogs and opossums, as well as edible plants and bulbs, showing that these living things developed with this *wondjina* in primeval times and that their souls have a habitat in this picture. Sometimes inexplicable longish figures are also to be found in the pictures, which the aborigines refer to as honey; these have a purely symbolic character. Honey is a sacred food; and certain painted ritual sticks are said to serve the purpose of helping to find honey. The representations of honey are in fact renderings of these ritual sticks. Close to the *wondjina* figures, in smaller niches, there frequently occur rather grotesque human figures called by the aborigines 'demons'. These are sometimes painted over the *wondjina*.

A *wondjina* picture ought to be painted afresh every year by the chief of the tribe appertaining to it. Even nowadays one comes across freshly painted pictures, although only in rare instances. From those that are not freshly painted it can be seen that they fade and flake comparatively rapidly, since the red and yellow mineral pigments consist of ochre, the white

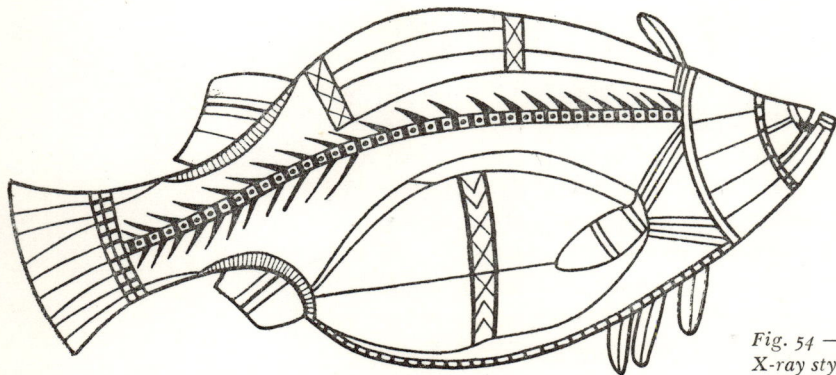

Fig. 54 — Fish. Painting in red in so-called X-ray style. Oenpelli, Unbalania, Northern Australia

Recumbent *wondjina* figure with plum-tree. Wonalirri, North-western Australia. *19 ft. 8 in.* ×
4 ft. 11 in.

pigment of white clay, and the black pigment of ground charcoal; and
these are applied after being mixed with water alone. At the site of the
picture one often still finds remains of chewed sticks that served as
brushes, sheets of bark that served as palettes, and pieces of charcoal. When
painting the figures afresh, the artists always keep to the same subject,
but not necessarily to the lines drawn by their predecessors. Thus under
a freshly-painted or relatively recent *wondjina* picture one can often
easily spot the contours of an older figure. One can then notice that the
painters vary a good deal in their artistic talents. Some paint with
vigorous sweeping strokes, whilst others compose the picture by labo-
riously adding one detail after another.

If one is fortunate enough to be taken to one of these sites by an aborigine,
he will not give a full logical explanation of the picture, but will impart
fragments of a mental outlook which to him seems quite self-explanatory.
But the older folk are (or at least were until recently) quite capable of
setting forth their conceptions in a logical manner in the course of a long
conversation. As a rule members of the younger generation cannot give
any information about the rock pictures; nor are they any longer interest-
ed in them, but go about their normal business, saddling and unsaddling
their donkeys and so on, in the shade of these overhanging rocks without
giving the pictures a single glance.

The aborigines usually begin explanations of the rock pictures with the *Mythology*
myth about the origin of the world. Members of the Unambal tribe in
north-western Australia, for example, tell the following myth about primeval times: "Heaven and earth existed from the very beginnings. They
have 'always been there'. In the bowels of the earth there lived, and still

From a geographical point of view the rock pictures of Australia can be divided into two groups. One group comprises the rock pictures of the north-western and northern coastal regions. These are naturalistic in style and derive from external influences that cannot be identified with any accuracy. To these may be added a stylistic group in the east and south-eastern part of Australia, which probably also traces its origin to external influences. In the case of the second major group, extending across the continent from the south-west to the south-east, the rock pictures are linear, sometimes even geometric, in style. In the mid-west and in several regions of the south-east both styles occur side by side or fused together.

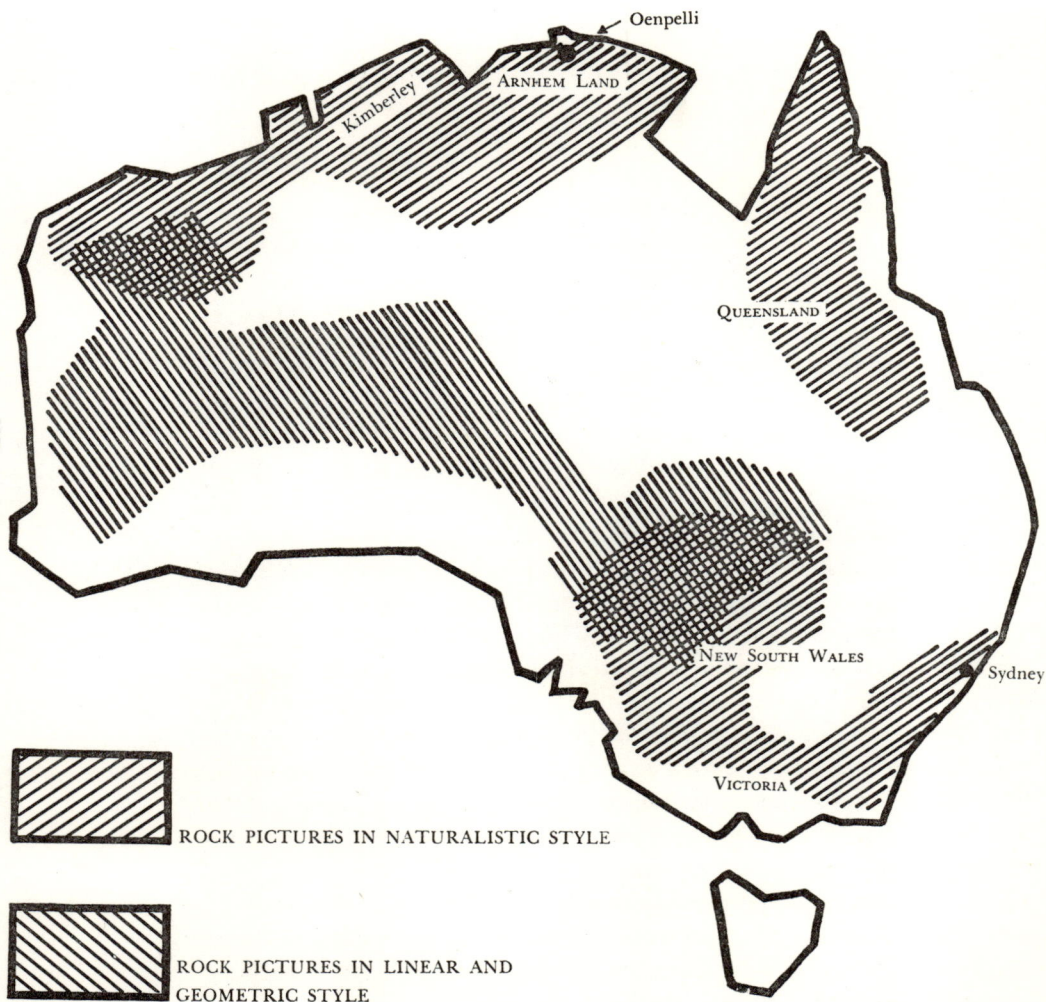

ROCK PICTURES IN NATURALISTIC STYLE

ROCK PICTURES IN LINEAR AND GEOMETRIC STYLE

lives, Ungud, in the form of a large snake. Ungud is the original creative force from which all life develops and to which it returns after death to be re-born." Ungud is often also identified with the earth. Everything that we see and regard as the earth is really only the back of Ungud; thus trees grow out of Ungud's back. Ungud is also identified with water, and often also regarded as the concept of time and as a state of mind, 'Lalai'. In the sky lives Walanganda, Lord of Heaven and at the same time the personification of the Milky Way. Of Walanganda it is said that "he has made everything". At first there was nothing on earth, and only Ungud who lived inside it. Walanganda poured fresh water upon earth, but Ungud "made the water deep." Ungud also made the rain, and so life on earth could begin. Walanganda and Ungud never carried out their work of creation by day, but always by night. When they did this they were in a dream-like state, 'lalai'. Whilst in this state Ungud was transformed into the being which he, or she (for Ungud can be either male or female at will, and also both at once) had created or was about to create.

Walanganda 'dreams up' the beings he creates in the same way. He is continually throwing down to earth, in a dream, 'soul force'. He fashions this 'soul force' into the image of whatever he wishes to create. He puts these pictures, painted in white, red and finally in black, on certain rock faces all over the world. This was the origin of the rock paintings to be found throughout the country, which are abodes for the souls of the beings they represent. The rock pictures are as 'fathers and brothers' to these beings. Only after the 'soul force' of these beings had taken shape in these pictures did Walanganda make the creatures themselves. Then he sent them out into all parts of the earth.

In those primeval days all the beings whose image Walanganda painted had neither mouth nor eyes. These they were still to receive from Ungud. Walanganda is still going on creating and dreaming, and never lets his creatures on earth die out. He is constantly sending fresh 'soul force' down from heaven.

In the rock pictures of the abodes of souls these figures of animals and plants form groups round the *wondjinas*. A *wondjina* is an anthropomorphic being and the personification of rain. Ungud 'finds' the first *wondjina* in a creative dream at the bottom of the water. And just as Ungud found the soul of a *wondjina* at the bottom of the water — the water which is at the same time himself — so also nowadays, the aborigines believe, every man finds in a vision the soul of his child in the water. The water-holes of the country are associated with certain *wondjinas*. Every watercourse, pond or spring in north-western Australia has its

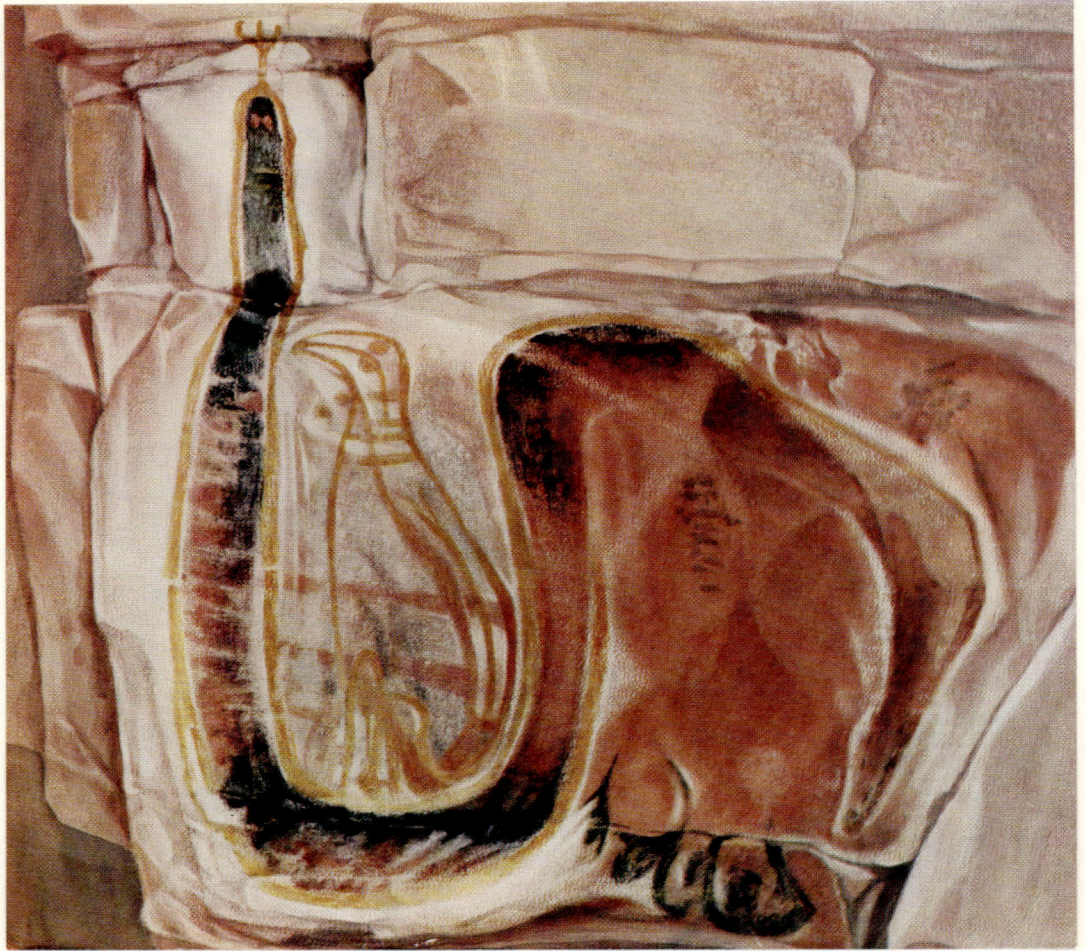

Snake with eagle. North-western Australia. *3 ft. 1 in. × 2 ft. 7¾ in.*

own *wondjina* figure situated nearby. Sometimes, however, it is a considerable distance away. A water-hole in a valley may have its *wondjina* figure painted on a rock face high up on the mountain side.

After they had been created in the early days of the world the *wondjinas* went forth across the land. They caused the rain to fall, fashioned the earth, drew the course of the rivers, pushed up the mountains and flattened out the plains.

At a time "when the stones were still soft" they built themselves "stone houses". When they 'died' they lay down upon the soft rock, leaving an impression behind. These 'impressions' are the rock pictures that exist today. To the aborigines it is of no consequence that these rock pictures are not impressions at all but paintings, and that they are located on sheer rock walls on which one cannot lie down. Of other *wondjinas* it is said that they stood in front of the rock faces and that one of their companions drew their silhouette, which was left behind as a shadow on the rock. At the spot where they left their 'impressions' behind the *wondjinas* disappeared into the earth, and ever since have lived at the bottom of the water belonging to the picture.[2]

The chief of the tribe which owes its origin to a certain *wondjina* and belongs to a certain rock picture is responsible for re-painting it before the rains come, to give fresh force to the soul substance contained in it and thus to assist in the propagation of men, animals and plants. In explaining how the pictures were painted, the aborigines set out their view of the world: talking to an aborigine in front of one of these pictures, one will hear him state over and over again that they only re-paint them, or 'touch' them, but did not paint them themselves in the first place — a statement that seems quite natural in the light of what has been said above. When they 'touch' figures of *wondjinas* and of Ungud, they do in fact seem merely to touch up paintings that already exist.

But they often paint afresh the animals, plants, fruit, celestial phenomena, etc., which belong to these pictures. According to information given by some aborigines in 1938 the fine representations of eagle-hawks at Kandjánlgari were only painted in very recent times. They say the same about a whole number of other paintings which strike one by the freshness of their colours. Thus it seems that the aborigines adopt a different attitude to the Ungud and *wondjina* figures on one hand and to the

Fig. 55 — Women running. Painting in red. Oenpelli, Unbalania, Northern Australia. After Ch. P. Mountford

accompanying pictures of natural phenomena on the other. The former they regard as the 'shadows' of primeval hero figures, their direct legacy, but not the latter, apparently, for in this case man has the ability to create them over and over again in the course of fertility rites. Processes of thought which we can only follow with difficulty may play some part in this. Undoubtedly the aborigine is imbued with the conception of a deep community between himself and life in nature and the cosmos. We have impressive evidence of this in his primeval traditions, his belief in spirits of fertility and procreation, and his totemistic outlook.[3]

The significance of the rock picture galleries of north-western Australia in religious cults can by and large be compared with that of the *tjurungas* of Central Australia, described in detail by Strehlow, Spencer and Gillen, as well as with related objects among other Australian tribes. Like these sacred objects of wood or stone, the rock paintings may be regarded as the legacy of primeval times. In both cases they transmit the life-giving forces of great mythical figures and play an important part in fertility rites. The rock galleries contain paintings of primeval tribal or clan heroes and of the local totem. Much the same is expressed in the engraved motifs on the *tjurungas*.[3a]

The *wondjina* figures almost always appear in combination with zoom-orphic and anthropomorphic representations, of which the latter seem to belong to different styles; in some cases they are definitely more recent than the *wondjina* figures, but in other cases they are older. Blending

Fig. 56 — Warriors running, with spears and spear-throwers. Oenpelli, Inagurdurwil, Northern Australia. After Ch. P. Mountford

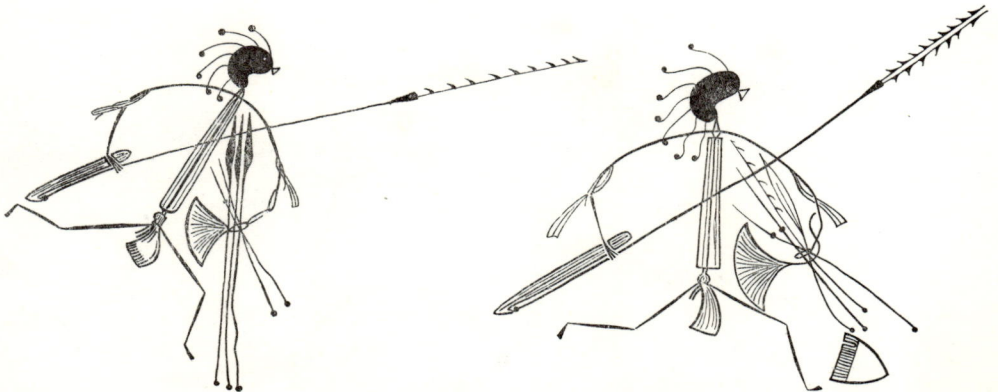

Fig. 57 — Warriors standing, with European axes. Oenpelli, Unbalania, Northern Australia. After Ch. P. Mountford

with other motifs is particularly frequent on the border of the area containing *wondjina* figures. For example, John Morgan [4] found a female squatting figure with the head of a *wondjina* by the middle reaches of Carson River, which flows to the west of Drysdale River: this is apparently a blending of two heterogeneous styles. The zoomorphic representations are only connected with the *wondjina* pictures in mythology. From a stylistic point of view they are different, for they are less rigid than the *wondjina* figures. In the re-touching of animal figures, too, greater licence is permitted, and the aborigines do not keep so closely to the older models still visible on the rock.

The impulse that led to the appearance of the *wondjina* figure may have come from some area outside the Australian continent where anthropomorphic representations were known.

PLATE P. 210

PLATE P. 215 There is perhaps a sign of such influence in the small elegant anthropomorphic figures which occur in north-western Australia as well as the
wondjina figures. These other representations are mostly monochrome
(from dark reddish brown to reddish yellow), and are frequently elegant
animated figures, or groups of figures, measuring between 12 and 27 in.
in height. Bradshaw [5] was the first to discover figures in this style on the
Upper Regent River and to publish sketches of them. Grey,[6] the discoverer of the *wondjina* figures, makes no mention whatsoever of this second
elegant style — which might be termed the 'Bradshaw' or 'elegant' style.
The reason for this omission is not that there are no such paintings in
the Glenelg River area, but that they are so indistinct and faded as to
be scarcely visible. Only by very thorough examination can one find traces
on the rock walls of such representations, which were overlooked by
Grey. Davidson [7] refers briefly to these pictures but refrains from passing
any judgment on them, considering that the information in his possession
was inadequate.

An attempt to classify stylistically the numerous anthropomorphic figures
in north-western Australia which do not belong to the *wondjina* style
would give a result roughly as follows:

PLATE P. 215 The first and most striking group comprises the few very elegant small
figures in profile or semi-profile; the very graceful lines convey a sense
of movement; and the mode of representation seems so 'un-Australian'
as to suggest that they are associated with some other culture.

Related to this group are the figures with very exaggerated hairdress.
They often appear to be clothed, have 'wide sleeves', and carry bags in
their hands. This group also includes the figures reproduced by Bradshaw.
At the rock picture sites in Eastern Kimberley in particular, but also in
Western Kimberley, there occur other figures which can be assigned
neither to the *wondjina* style nor to any of the groups of the so-called
'Bradshaw style'. They are rather grotesque figures, sometimes male but
generally female, which are still painted nowadays. These 'demon
figures' are the last remnant of a tradition which one comes across quite
frequently. These are the so-called 'squatting figures' (mostly female, as
already mentioned), which seem to degenerate in the course of time from
rather strict stylization to grotesqueness. In addition to reproductions

Small figures with arcs over their heads. An illustration of the 'elegant style'. Wonalirri, North- ▶
western Australia. *1 ft. 1¾ in. × 7 in.*

of this kind, obviously quite recent, there are also a large number of older figures — e.g., on the roof of one site containing rock pictures, and even older ones at the foot of one *wondjina* figure.

PLATE P. 219 At Ngungunda 2 a strictly stylized squatting figure is portrayed, with beams radiating from the head and the body filled in with parallel stripes; aborigines who saw it eventually designated it a 'she-devil', "because she-devils are always in the habit of lying down in this indecent manner" — the indecency being indicated by contemptuous laughter on the aborigines' part.[8] They said that the squatting figure actually represented the act of coitus, a woman lying on her back with her legs wide apart. In Western Kimberley Mrs. Schulz [9] came across similar pictures and received the same sort of information from the aborigines.

A fourth group comprises all those figures that defy classification because they are unique.

Common to all groups, apart from the fact that they differ distinctly from those in the *wondjina* style, is the almost complete absence of zoomorphic representations. Bradshaw was the only investigator to find his figures together with those of animals — but judging from the sketches he published the animals may be later addenda.

Worms [10] holds the view that there must once have been far more pictures than there are now, since only those in protected places could be preserved, and innumerable others must have been effaced by weathering — by the heavy monsoon storms and the glowing sunshine. Worms compares these representations with the *wondjina* pictures and comes to the conclusion that the latter served a mythological purpose whereas the *giro giro* pictures (a native term for the graceful paintings with the small figures) were representations of the daily life of an older race now extinct. He has in mind a pre-australoid, perhaps negrito-tasmanoid race.

If, therefore, one attempts to establish the connection between the two styles in north-western Australia from the standpoint of historical evolution, one finds that an important process took place — despite the fact that the anthropomorphic *wondjina* figures became more primitive in the course of time as compared with the 'elegant (Bradshaw) style' paintings. The latter do not give the impression of having been the focus of a cult, but appear to have been produced to satisfy pleasure in art for its own sake. The *wondjinas*, on the other hand, with their naive naturalism, are often painted in beautiful colours and are well adapted to the uneven surface of the rock; the whole mental outlook of the aborigines revolves around them. Here an antropomorphic style has been introduced from outside Australia and incorporated into an ancient conceptual

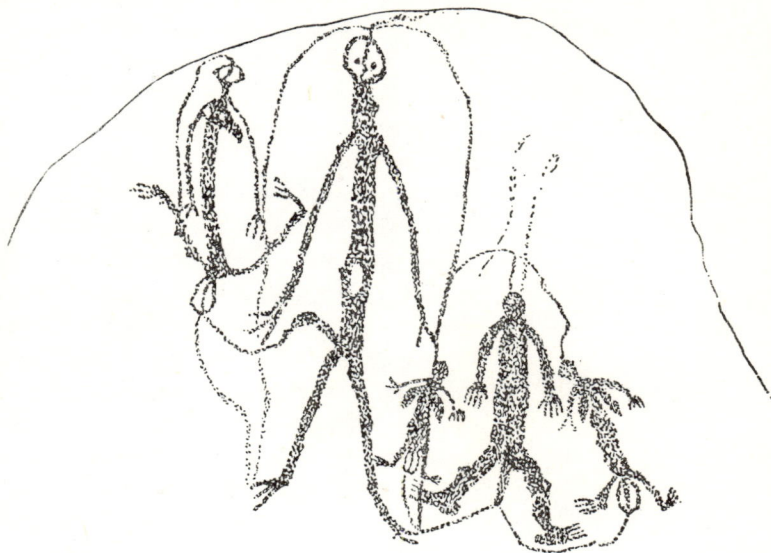

framework, in which this style of painting was originally unknown. The creative force Ungud, still today thought of as a snake, was originally also represented as one; and it was only under the influence of some external model that it was also conceived of and portrayed in human form. Although the anthropomorphic style became much more primitive as a result of this process of assimilation, this process shows that the aborigines of north-western Australia manifested very great aptitude in absorbing these influences from abroad and maintaining the new style for a long time afterwards. The development of the *wondjina* figures out of the 'elegant style' figures must have taken place a fairly long time ago. This is clear from the mere fact that a comparison between the present *wondjina* figures and those discovered by Grey in 1838 shows that no stylistic changes took place during the intervening century. It is unlikely that, once the 'elegant style' had developed into the *wondjina* style, one element of the former style should have continued to exist. The numerous animated human figures in a degenerate style that are still being painted nowadays, and which can be found around (and sometimes in) the *wondjina* pictures, cannot be derived from the 'elegant style'. They were more probably stimulated from the east, by the influences radiating from the second great centre of rock art on the northern periphery of the Australian continent, Oenpelli, in Arnhem Land.

To the east of the Kimberleys, by Forest River, there are still traces of the *wondjina* style. Basedow,[11] who studied these rock pictures, published a reproduction of a *wondjina* head and animal paintings which invite comparison with those of the Kimberleys, as well as anthropomorphic figures which can only be equated with the last degenerate paintings of the north-west.

Towards the east the *wondjina* style no longer appears in its pure form, and in the Northern Territory we only find sporadic sites where the style of the pictures can be related to that of the paintings of the Kimberleys. We are again indebted to Basedow[12] for some re-touched rock pictures from the area of Humbert River, a tributary of Victoria River, and from Pigeon Hole. They are represented in a curious vigorous style and are probably not related to the Kimberleys paintings. The figure of a squatting or running woman from Blunder Bay can at best be regarded as equivalent to the demon figures from the Kimberleys.

Distinct affinities with the Kimberleys paintings are, however, again found at Delamere, the site discovered and studied by Davidson. The affinities with the *wondjina* pictures of the west are not only external, in the arrangement and placing of the pictures, but, as Davidson has established, also extend to the myths they represented. The anthropomorphic figures are known as 'lightning brothers'. The resemblance to the *wondjinas* also extends to characteristics such as the filling in of the body with stripes, the absence of a mouth, and the beams or rays framing the head. This site contains very primitive animal figures and both from a geographical as well as from a stylistic point of view seems to lie between the two art centres of the north, the Kimberley area and Arnhem Land.

Apart from Delamere and probably some eastern *wondjina* sites as well, the influence of the great centre of rock art at Oenpelli makes itself felt in the Victoria River and Humbert River area, and still more in the Katherine River area further to the east. In 1947-8 C. P. Mountford,[13] leader of a joint Australian-American expedition, discovered near this missionary station several large rock art sites. They contain representations of animals, especially fish, turtles and snakes, most of which have a marked 'X-ray style', i.e. internal organs not normally visible, such as the stomach, heart, lungs or spine, are painted as well. With these pictures the aborigines still have an active relationship, but this is less the case with the innumerable anthropomorphic figures covering the rock walls, which they believe to be the work of spirits. The style of these figures is curiously diversified — at once vivid and degenerate. The representations comprise human beings in profile, running carrying a spear and spear-

FIG. 54

FIGS. 55, 56

Squatting figure. Ngungunda 2, North-western Australia. 2 ft. 1/2 in. × 1 ft. 7 in.

thrower, and also groups of men standing or dancing, often with spindly limbs. In most cases several layers and styles are superimposed upon one another. It is, however, scarcely possible to establish a chronological sequence at Oenpelli; at one site certain types can be identified as more recent, but at others the evidence points the other way and upsets one's tentative conclusions. Nor can the style in which animals are represented automatically be regarded as more recent, because there are some representations of animals on which human figures are superimposed and which must therefore be older. One approach to an understanding of this style may perhaps be by way of the bark paintings still executed today in Arnhem Land.

Influences radiating from Oenpelli

Apart from the rock pictures closely related in style to those of Oenpelli there are others to the south, south-west and probably also east of this centre where the anthropomorphic influences radiating from it are less marked, and finally are no longer to be found at all. The border of the zone influenced by Oenpelli seems to lie along the Roper River in the south and the Katherine River in the west. Further east, on Groote Eylandt, Tindale [14] discovered further rock pictures, composed of anthropomorphic and zoomorphic motifs. They can be compared with the bark paintings still produced nowadays on the island and do not appear to be very old. They could, however, be regarded as a last eastern offshoot of the Oenpelli anthropomorphic representations, but the reasons for

Fig. 59 — Figures resembling human beings, pecked out on rock. Depuch I., Western Australia

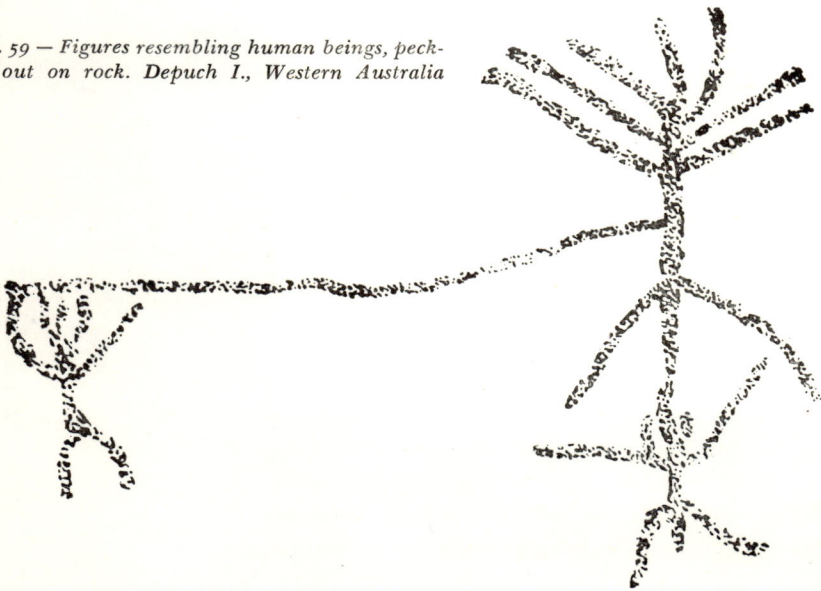

Fig. 60 — Hunting scene. Rock engraving. Gosford near Sydney, N.S.W. After D. S. Davidson

supposing that such a link existed are based on geographical considerations rather than stylistic affinities. All the rock pictures are merely primitive full-face figures such as are also found in south-eastern Australia. McCarthy [15] found animal pictures on Groote Eylandt. These are also comparable stylistically to the bark paintings in which hunting and fishing scenes are depicted, but are more advanced.

A fruitful comparison may be drawn between the rock art of the Oenpelli area and that of the area in the south subject to its influence, as well as that of the north-west; a detailed comparison between the 'elegant style' of the Kimberleys and some pictures from Oenpelli shows that they have common features. But at the same time some vital differences must be pointed out, which show that although the two areas may have responded to identical stimuli from without they followed completely different lines of development. South of King Leopold Ranges pictorial art as found in the north-west and the Kimberley area suddenly comes to a stop. Only in the northern part of Western Australia, particularly in the Yule River area, do we still find engravings or peckings of anthropomorphic and zoomorphic figures. In the south aboriginal art is represented only at isolated sites by increasingly abstract linear figures, often very primitive in style. Both styles, the abstract and the realistic, occasionally overlap. South-east of Arnhem Land, in the north of Queensland, we only come across occasional engravings or paintings of importance, and their quality can no longer be compared with those of northern and western Arnhem Land.

In New South Wales the best-known works are the rock engravings, some of them of gigantic size, not far from Sydney. These simple outline drawings are very plentiful, often measure as much as 20 to 30 feet in length, and are for the most part situated on broad ledges at a high altitude. They are among the first rock pictures to have been studied, and there is

New South Wales

221

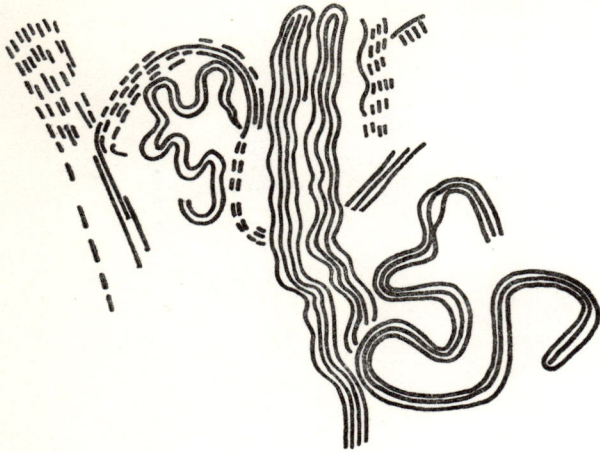

FIG. 60

already a considerable literature on the subject. McCarthy[16] has recently been engaged in compiling an exact catalogue of these rock pictures, the number of which is constantly growing as new finds are made. For the most part they represent living creatures (fish, kangaroos, ostriches and birds), utensils and weapons (boomerangs and shields), and numerous anthropomorphic representations, mostly male — all executed in a primitive yet spirited manner. Sometimes the bodies are filled in with vertical lines; the faces are generally suggested by eyes and the hair by disconnected radiating lines; mouth and nose are absent. One particular posture — the legs wide apart and 'squatted off' — is obviously intended to express movement, probably in dancing. There can scarcely be any doubt that the rock engravings near Sydney had a ritual significance and that the large compositions to be found here represented mythological concepts. But it has not been possible to obtain information about the rock pictures from the aboriginal population, since in this area they died out long ago. In addition to these engravings paintings are also found in New South Wales, but these are scarce and very primitive in their manner of execution. Davidson[7] gives some examples of those found in Milton District. In the eastern part of New South Wales extraordinarily large and rather ungainly paintings have been found, which in all probability represent deified culture heroes and progenitors of tribes that are now extinct.

In the western part of New South Wales there is a wealth of rock engravings and paintings. An account of these sites has been published by Lindsay Black.[17] McCarthy is covering this region as well in his detailed inventory.

Victoria In Victoria, according to Davidson, paintings are very rare and no engravings at all have as yet been discovered. But the paintings that exist are nevertheless noteworthy. In the first place there is the site of Glen Isla, where the pictures were copied by Matthew in 1897 and are reproduced by Davidson.[7] But Matthew's copies are apparently not faultless. This opinion is endorsed by Adam,[18] who has studied this site in detail; but it would be difficult to improve on them now, since the colours have obviously faded very much since 1897.

The other site of rock pictures in Victoria is at Mount Langi Ghiran.[7] It represents a figure holding a "disproportionately large" boomerang. Davidson sees no reason why this site should be called 'the cave of the snake' by the aborigines, but Mrs. Schulz, who visited this site in 1956, provisionally identified the 'boomerang' as a snake, which would explain this designation.

The most important site in Victoria is the Conic Range rock-shelter,

Lizard-like animal. Rock painting. Hawker, Southern Australia. *3 ft. 2 in.*

FIG. 64

an account of which has been published by Tugby.[19] These figures of slender human beings, painted in dark red, bear a strong resemblance to those in the 'elegant style' in north-western Australia. But there, too, the picture seems to have been badly damaged by weathering, and it is difficult to make out the details. It must be recognized that the three sites of rock art in Victoria are unusual from a stylistic point of view, and cannot simply be grouped together with the rock pictures of nearby New South Wales or of Southern Australia.

Southern and Central Australia

FIG. 65

In Southern Australia — at Devon Downs, for example — there are labyrinth-like engravings. Type B from Devon Downs has been subjected to radio-carbon analysis and gave the date of approximately 2200 B.C.[20] A more recent development at the same site has finer simpler lines and, perhaps, also human figures reduced to symbols, such as are frequently found in rock pictures in Southern and Central Australia.

Labyrinth-like forms also occur as engravings or peckings at Burra and in the Flinders Ranges in Southern Australia, and extend to the centre of the continent.

FIGS. 62, 63

In the Flinders Ranges peckings of animal or (apparently) human figures are also met with. They might perhaps be described as a reminder of the figure at Mootwingee in the west of New South Wales. But in addition we find here concentric circles with cross-lines such as are also to be seen at Devon Downs. Perhaps these suggest that the influence of Central Australia was felt here. The large sites at Eucolo Creek near Pimba contain concentric circles, the comb motif, plant motifs and what are clearly anthropomorphic figures.[21]

Anthropomorphic representations in cruder form are to be found at South Para River and in a simplified abstract form at Malkaia.[7] It is not clear whether the human figures in the paintings of Southern Australia should be traced back to the influence of anthropomorphic art from Victoria or New South Wales, or whether they denote influences from the north, which might have reached Southern Australia *via* the centre, bypassing the west, where there are no anthropomorphic representations.

PLATE P. 227

If that is so, a connecting link would be provided by the head with beams radiating from it at Ayers Rock. The rather clumsy figures from South Para River are reminiscent of those at Delamere as well as the animal figures at Ayers Rock. It seems clear enough that influences from the north reached the centre and the south by way of the Western Australian desert. The mythological evidence goes to show that in Western Australia the aborigines still recollect a cultural movement from the west across the desert to the coast of the Great Australian Bight.[22]

*Fig. 62 — Human and animal
figures. Euriowie, western N.S.W.*

The fact that such striking implements as the threadcross were used both
by the tribes of Western Australia, as well as the linguistic affinities that
exist between them, suggest that they are related to one another.

It would also be possible to link the labyrinth-like representations in
Western with those in Southern Australia, thus making for a homogeneous area in the south-west of the continent where this motif appears.
It can be assumed that influences radiated from the centre to the north-
west and north. In this region the representation of a snake in the form
of a spiral seems to be derived from the spiral style of the centre. Paintings
of this kind are to be found at Yule River in Western Australia, in the
McDonnel Ranges, in Central Australia, at Ooraminna, at Delamere,
on a painted sheet of bark from Liverpool River and at Ngungunda in
the Kimberleys.[8]

In Central Australia, and in a similar form in Western Australia as well,
there is a style of rock art that involves abstract lines. The meaning of
these drawings cannot be established. It is clear that in Central Australia,
as well as in the centre of Western Australia under the influence of the
centre, concentric circles often serve as the starting point of such lines,
but already in the western part of Central Australia such spirals and
circles are driven into the background: here a drawing may often have
no more than one spiral or circle. In the southern part of Western

Australia no spirals are found at all, but only labyrinth-like lines, arranged in an apparently arbitrary fashion.

Conclusions This general survey of Australian art leads to certain interesting results. In the first place we see that the group of rock pictures consisting of naturalistic anthropomorphic and zoomorphic figures can be contrasted with a second group that gives preference to geometric signs, which is to be found in Western, Central and Southern Australia. There are, of course, points of transition between these two groups, and for this reason no hard-and-fast geographical dividing-line can be drawn between them. But the geometric style of the rock pictures of the south and west seems to be concentric, and is perhaps older. It must be borne in mind that at the present day the style of the human figures on the bark paintings in the north is steadily being superseded — smothered, so to speak — by a geometric style, the main motif of which is a rhomb, but which also includes the herring-bone pattern. In the ceremonial style of the bark-paintings in Arnhem Land, which differs from the 'ordinary' style chiefly by the use of geometric motifs, a preference seems to be shown for geometric symbols, as is also the case with the *tjurungas* in Central Australia. These motifs to be found on the northern periphery of the continent are thought to be older, since they are ceremonial — particularly the so-called herring-bone and the lozenge patterns. It is quite clear that these motifs are not merely supplementing anthropomorphic and zoomorphic ones, but are gradually crowding them out. The old ceremonial motifs are gaining the ascendancy and the naturalistic-realistic style is giving way to one that is geometric and abstract.

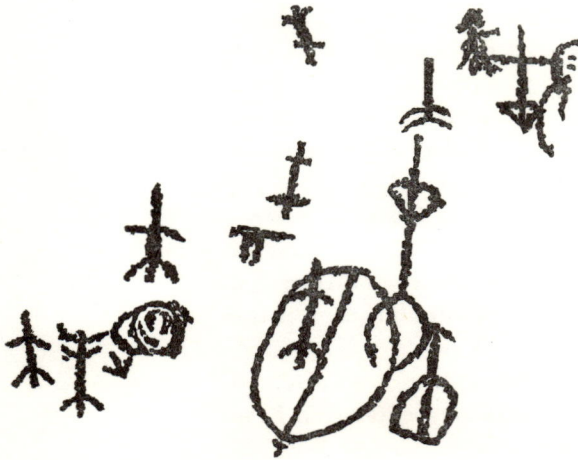

Fig. 63 — Human and animal figures. Euriowie, western N.S.W.

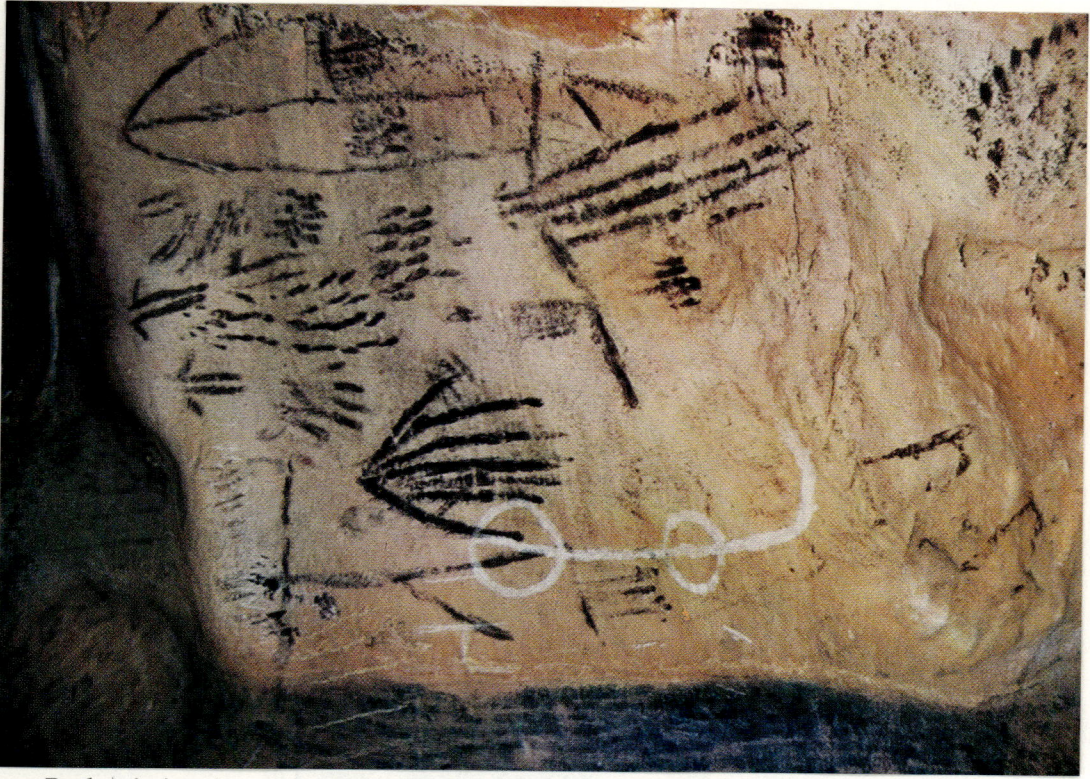

Rock painting. Ayers Rock, Central Australia. *Width 3 ft. 11¼ in.*

The naturalistic style of rock art extends in an arc from the furthermost north-west to the east and south-east of the continent. On both sides of this stylistic 'bridge', which is clearly weaker in the middle than at either end, there are paintings and engravings in which the two styles are merged — as, for example, in the few rock paintings of Queensland and the eastern part of New South Wales, and in the engravings in the eastern part of Southern Australia.

The naturalistic rock paintings can be divided into different sub-groups according to their motifs and their quality as works of art. In the Kimberleys two styles can clearly be distinguished: the *wondjina* style and the so-called 'elegant style'; it seems possible that the former, which still survives today, is derived from the latter. Traces of the *wondjina* style are met with far away in Southern, Western and Central Australia. The style of the second artistic centre in the north, Oenpelli, is comparable in some phases to the 'elegant style'. There is no reason to dispute the view that these rock pictures were the focal point of cults, as we may do in the case of the Kimberleys paintings. The sites in Victoria and in the western part of New South Wales resemble in style those of Oenpelli. But there are no intermediate stations which could lend support to the theory that this style spread over the whole of Australia.

In both areas, the Kimberleys and Oenpelli, zoomorphic motifs appear together with anthropomorphic ones, but it seems that they only do so at a stage when anthropomorphic representation begins to flag. In the Kimberleys they seem to be connected with the *wondjinas*; but the mythological evidence suggests that this connection has not always existed and that in recent times anthropomorphic figures have been superseded by zoomorphic ones, particularly snakes.

It is also clear that these two areas occupied a special position as centres from which foreign influences were transmitted to the rest of the continent. Anthropomorphic representation spreads outwards from the Kimberleys and Oenpelli. Perhaps in both cases the original stimulus may have come from without. But Oenpelli is unique as regards the

FIG. 54 representation of animals in 'X-ray style'. In the south-east a similar sub-division can be made, although the rock pictures never attain the same level of artistic accomplishment as do those of the north-west. But here, too, in Victoria and the western part of New South Wales, we occasionally find small anthropomorphic paintings. The large anthropomorphic figures (paintings in Victoria and at isolated sites in the north-eastern part of New South Wales, and engravings in the vicinity of Sydney) are found in combination with primitive animal figures and are clearly degenerate forms of a more advanced art, probably the older style with the small figures.

These conclusions are, moreover, substantiated by study of the quality

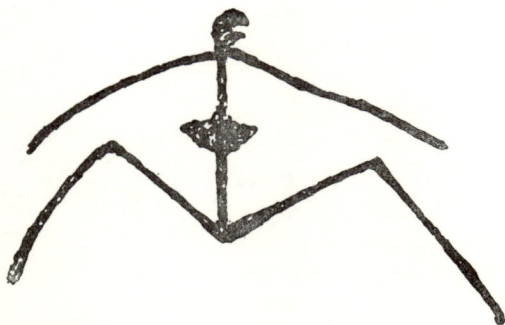

Fig. 64 — Squatting figure. Painting in red, Conic Range, eastern Victoria. After D. J. Tugby

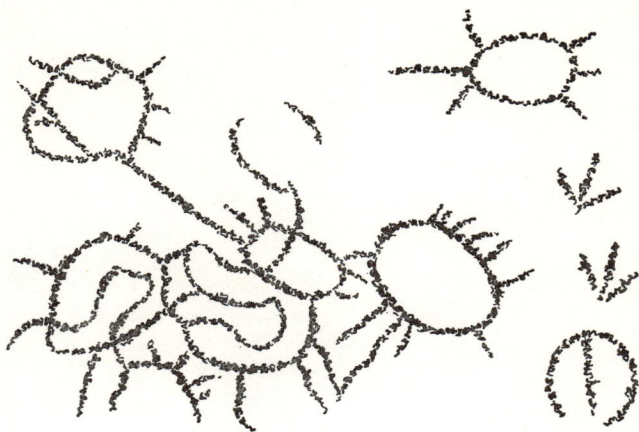

*Fig. 65 — Rock engraving. Devon Downs,
Southern Australia. After D. S. Davidson*

of the works. As a rule it may be said that nowadays Australia appears to be in the grip of a tendency towards schematization, which is cramping all artistic expression, so that works of art charged with living tension are very rare. A map could be drawn showing the location of these few inspired works. One would then see that in the sphere of geometric or abstract art such motifs only occur — or occurred until about a century ago — in the extreme west and south-west on ceremonial staffs. Perfect specimens of these could still be collected by Europeans. In the centre, north-east and north they are extremely rare. But in the centre a few rock paintings have been preserved in which the geometric or abstract style is shown to perfection. The only rock engraving of ascertainable date — that at Devon Downs — which was produced in the third millennium B.C., is markedly inferior.

FIG. 65

In anthropomorphic art this tension was only able to survive in the oldest examples and in the north-west, the area where contact is thought to have been made with the outside world. Anthropomorphic art continues up to the present day, but all of it, both rock art and bark paintings, seems degenerate, lacking in inspiration and vigour of artistic expression.

*Fig. 66 — Rock painting. Malkaia, Southern
Australia. After D. S. Davidson*

[1] Elkin, A.P., *Grey's Northern Kimberley cave-paintings re-found*, in: *Oceania*, Vol. XIX, No. 1, pp. 1—15, Sydney, 1948.

[2] Lommel, Andreas, *Die Unambal, ein Stamm in Nordwest-Australien*, in: *Monographien zur Völkerkunde, herausgegeben vom Hamburgischen Museum für Völkerkunde*, No. II, Hamburg, 1952.

[3] Petri, Helmut, *Sterbende Welt in Nordwest-Australien*, in: *Kulturgeschichtliche Forschungen*, Vol. 5, Brunswick, 1954.

[3a] Ibid., pp. 129—216.

[4] Morgan, John, Unpublished sketches for a new map of North-western Australia.

[5] Bradshaw, Jos., *Notes on a recent trip to Prince Regent River*, in: *Proceedings of the Royal Geographical Society of Australasia, Victoria Branch*, Vol. 9, pp. 99—100, Melbourne, 1892.

[6] Grey, George, *Journals of two expeditions of discovery in North-west and Western Australia during the years 1837, 1838 and 1839*, London, 1841.

[7] Davidson, D. Sutherland, *Aboriginal Australian and Tasmanian rock carvings and paintings*, in: *Memoirs of the American Philosophical Society*, Vol. V, Philadelphia, 1936.

[8] Lommel, Andreas and Katharina: *Die Kunst des fünften Erdteils*, Museum für Völkerkunde, Munich, 1959.

[9] Schulz, Agnes Susanne, *North-west Australian rock paintings*, in: *Memoirs of the National Museum of Victoria*, No. 20, pp. 7—57, Melbourne, 1956.

[10] Worms, Ernest A., *Contemporary and prehistoric rock paintings in Central and Northern North Kimberley*, in: *Anthropos*, Vol. 50, Nos. 4—6, Fribourg, 1955.

[11] Basedow, H., *The Australian aboriginal*, Adelaide, 1925.

[12] Basedow, H., *Anthropological notes on the West Coastal tribes of the Northern Territory of Australia*, in: *Transactions of the Royal Society of South Australia*, Vol. 31, 1907.

[13] Mountford, Charles P., *Art, myth and symbolism*, in: *Records of the American-Australian Scientific Expedition to Arnhem-Land, 1948*, Vol. I, Melbourne, 1956.

[14] Tindale, Norman B., *Natives of Groote Eylandt and of the West Coast of the Gulf of Carpentaria*, in: *Records of the South Australian Museum*, Vol. II, No. 2, 1946.

[15] McCarthy, Frederick D., *The cave paintings of Groote and Chasm Islands*, in: *Records of the American-Australian Scientific Expedition to Arnhem-Land, 1948*, Vol. II, Melbourne, 1959.

[16] McCarthy, Frederick D., Various articles.

[17] Black, Lindsay, *Aboriginal art galleries of Western New South Wales*, Pt. III, Melbourne, 1943.

[18] Adam, Leonhard, *Rock paintings near Glen Isla, Victoria*, in: *Mankind*, Vol. IV, No. 8, pp. 343—345, Sydney, 1952.

[19] Tugby, Donald J., *Conic Range Rock Shelter: a preliminary account of rock paintings in North-east Victoria*, in: *Mankind*, Vol. IV, No. 11, pp. 446–450, Sydney, 1953.

[20] Tindale, Norman B., *Culture succession in South-east Australia from Late Pleistocene to the present*, in *Records of the South Australian Museum*, Vol. XIII, No. 4, pp. 1–49, Adelaide, 1957.

[21] Hall, F.J.; McGowan, R.G.; Guleksen, G.F.; *Aboriginal rock carvings: a locality near Pimba, S.A.*, in: *Records of the South Australian Museum*, Vol. IX, No. 4, Adelaide, 1951.

[22] Basedow, H., *Anthropological notes made on the South Australian Government North-west Prospective Expedition, 1903*, in: *Transactions of the Royal Society of South Australia*, Vol. 28, 1904.

APPENDICES

BIBLIOGRAPHY

FRANCO-CANTABRIAN ROCK ART

Alcalde del Rio, H., Breuil, H. and Sierra, L., Les cavernes de la région cantabrique, 2 vols., Monaco, 1911.

Bégouen, Cte. H., La grotte de Baume-Latrone, in: Mém. de la Soc. Arch. du Midi de la France, XX, 1941, pp. 101—130.

Breuil, H., Les peintures de la caverne de Niaux (Ariège), in: Bull. de la Soc. préhist. de l'Ariège, 1950.

Breuil, H., La caverne ornée de Rouffignac (Dordogne), in: Mémoires de l'Académie des Inscriptions et Belles-Lettres, vol. XLIV.

Breuil, H., Obermaier, H. and Alcalde del Rio, H., La Pasiega à Puente Viesgo (Santander), Monaco, 1913.

Breuil, H. and Obermaier, H., The cave of Altamira at Santillana del Mar, Spain, Madrid, 1935.

Breuil, H., Obermaier, H. and Verner, W., La Pileta, Monaco, 1915.

Capitan, L., Breuil, H. and Peyrony, D., Les figures gravées à l'époque paléolithique sur les parois de la grotte de Bernifal (Dordogne), in: Revue de l'Ecole d'Anthrop., 1903, pp. 202—209.

Capitan, L., Breuil, H. and Ampoulange, Une nouvelle grotte paléolithique à parois gravées: la grotte de la Grèze, in: Revue de l'Ecole d'Anthrop., 1904, pp. 487—494.

Capitan, L., Breuil, H. and Peyrony, D., La caverne de Font-de-Gaume aux Eyzies (Dordogne), Monaco, 1910.

Capitan, L., Breuil, H. and Peyrony, D., Les Combarelles aux Eyzies (Dordogne), Monaco, 1924.

Capitan, L., Breuil H., Peyrony, D. and Bourrinet, Les gravures sur cascade stalagmatique de la grotte de la Mairie à Teyjat, in: XIVe Congrès Intern. d'Anthrop. et d'Arch. Préhist., Geneva, 1912.

Cartailhac, E. and Breuil, H., Les peintures et gravures murales des cavernes pyrénéennes, IV: Gargas, Aventignan (Hautes-Pyrénées), in: L'Anthropologie, 1910, p. 129.

Daleau, F., La grotte de Pair-non-Pair, Association Française pour l'Avancement des Sciences, Montauban, 1902, pp. 786—789.

Graziosi, P., Les gravures de la grotte Romanelli, in: IPEK, VIII, 1932-3.

Graziosi, P., Le Pitture e graffiti preistorici dell' isola di Levanzo nell'Arcipelago delle Egadi (Sicilia), in: Rivista di Scienze Preistoriche, 1950.

Lalanne, G., Bas-Relief à figurations humaines de l'abri sous roche de Laussel (Dordogne), in: L'Anthropologie, 1912, pp. 129—148.

Lalanne, G. and Breuil, H., L'abri sculpté du Cap Blanc à Laussel (Dordogne), in: L'Anthropologie, 1911, pp. 385—402.

Lémozi, A., La grotte-temple du Pech-Merle, Paris, 1929.

Martin, H., Les sculptures du Roc de Sers, in: Préhistoire, I, 1932, pp. 1—8.

Passemard, E., La caverne d'Isturitz en pays basque, in: Préhistoire, September 1944.

Trombe, F. and Dubuc, G., Le centre préhistorique de Gantier-Montespan, in: Arch. de l'Inst. de Paléont. Humaine, Paris, 1947.

Vézian, J., La grotte du Portel, in: Bull. de la Soc. Préhist. du Languedoc, no. 2, 1945, pp. 2—11.

Windels, F., Lascaux: 'Chapelle Sixtine' de la préhistoire, Montignac (Dordogne), 1949.

THE ROCK PICTURES OF THE SPANISH LEVANT

Almagro, M., La cronologia del arte levantino de España, in: Congrès Int. des Sciences Préhistoriques et Protohistoriques, Actes de la IIIe Session, Zurich, 1950, Zurich, 1953, pp. 142-9.

Almagro, M., El Covacho con Pinturas rupestres de Cogul (Lérida), Lérida, 1952.

Almagro, M., Las pinturas rupestres levantinas, Madrid, 1954.

Bandi, H.-G. and Maringer, J., Kunst der Eiszeit, 2nd ed., Basle, 1955.

Breuil, H., Les roches peintes de Minateda (Albacete), in: L'Anthropologie, vol. 30, 1920, pp. 1—50.

Breuil, H., Serrano Gomez, P. and Cabré Aguiló, J., Les Abris del Bosque à Alpera (Albacete), in: L'Anthropologie, vol. 23, 1912, pp. 529—562.

Cabré Aguiló, J., El arte rupestre en España, Madrid, 1915.

Hernandez-Pacheco, E., Las pinturas prehistoricas de las cuevas de la Araña (Valencia), Madrid, 1924.

Kühn, H., Kunst und Kultur der Vorzeit Europas, Vol. I: Das Paläolithikum, Berlin, 1929.

Lindner, K., Die Jagd der Vorzeit, Berlin and Leipzig, 1937.

Narr, K. J., Das höhere Jägertum: Jüngere Jagd- und Sammelstufe, in: Historia Mundi, Vol. I, Berne, 1952.

Narr, K. J., Interpretation altsteinzeitlicher Kunstwerke durch völkerkundliche Parallelen, in: Anthropos, Vol. 50, 1955, pp. 513—545.

Narr, K. J., Vorderasien, Nordafrika und Europa, in: Abriss der Vorgeschichte, Munich, 1957.

Obermaier, H., Nouvelles études sur l'art rupestre du Levant Espagnol, in: L'Anthropologie, Vol. 47, 1937, pp. 477—498.

Obermaier, H. and Breuil, H., Las pinturas rupestres de los alrededores de Tormón (Teruel), Madrid, 1927.

Obermaier, H. and Wernert, P., Las pinturas rupestres del Barranco de Valltorta, Castellón, Madrid, 1919.

Obermaier, H. and Wernert, P., La edad cuaternaria de los pinturas rupestres del Levante Español, in: Mem. de la Real Sociedad Española de Historia Natural., Vol. XV, Madrid, 1929, pp. 527—537.

Pericot-Garcia, L., La cueva del Parpalló (Gandia), Madrid, 1942.

Pidal, R. M. (ed.), Historia de España, Vol. I, Madrid, 1954.

Porcar, J. B., Obermaier, H. and Breuil, H., Las pinturas rupestres de la Cueva Remigia, Castellón, Madrid, 1936.

Vilaseca, S., Las pinturas rupestres de la cueva del Polvorín, Madrid, 1947.

ROCK ART OF THE MAGHREB AND SAHARA

Almagro, M., Prehistoria del Norte de Africa y del Sahara español, Instituto de Estudios africanos, Barcelona, 1946.

Breuil, H., in collaboration with Henri Lhote, Les roches peintes du Tassili-n-Ajjer, Paris, Arts et Métiers graphiques, 1954.

Chasseloup-Laubat, F. de, Art rupestre au Hoggar, Paris, Plon, 1938.

Dalloni, M., Mission du Tibesti, in: Mém. Ac. Sciences, Pt. II, Paris, 1935.

Flamand, G. M. B., Les Pierres écrites, Paris, 1921.

Frobenius, L. and Obermaier, H., Hadschra Maktuba, Munich, 1925.

Frobenius, L., Ekade Ektab: die Felsbilder Fezzans, Leipzig, 1937.

Graziosi, P., Arte rupestre della Libia, Naples, 1942.

Lhote, H., Gravures, peintures et inscriptions rupestres du Kaouar, de l'Aïr et de l'Adrar des Iforas, in: Bull. Inst. Franç. Afrique Noire, Vol. XIV, no. 4, Oct. 1952, pp. 1268—1340.

Lhote, H., Peintures rupestres de l'oued Takéchérouet (Ahaggar), in: Bull. Inst. Franç. Afrique Noire, Vol. XV, no. 3, 1953, pp. 283—291.

Lhote, H., Le cheval et le chameau dans les peintures et les gravures rupestres du Sahara, in: Bull. Inst. Franç. Afrique Noire, Pt. XV, no. 3, July 1953, pp. 1136—1228.

Lhote, H., La route antique du Sahara Central, in: Encyclopédie mensuelle d'Outre-Mer, Vol. I, Nov. 1951, p. 300.

Lhote, H., Die Felsbilder der Sahara, Würzburg-Vienna, 1958.

Monod, Th., L'Adrar Ahnet, Institut d'Ethnologie, Paris, 1932.

Rhotert, H., Libysche Felsbilder, Darmstadt, 1952.

Vaufrey, R., L'art rupestre nord-africain, Arch. Inst. Paléont. Humaine, Paris, 1939.

ROCK ART OF SOUTH AFRICA

Most of the studies of South African prehistoric art are articles in learned journals; they are listed here without the title being given. This is done only in the case of book-length works.

Armstrong, A. I., Journ. Roy. Anthrop. Inst., 1931, Vol. 61, pp. 239—276.

Bartels, M., Zeitschr. f. Ethnol., 1892, Vol. 24, pp. 26-7; Vol. 25, p. 32.

Battiss, W. W., The Amazing Bushman, Pretoria.

Battiss, W. W., The Artists of the Rocks, Pretoria, 1948.

Bleek, D. F., S. Afr. Journ. Sci., 1932, Vol. 29, pp. 72—83.

Bleek, W. H. I. and Bleek, D. F., The Mantis and his Friends, Cape Town, 1923.

Bleek, W. H. I. and Lloyd, L. C., Specimens of Bushman Folklore, London, 1911.

Bleek, W. H. I., Cape Monthly Mag., N.S., 1874, Vol. 9, pp. 10—13.

Breuil, H., The White Lady of the Brandberg, London, 1955.

Breuil, H., Les Roches Peintes d'Afrique Australe, Paris, 1954.

Breuil, H., Philipp Cave, London, 1957.

Breuil, H., The Tsisab Ravine, Clairvaux, 1959.

Breuil, H., Man, 1930, Vol. 30, pp. 149—151; S. Afr. Arch. Bull., 1945, Vol. I, No. 1, pp. 5—7; S. Afr. Journ. Sci., 1945, Vol. 41, pp. 353—5; Man,

1946, Vol. 46, p. 84; L'Anthropologie, 1949, Vol. 53, pp. 377—406; France Abroad, Vol. 3, No. 9; S. Afr. Arch. Bull., 1949, Vol. 4, No. 13, pp. 14—18; id., pp. 19—27; Vol. 4, No. 14, pp. 39—50; etc.

Burkitt, M. C., South Africa's Past in Stone and Paint, Cambridge, 1928.

Christol, F., L'Art dans l'Afrique Australe, Paris, 1911.

Dart, R. A., Nature, 1925, Vol. 115, pp. 425—9; S. Afr. Journ. Sci., 1931, Vol. 28, pp. 475—486.

Dornan, S. S., Pygmies and Bushmen of the Kalahari, London, 1925.

Dornan, S. S., Journ. Roy. Anthrop. Inst., 1917, Vol. 47, pp. 37—112.

Fritsch, G., Zeitschr. f. Ethnol., 1878, Vol. 10, pp. 15—21; 1880, Vol. 12, pp. 289—300; 1887, Vol. 19, pp. 195—202.

Frobenius, L., Madzimu Dsangara, Berlin, 1932.

Gardener, W. E., Scientific American, 1912, Vol. 107, p. 370.

Goodall, E., Proc. Rhod. Sci. Ass., 1946, Vol. 41, pp. 63—73; Pan Afr. Congr., 1955, pp. 295—9.

Goodwin, A. J. H., Annals S. Afr. Mus., 1936, Vol. 24, Pt. 4, pp. 163—210.

Hall, R. N., Proc. Rhod. Sci. Ass., 1912, Vol. 11, pp. 140—154.

Houghton, S. H., Trans. Roy. Soc. S. Afr., 1926, Vol. 13, pp. 105—6; 1927, Vol. 14, p. 315.

Hewitt, J., Trans. Roy. Soc. S. Afr., 1931, Vol. 19, pp. 185—196; Records Albany Museum, 1931, Vol. 4, pp. 1—63.

Halm, T., Zeitschrift f. Ethnol., 1879, Vol. 11, pp. 307—8.

Holub, E., Sieben Jahre in Südafrika, 1880.

Holm, E., S. Afr. Arch. Bull., 1956, Vol. 11, No. 41, pp. 12—21; Vol. 13, No. 49, pp. 34 ff.; Paideuma, Vol. 6, Sept. 1957, Pt. 5, pp. 297—300; IPEK, 19, pp. 77—84; Antaios, I, 5.

Holm, E., Südafrikas Urkunst, Pretoria, 1957.

Hübner, A., Zeitschrift f. Ethnol., 1871, Vol. 2—3, pp. 51—3.

Impey, S. P., Origin of the Bushmen, Cape Town, 1926.

Johnson, J. P., The Prehistoric Period in South Africa, London, 1910.

Jones, N., The Stone Age in Rhodesia, Oxford, 1926.

Jones, N., The Prehistory of Southern Rhodesia, Cambridge, 1949.

Leakey, L. S. B., Stone Age Africa, Oxford, 1926.

Lowe, C. van Riet, S. Afr. Journ. Sci., 1933, Vol. 30, pp. 525—6; Arch. Series, No. 1, 1938; No. 5, 1941; S. Afr. Journ. Sci., 1945, Vol. 41, pp. 329—344; Trans. Roy. Soc. S. Afr., 1937, Vol. 24, pp. 253—261; Bantu Studies, 1929, Vol. 3, pp. 385—393; S. Afr. Arch. Bull., 1947, Vol. 2, No. 6, pp. 41—5; Vol. 1, No. 2, pp. 38—40.

Luschan, F. von, Zeitschrift f. Ethnol., 1908, Vol. 40, pp. 665—685.

Mason, A. Y., Bantu Studies, 1933, Vol. 7, pp. 131—158.

Moszeik, O., Die Malereien der Buschmänner in Südafrika, Berlin, 1910.

Obermaier, H. and Kühn, H., Buschmannkunst (English and German), 1930.

Orpen, J. M., Cape Monthly Mag., N.S., 1874, Vol. 9, pp. 1—10.

Passarge, S., Die Buschmänner der Kalahari, Berlin, 1907.

Pöch, R., Zeitschrift f. Ethnol., 1910, Vol. 42, pp. 357—361.

Prozesky, H., Zeitschrift f. Ethnol., 1906, Vol. 38, pp. 908—910.

Peringuey, L., Trans. Roy. Soc. S. Afr., 1914—5, Vol. 4; 1919—1920, Vol. 8.

Riet, J. and M. v. d. and Bleek, D. F., More Rock Paintings in South Africa, London, 1940.

Schapera, I., S. Afr. Journ. Sci., 1925, Vol. 22, pp. 504—515.

Stow, G. W. and Bleek, D. F., Rock paintings in South Africa, London, 1930.

Tongue, M. H. and Bleek, D. F., Bushman Paintings, Oxford, 1909.

Willcox, A. R., Rock Paintings of the Drakensberg, London, 1956.

Wilman, M., The Rock Engravings of Griqualand West and Bechuanaland, South Africa, Cambridge, Kimberley, 1933.

Zelizko, J. V., Felsgravierungen der südafrikanischen Buschmänner, Leipzig, 1925.

ROCK ART OF AUSTRALIA

The bibliography relating to this chapter is on p. 230.

Annals S. Afr. Mus.: Annals of the South African Museum.

Arch. Series: Archaeological Survey Series.

Cape Monthly Mag.: Cape Monthly Magazine (New Series).

Bull. de la Soc. préh.: Bulletin de la Société préhistorique.

IPEK: Jahrbuch für Prähistorische und Ethnologische Kunst.

Journ. Roy. Anthrop. Inst.: Journal of the Royal Anthropological Institute.

Mém. Ac. Sciences: Mémoires de l'Academie des Sciences.

Pan Afr. Congr.: Proceedings of the Pan-African Congress.

Proc. Rhod. Sci. Ass.: Proceedings of the Rhodesian Scientific Association.

S. Afr. Arch. Bull.: South African Archaeological Bulletin.

S. Afr. Journ. Sci.: South African Journal of Science.

Trans. Roy. Soc. S. Afr.: Transactions of the Royal Society, South Africa.

Zeitschr. f. Ethnol.: Zeitschrift für Ethnologie.

CHRONOLOGY

Comparative table showing the duration of rock art in the various centres treated in this volume.
N.B.: The scale changes after 10,000 B.C. and the beginning of the Christian era.

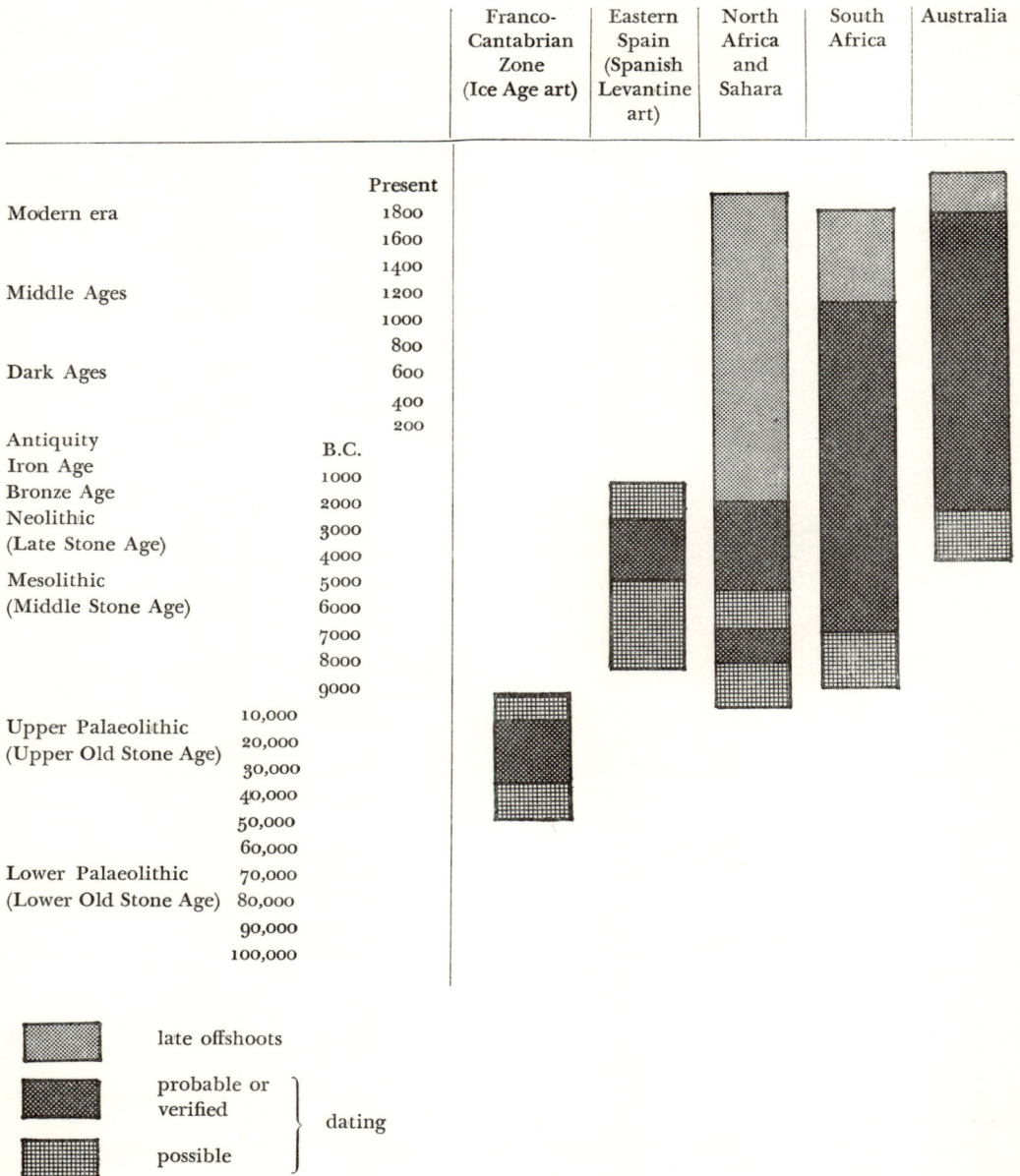

	Franco-Cantabrian Zone (Ice Age art)	Eastern Spain (Spanish Levantine art)	North Africa and Sahara	South Africa	Australia

	Present
Modern era	1800
	1600
	1400
Middle Ages	1200
	1000
	800
Dark Ages	600
	400
	200
Antiquity	B.C.
Iron Age	1000
Bronze Age	2000
Neolithic	3000
(Late Stone Age)	4000
Mesolithic	5000
(Middle Stone Age)	6000
	7000
	8000
	9000
Upper Palaeolithic	10,000
(Upper Old Stone Age)	20,000
	30,000
	40,000
	50,000
	60,000
Lower Palaeolithic	70,000
(Lower Old Stone Age)	80,000
	90,000
	100,000

late offshoots

probable or verified ⎤
⎥ dating
possible ⎦

238

GLOSSARY

Acheulean culture

Culture of the Lower Old Stone Age (Lower Palaeolithic), named after the site of St. Acheul, near Amiens. The most characteristic tool is the hand-axe, a rather crude implement made of a flint nodule. Dating: second and third interglacial periods (approx. 480,000–150,000 B.C.).

Addax

Species of African antelope.

Adrar

Berber for mountainous region.

Atlanthropos mauretanicus

Primitive type of man from the Lower Pleistocene, of which evidence has been found at Palikao, near Ternifine, western Algeria.

Aurignacian culture

Earliest stage of the Upper Palaeolithic (Upper Old Stone Age), named after the cave of Aurignac (Haute-Garonne Dép.). Advanced stage of hunter culture. Blade industry (manufacture of long flint flakes worked into scrapers, burins, borers, etc.). Implements made of bone, antlers and (mammoth) ivory. Portable and mural art. Approx. 60/40,000—20,000 B.C. Nowadays Aurignacian is divided into several sub-periods: Lower Perigordian or Châtelperronian, Aurignacian proper, Upper Perigordian or Gravettian. Main areas of distribution: Western Europe, Asia Minor, Russia. Most important human type: Cro-Magnon.

Boskop type

In South Africa, most important Upper Pleistocene representative of *homo sapiens diluvialis*, named after the find of a skeleton near Boskop, South-western Transvaal.

Bovidae

(From Latin *bos*). Collective term for wild and domesticated cattle.

Campignian culture

Late Mesolithic culture in northern France, forming a transition to Neolithic culture. Named after the hill of Campigny (Seine-Inférieure Dép.).

Canna

Term applied by Bushmen to a genus of plant favoured by elands, and also to this species of antelope.

Capsian culture

Mesolithic culture in North Africa with origins in the Upper Palaeolithic. Named after Capsa (now Gafsa) in southern Tunisia.

Cervidae

Collective term for all species of deer (incl. reindeer).

Chellean culture

Earliest stage of the Lower Old Stone Age (Lower Palaeolithic), characterized by hand-axes. Named after the site of Chelles, near Paris. Nowadays the term Abbevillian is preferred (after Abbeville on the Somme). Dating: first interglacial period (approx. 540,000—480,000 B.C.).

Climatic optimum

Postglacial phase of particularly warm climatic conditions (approx. 4th and 3rd millennia B.C.).

Cro-Magnon man

Most important representative of the late glacial *homo sapiens diluvialis*. Named after the cave of Cromagnon at Les Eyzies (Dordogne). Associated with Upper Palaeolithic cultures.

Diabase

or dolerite: an igneous rock, dark green to black in colour.

Epipalaeolithic

Transitional period between Palaeolithic and Mesolithic.

Equidae

Animals of the horse family, including ass, zebra and wild ass.

Equus capensis

(Cape horse). One of the extinct animal species testifying to the antiquity of Bushman art, others being the prehistoric gnu, the warthog, a tapir-like animal and a llama-like species. The *equus capensis* has been described by R. Broom on the strength of fossil finds as a gigantic horse with a large head and crooked nose.

Fauresmith culture

In South Africa, Lower Palaeolithic culture of the Middle Pleistocene with an improved method of producing flakes. Named after the site of Fauresmith, in the Orange Free State.

Felidae

Animals of the cat family (lion, tiger, etc.).

Haematite

or hematite: a mineral containing ferric oxide,

which can be used as a red paint pigment.

Homo sapiens

Collective term for all the races of mankind existing at present. *Homo sapiens* was preceded by *homo sapiens diluvialis,* who succeeded Neanderthal man in the Upper Palaeothic.

Levalloisian culture

Lower Palaeolithic culture with an improved method of producing flakes. Approx. 150,000—80,000 B.C., found especially in northern France and southern England. Named after the site of Levallois-Perret, near Paris.

Levalloisian technique

('tortoise core' technique): improved method of producing flakes in the Late Lower Palaeolithic. The raw material (usually a flint nodule) is prepared by blows dealt in a certain adroit manner until a relatively large flake is struck off. Widely diffused.

Limonite

Mineral containing ferric oxide of brownish colour, which can be used as a paint pigment.

Macaroni

Term for Early Upper Palaeolithic wall drawings executed with the fingers or a pronged instrument. At first they are merely an indecipherable tangle of lines, but later they form primitive animal figures.

Magdalenian culture

Late Upper Palaeolithic culture named after the rock-shelters at La Madeleine (Dordogne). Climax of Ice Age reindeer-hunting culture. Engravings, polychrome paintings, portable art. Approx. 20,000—10,000 B.C. Diffused eastwards from Western Europe.

Maglemosian culture

Stage of culture in the Mesolithic, named after a moor near Müllerup on the western coast of Zealand (Denmark), where Mesolithic settlements were excavated in 1900.

Magosian culture

In East Africa, a culture of the fourth interpluvial epoch (approx. 10,000—8000 B.C.), named after Magosi in Kavamodja.

Mesolithic

(Middle Stone Age). Transitional stage from Palaeolithic to Neolithic. Dating in Europe approx. 10/8000—3000 B.C. (ending earlier in the Near East and Egypt). Several sub-groups such as Azilian, Sauveterrian, Tardenoisian, Maglemosian, Campignian, Capsian (North Africa), Natufian (Asia) cultures. The Mesolithic period commences approximately at the close of the Pleistocene. Implements (tools and weapons) differ only slightly from those of the Upper Palaeolithic, but the stone implements are smaller (microliths, often geometric in form). Fishing and catching birds begin to be important means of livelihood in addition to hunting. The dog becomes man's first domesticated animal.

Microlithic artefacts

(microliths): small stone implements, often geometric in form (triangles, trapezoids, crescents, etc.), the appearance of which is characteristic of Mesolithic cultures (both in the chronological sense and from the standpoint of cultural history). Rows of these microliths were often inset into shafts of bone, antlers or wood.

Mousterian culture

Important culture of the Late Lower Palaeolithic, characterized by an improved method of producing flakes (similar to the Levalloisian technique) and such types of stone implement as flint points and scrapers. It is distributed over wide areas of the eastern hemisphere. Mousterian is divided into numerous sub-stages and sub-groups, so that nowadays it serves only as a collective term. This epoch is characterized by Neanderthal man.

Natufian culture

In Syria and Palestine, a culture of Mesolithic hunters, fishermen and food-gatherers. Approx. 8000—6000 B.C.

Neanderthal man

(*homo neandertalensis*). Early man of the Upper Pleistocene. Named after the first skeleton find of this type in the Neanderthal, near Düsseldorf (1856). Remains of Neanderthal man are distributed over wide areas of the eastern hemisphere. This type of man, representative of Lower Palaeolithic cultures with an improved method of producing flakes, died out with the beginning of the Upper Palaeolithic.

Neolithic

(New Stone Age). In Europe, dating from 3000—1800 B.C. (in the eastern Mediterranean area beginning as early as 5000 B.C.). First elements of a farming economy with fixed settlements, keeping of domesticated animals (dogs, pigs, sheep, goats, cattle) and cultivation of crops. Other innovations in this period are pottery, polished stone implements and weaving.

Oryx

Species of African antelope with horns about 4 ft. long.

Palaeolithic

(Old Stone Age). This is sub-divided into the Lower Palaeolithic, approx. 600,000—60/40,000 B.C., and the Upper Palaeolithic, to 10/8000 B.C. Order of the individual cultures, which often overlap: Abbevillian (formerly Chellean), Clactonian, Acheulian, Tayacian, Levalloisian, Mousterian, Aurignacian, Solutrian, Magdalenian; the last three are Upper Palaeolithic. The first art finds date from the Aurignacian (60/40,000—20,000 B.C., the middle of the last glacial period). Lower Palaeolithic man was a nomadic hunter (food-gatherer, hunter, fisherman), but Upper Palaeolithic man was a specialized hunter (a so-called advanced hunter). Implements were made of stone, antlers, bone, ivory and wood.

Perigordian culture

Upper and Lower Perigordian are sub-stages of Aurignacian. Named after the Périgord region in south-western France.

Perspective, twisted

With animal bodies depicted in profile, representation of the horns and antlers not viewed from the side, but from the front.

Pleistocene

(Ice Age or *diluvium*). Period characterized by great climatic changes (Ice Age and interglacial periods) between the Pliocene (Late Tertiary period) and the Holocene (in geological reckoning, the present day), approx. 600,000—10/8000 B.C.

Pschent

Egyptian head-dress. Emblem of royalty.

Quagga

(*equus quagga*): species of zebra which became extinct in South Africa in historical times.

Rock-shelter

(*abri*): protected site beneath overhanging rock which can serve as a place of settlement.

Sangoan culture

In Rhodesia and the Congo, a Middle or Late Pleistocene culture of the Lower Palaeolithic, having affinities with Fauresmith culture.

Scalariform signs

Rock engravings in the form of rows of bands, resembling a ladder.

Solutrian-Magdalenian

cf. Solutrian and Magdalenian.

Solutrian

Upper Palaeolithic culture between Aurignacian and Magdalenian and differing from these cultures in essentials. Characteristic are the so-called leaf-shaped spear-heads (*feuilles-de-laurier*) and barbed arrow-heads. Approx. 30,000—20,000 B.C. Origin still disputed. Radiation eastwards from Western Europe. Named after the site of Solutré, near Mâcon.

Stellenbosch culture

In South Africa, hand-axe industry of the Lower Pleistocene, having affinities with Abbevillian (Chellean). Named after Stellenbosch, about 30 miles from Capetown.

Tati Bushmen

Group of Bushmen in north-western Bechuanaland and Southern Rhodesia.

Tectiforms signs

Rock pictures believed to represent hut- or tent-like constructions or traps.

Tjurunga

(*churinga*): longish objects, oval and flat, made of stone or wood, usually decorated, used in rites by Australian aborigines.

Totem

(derived from *ototeman,* a word used by the Ojibway Indians on Lake Superior): a term employed by ethnologists to express the idea that a mystical connection exists between a group of men and an animal, or more rarely a plant or natural phenomenon.

Wild ass

(*equus hemionus*): independent sub-species of the species *equus* (other sub-species being the horse, ass and zebra). The most important breed is the *kulan,* found in Western Asia.

Wilton culture

Group of hunter cultures with microlithic stone implements in the northern part of South Africa and the Congo. After 8/7000 B.C.(?). Named after Wilton, in Cape Province.

Zimbabwe

Extensive ruins in Southern Rhodesia, dating mainly from the 9th—13th and 17th centuries A.D. Their origin and cultural attribution are still a mystery.

INDEX